# World Trends Since 1900

# A Friend's Guide to Chamber Music
## World Trends Since 1900

## Nancy Monsman

CATHEDRAL ROCK ART 2022

Published by Cathedral Rock Art
Printed in the United States of America
Typeset by Openform

ISBN: 978-0-578-99903-6
First Edition
This publication is made possible by a subvention from
the Arizona Friends of Chamber Music

For information on purchasing additional copies, please contact:
Arizona Friends of Chamber Music
P.O. Box 40845
Tucson, Arizona 85717
Phone: 520-577-3769
Email: office@arizonachambermusic.org

*To Max*

# Contents

## Chapter Three
## Revolutionary France

Chapter Four
Czech Dialogues

Chapter Five
Hungarian Quests . . . . . . . . . . . . . . . . . . . . . . . . . . . . . . . . . . . . . . . . 85

## Chapter Nine
## The Mediterranean

## Chapter Ten
## British Soundscapes

## Chapter Eleven
## Cultural Fusion in Latin America

## Chapter Fourteen
## American Pathfinders . . . . . . . . . . . . . . . . . . . . . . . . . . . . . . . . . . . . . 293

# An Introductory Word

*A Friend's Guide to Chamber Music: World Trends Since 1900* is a companion to the earlier guide, *European Trends From Haydn to Shostakovich.* The new volume explores international developments of this unique form, an exhilarating collaboration among equals in a small group pared to fit the space of a "chamber." Intended for performers, listeners, students, and chamber programmers, *World Trends* offers a survey of works created for three or more concert instruments. It can be used either as a reference or as a glimpse of cultural history—which can effectively be viewed through the lens of chamber music, a multi-faceted genre that reveals many fascinating narratives.

The date of 1900 marks the approximate moment when musical concepts began to change rapidly during the eventful years leading up to World War I. The great chamber works of the 1890s, particularly the late Brahms compositions for clarinet and the final quartets of Dvořák, essentially offer a summation of classic/romantic practice. Rather than plotting a strong new path, these works mark the end of a long span of harmonic and melodic tradition that began with Haydn in the eighteenth century. Arguably, twentieth-century composers continued the line that began with Richard Wagner's ineffable *Tristan und Isolde* (1859, premiered in 1865). The extreme chromaticism and long-range suspension heard in the opera's Prelude, troubling to much of that era's musical establishment, suggested a new tonal world. Later Romanticists such as Richard Strauss and Gustav Mahler exploited this expanded harmonic freedom as a stylistic basis. They did not abandon traditional tonality, but Tristan's influence became decisive.

Modernism, a term coined by its literary practitioners but encompassing all arts, became an international movement at the beginning of the twentieth century. Largely experimental in its early phase, as the century progressed Modernism often resembled a collection of ideas rather than a coherent style. In the aftermath of World War I, Modernism assumed utopian overtones; its followers asserted that art and technology could transform society. New performance venues—exhibitions, cafés, outdoor events—became laboratories for exploring modernist concepts. Three musical characteristics prevailed: the expansion or abandonment of tonality; extended technical requirements for its performers; and the exploration of novel sonorities. Modernism's dominance began to wane in the 1960s and 1970s as Postmodernism emerged—a populist reaction to cultural authority characterized by skepticism of grand theories and expanded structural freedom. Near the end of the century this latest trend arrived at the unsustainable for many composers, who happily became czars of their own epiphanies. What comes next? A review of music history indicates that major shifts happen about every 150 years. If that holds true, we are at the cusp of another major arts development, perhaps one that builds on the stylistic fusion already at play in our global society. Advanced technologies stand ready to serve.

For two hundred years Central Europe, especially Austria and Germany, maintained status as the wellspring of chamber music. In the years leading up to World War I Vienna continued its preeminence with the Second Viennese School, comprised of Arnold Schoenberg, Alban Berg, and Anton Webern (the First School includes the great Viennese composers from the era of common harmonic practice—Haydn, Mozart, and Beethoven). After the cataclysm of World War I, geographic coherence loosened as composers migrated to new centers. Paris became the magnet that attracted musicians of various nationalities. Composers such as

Francis Poulenc and Igor Stravinsky shared ideas and drew from their diverse cultural traditions. As World War II approached during the 1930s, the chamber mainstream devolved to ever more distant centers, especially the United States. Numerous composers relocated because of improved opportunities as well as basic survival, creating a diaspora that enriched musical development for their host countries. When peace was restored, individual traditions began to flourish in Latin America, Australia, and (most recently) China.

Because of the rapid development of new harmonic, rhythmic, and textural practices after 1900, composers of necessity began to write ever more elaborate explanations for their works; this volume directly quotes their commentary. Composers of the eighteenth century most often produced chamber works in coherent sets to satisfy a patron; those of the nineteenth century continued this practice to satisfy publishers. With the exceptions of Shostakovich and Bartók, modernists who desired to emulate the chamber productivity of Beethoven, composers after 1900 most often wrote single works for specific purposes. All appear chronologically within regions so that influences and developments can be discerned over the decades surveyed.

*World Trends* developed from my program notes written over two decades for the Arizona Friends of Chamber Music concerts, both the Evening Series and the Winter Chamber Music Festivals. Several works discussed in this study were created through their active commissioning program, an ongoing contribution to the genre.

## Acknowledgements

With much appreciation, I thank the Arizona Friends of Chamber Music for their generous subvention of this book. The Friends' active Board and especially its President Emeritus, Jean-Paul Bierny, have been a steady inspiration for their dedication and support of this special genre. Elizabeth Rosenblatt deserves particular acknowledgment for her careful proofing and editorial insight. I appreciate my long and continuing association with Professor Jay Rosenblatt, whose critical eye has been invaluable for the editorial process of this study and past AFCM projects as well.

Since one often judges a book by its cover, I sincerely thank Andrea Bertassi, Professor of Architecture at SCAD in Savannah, Georgia for his beautiful design work. I also thank Wilson Graham Photography for the author's photo and Azure Photography for its image of the cover painting.

Suzanne Stephens-Janning, Chair of the Stockhausen Institute Board of Directors, deserves appreciation for her contributions to the material on the composer's works. I thank cellist Nicholas Tzavaras for his guidance as I explored recent compositions from China. My violinist friend Lincoln Brown offered astute commentary as chapters emerged. Readers from the AFCM Board, Elaine Rousseau and Alan Hershowitz, offered comments and corrections at the proof stage.

In a quiet Covid year, I express gratitude to my chamber music partners for daring to play through the fifteen Shostakovich string quartets while outdoors, masked, and socially distanced. Last but most importantly, I thank my husband Gerald, who gave wise observations and consistent encouragement during this chamber music journey.

*Nancy Monsman*
*Tucson, Arizona*

# ONE

# The Twilight of Empires

Glittering opulence illuminated fin-de-siècle Europe's visible national life. Significant achievements both artistic and scientific—such as the perfection of the moving picture (1888–95) by Louis Le Prince and the brothers Auguste and Louis Lumière in France—as well as general prosperity buoyed confidence. Yet restless undercurrents could be detected. Europe's two dominant forces, the German Empire (1871–1918) and the Habsburg Empire (1526–1918) formally disbanded only after the Great War, but signs of fatal weakness could be detected decades earlier. Germany had set a disastrous course of *Weltpolitik*, an imperialist foreign policy that in its "search for the sun" prepared the stage for World War l. Political shifts happened simultaneously in Vienna, the Habsburg cultural center and home of its Emperor. In 1895 the charismatic anti-Semite Karl Lueger was easily elected Vienna's mayor—an "appalling madness" to liberal thinkers such as Johannes Brahms. This sentiment was echoed by Emperor Franz Joseph, who feared Lueger and blocked his appointment for two years. Later an inspiration for Adolf Hitler, Lueger in his prime was "the Handsome Karl," praised for his creation of parks and improvements of services. Life continued with deceptive peace.

In this ostensibly encouraging environment, Brahms and other late romantic composers continued to create masterpieces as they listened for successors. The young prodigies Enescu, Wolf, Mahler, Dohnányi, and Korngold (see all below) showed promise of continuing the romantic tradition. However, Wolf suffered incapacitating illness and the others relocated to the United States to follow diverging paths. Dvořák recognized a fellow romanticist in his son-in-law Josef Suk, who unfortunately composed little because of his intense performing and teaching schedule; Dvořák's most significant influence arguably resulted from his three-year residency in the United States (see chapter fourteen). Brahms, who regularly attended concerts of new music at the Vienna Conservatory, hoped to sustain Europe's strong tradition of composition, romantic or otherwise. He listened to the early efforts of his admirer Arnold Schoenberg with interest, and he encouraged the work of Alexander Zemlinsky through ongoing financial support.

When Brahms died on April 3, 1897, Vienna's cultural dynamics began to change with lightning speed. On that same day painter Gustav Klimt called a meeting of "The Secession," an avant-garde movement proclaiming the motto "To the Age its Art, To the Art its Freedom." Hosted in a building designed by the revolutionary architect Joseph Olbrich, who proclaimed that "everything measured by traditional aesthetics appears foolish and awkward," Secession members then declared their official separation from the conservative Association of Austrian Artists—effectively launching twentieth-century Modernism.

The Secessionists' expanded artistic freedom led to the creation of stunning visual masterpieces such as Klimt's *Portrait of Adele Bloch-Bauer* (completed in 1907). New liberties were soon insinuated into musical composition, long grounded by coherent systems of counterpoint and common harmonic practice. Heard in the atonality of Schoenberg and Anton Webern, as well as the Expressionism of Alban Berg, Modernism soon prevailed in the new century.

The following end-of- empire chamber works are late romantic statements that stand at the cusp of Modernism.

HUGO WOLF
B. MARCH 13, 1860 IN WINDISCHGRAZ, SLOVENIA,
D. FEBRUARY 22, 1903 IN VIENNA

## Italian Serenade (1887)

Although renowned as a composer of art songs, the Viennese late romanticist Hugo Wolf also wrote a small number of purely instrumental works. The perennial favorite is his *Italian Serenade*, a charming miniature that he scored for string quartet or small orchestra. Wolf had conceived his *Serenade* as a four-movement suite, but he had completed only the first movement by the onset of his mental illness. Although he attempted to write both a slow movement and a tarantella during the six years of his asylum commitment, only fragments survive.

Wolf most probably never visited Italy, but his delightful *Serenade* conjures its buoyant spirit. He wrote that he gave careful thought to the title word "serenade," which originally suggested night music sung beneath a lady's window but by his own time implied genial entertainment appropriate for informal concerts or the outdoors. Wolf's essentially lighthearted and melodious work develops with subtle color inflections and inventive declamation that perhaps did conjure a story for this most poetically sensitive of all composers.

GUSTAV MAHLER
B. JULY 7, 1860 IN KALIŠTĚ, BOHEMIA,
D. MAY 18, 1911 IN VIENNA

## *Adagietto for Harp and Strings from Symphony No. 5 (1902)*

One of the leading exponents of the German post-Romantic movement and among its last, Gustav Mahler most often used vast musical forces to convey large philosophical and poetic concepts. Yet he was fundamentally a melodist who could also create an intimate atmosphere that suggested Schubert. The Adagietto, the fourth movement of his Symphony No. 5 (1902), is a graceful song scored simply for harp and strings. The movement, a stylistic and emotional contrast to the three earlier movements of Symphony No. 5, was said to be written for his brilliant new wife Alma, a musician for whom he felt "an immense and superhuman love." Mahler sent it to her as a bouquet with no accompanying words.

Marked "very slow" (Sehr langsam), the F major Adagietto unfolds in three-part song form. The central section develops the contemplative opening theme with poignant harmonic modulations. The harp throughout provides gentle accompaniment for the strings. Frequently programmed independently of the other Symphony No. 5 movements, the Adagietto has become one of Mahler's best-known compositions.

## *Piano Quartet in A Minor (1875)*

Nicht zu schnell
Scherzo (fragment extended by Alfred Schnittke)

Mahler began the A Minor Piano Quartet, his sole surviving chamber work, when he was a fifteen-year-old student at the Vienna Conservatory. Since a scherzo fragment of twenty-four measures exists with the manuscript, Mahler most probably had projected a larger four-movement composition. Mahler was pianist at both its 1876 premiere and its subsequent performance at the home of Dr. Theodor Billroth, a close friend of Brahms. Although Mahler considered publication, he filed away the quartet and it was assumed lost. The composer's widow Alma recovered it in the 1960s, and it has since been performed in numerous venues together with the scherzo fragment, extended by Alfred Schnittke.

The opening movement, Nicht zu schnell (not too fast), reveals the opulent scoring and dramatic pacing heard throughout Mahler's career. The pulsing piano introduction foreshadows the two darkly expressive themes, both developed imitatively with expressive late romantic harmonies. A violin cadenza referencing the movement's themes leads to the hushed conclusion.

The fragmentary Scherzo, extended by Schnittke to create a complete movement, develops in a spectral atmosphere. Dissonant harmonies and diaphanous textures conjure a modernist world. As a mirror of the opening movement, the Scherzo ends with a whisper.

ERNŐ DOHNÁNYI
B. JULY 27, 1877 IN POZSONY, HUNGARY,
D. FEBRUARY 9, 1960 IN NEW YORK CITY

*Piano Quintet in C Minor, Opus 1 (1895)*

Allegro
Scherzo: Allegro vivace
Adagio, quasi andante
Finale: Allegro animato

One of Hungary's most influential musicians, Dohnányi was honored throughout Europe as a preeminent pianist, conductor, and composer. A prodigy, by the time he wrote his Opus 1 Quintet at age 17 Dohnányi had already composed sixty-five student works. The quintet won high praise from Brahms, who arranged for the work's Vienna premiere in 1895. The work shows strong influences of both Brahms and Schumann in its richly romantic harmonies and sweeping lyrical lines.

The opening motif, introduced by the piano, dominates the quintet since it recurs in a variety of forms throughout. The strings offer a contrasting theme in E flat major. The Scherzo is constructed in ABA form with vivacious outer sections and a songful center that suggests Schubert. The Adagio provides a gentle contrast. The Finale, based on an idea closely related to the main theme of the first movement, recalls the dramatic aura of the opening Allegro. A fugal section based on a variation of this theme leads to a bold restatement of the original motive. The movement concludes with a brilliant coda.

GEORGE ENESCU

B. AUGUST 19, 1881 IN LIVENI, ROMANIA,
D. MAY 4, 1955 IN PARIS

*Octet for Strings in C Major, Opus 7 (1899–1900)*

Très modéré
Très fougueux
Lentement
Mouvement de valse bien rythmée

The prodigious Romanian composer, violinist, and conductor George Enescu began his musical studies at age five with Nicholas Chioru, a noted Roma violinist. Youthful studies followed in Vienna, where Enescu won first prizes in violin and harmony. The much honored thirteen-year-old then enrolled in the Paris Conservatory as a student of Gabriel Fauré and Jules Massenet. Two years later, Enescu presented a Paris debut concert of his own works, an event that attracted the attention of influential publishers. The multi-talented Enescu then embarked on an energetic international performing career and (more occasional) composing career while based in Bucharest, where he served as court violinist to the Queen of Romania. After relocating to Paris, he travelled to the United States as conductor for both the Philadelphia Orchestra and the New York Philharmonic. In his New York farewell concert in 1946, the versatile Enescu conducted his popular Romanian Rhapsody No. 1 and performed both Bach's Concerto for Two Violins (as violinist) and his earlier violin sonata (as pianist) with his student Yehudi Menuhin. He returned to Paris, but his final years were marred by poverty and poor health.

Enescu began his Octet as an eighteen-year-old and completed it in 1900 following a year and a half of steady effort. This remarkable neo-Romantic work has been compared to Mendelssohn's early Octet both as an outstanding composition and as a significant accomplishment by one so young. Unlike Mendelssohn, who premiered his works in the security of his musically nurturing home, Enescu was directed by the impresario Édouard Colonne, who presented a public concert series in Paris. After five rehearsals of the Octet, Colonne decided to withdraw it from the program—a decision that devastated Enescu. The Octet was finally premiered nine years later.

Enescu wrote about the challenging creation of his Octet: "I wore myself out trying to make work a piece of music divided into segments of such length that each of them was likely at any moment to break. An engineer launching his first suspension bridge over a river could not feel more anxiety than I felt when I set out to darken my paper." Enescu described the Octet as a cyclic form, one in which motifs recur throughout to unify the composition. He stated that the four movements are linked so that together they form a single, large-scale sonata form movement. The first movement ("Very moderate") should be perceived as the exposition, and the Octet's inner two movements ("Very fiery" followed by "Slowly") heard as the development section. The finale ("Moving in waltz rhythm") functions as the recapitulation, and an extended coda concludes the work. The Octet develops a wealth of themes, several of which suggest Roma influence in their freely improvisatory style.

ERICH WOLFGANG KORNGOLD
B. MAY 29, 1897 IN BRÜNN, MORAVIA,
D. NOVEMBER 29, 1957 IN LOS ANGELES

*Sextet for Strings in D Major, Opus 10 (1914)*

Moderato—Allegro
Adagio
Intermezzo
Finale: Presto

Born into a musical family in Brünn (present-day Brno, Czech Republic), Korngold was a remarkable child prodigy. At the age of nine he performed his cantata *Gold* for Gustav Mahler, who pronounced him a genius. Soon after, Richard Strauss remarked: "That these compositions are by a child provokes awe. This assurance of style, this mastery of form, this bold harmony is truly astonishing!" Korngold was fourteen when he wrote his first orchestral works, which caused a sensation in Vienna, and soon he began to write operas. His fame reached its zenith in 1920 with the premiere of his opera *Die tote Stadt* (The Dead City). He then began a teaching career at the Vienna Staatsakademie and was awarded the title Professor Honoris Causa by the President of Austria.

In 1934 Korngold was invited to Hollywood to write film music, and because of the war he chose to remain in California. A pioneer of the symphonic film score, a significant influence on later Hollywood composers such as John Williams, Korngold treated each as "an opera without singing." He intended that scores such as the fervently romantic *Captain Blood* could stand alone as serious works. After the war, Korngold again composed for the concert hall.

Korngold wrote his Sextet on a summer holiday in 1914, when he was seventeen years old; delayed by war, the premiere was held three years later. Considered to be his finest chamber work, the intensely romantic Sextet suggests the influence of Richard Strauss because of its dramatic lyricism and rich harmonic resources. The opening movement, in sonata form, develops two ardent themes with restless harmonies and sonorous textures. After a brief introduction, the solo cello introduces the main theme of the fervent Adagio; as it develops, double and triple-stop chords create an orchestral effect. The Intermezzo, one of Korngold's most popular movements, unfolds with Viennese grace. The good-natured Finale contains thematic references to the earlier movements.

TWO

# Viennese Symbolism

Vienna's heirs to its great musical past suffered a crisis of confidence at the beginning of the twentieth century. The post-Wagnerians Bruckner, Strauss, and Mahler had created an expressive late Romantic style based on the harmonic and melodic freedom that began with Wagner's bold experiments in his opera *Tristan und Isolde* (1859) more than a generation earlier. Wagner's dramatic expansion of chromatic inflections—half step departures from pivotal scalar tones that delay gravitational pull to the cadence—denied expected harmonic resolutions, shocking the musical establishment. In earlier decades chromatic (its root meaning "color") inflections had been a vital feature both as decoration and as the genesis for modulations to new tonal areas. But in the late nineteenth century, free chromaticism loosened tonal centers and expanded both melodic phrases and chords with "color" notes exterior to the scale.

Borrowing a concept from Vienna's lively visual arts community, composer Alban Berg became the leading exponent of Expressionism, a genre that achieved heightened emotional experience through fervent pulsations of color and tone. Often called "the final convulsion of Romanticism," Expressionism demanded new harmonic procedures to sustain its wide emotional range. Schoenberg had already been creating über-romantic works based on chromatically expanded scales. His tireless refinements soon led to solidification of the twelve-tone scale system and the revolutionary concept of atonality.

Composers Zemlinsky, Schoenberg, Berg, and Webern—the latter three the constituents of the Second Viennese School— became obsessed with numerology as a symbolic method. Numbers relating to personal events were translated into both intervals and note clusters to create motifs, all developed according to rules derived from their philosophies of religion or their own psychology. That these inward journeys were launched in the City of Freud carries its own significance.

ALEXANDER ZEMLINSKY
B. OCTOBER 14, 1871 IN VIENNA,
D. MARCH 15, 1942 IN LARCHMONT, NEW YORK

Austrian composer, conductor, and teacher Alexander Zemlinsky has often been linked to the revolutionary Second Viennese School, the early twentieth-century group (comprised of Schoenberg, Berg, and Webern) that brought harmonically luxuriant late Romanticism into atonal realms. However, Zemlinsky's intensely expressive, finely crafted music never reached those harmonic extremes. He objected to his pupil Schoenberg's atonal experiments. Zemlinsky wrote to him: "A great artist, who possesses everything needed to express the essentials, must respect the boundaries of beauty, even if he extends them further than hitherto."

Zemlinsky carried a burden of guilt because of a family tragedy that directly involved Schoenberg. Zemlinsky's sister was Mathilde, famously portrayed as the unmarried pregnant woman in Schoenberg's *Verklärte Nacht* (1899). Like his unnamed protagonist, Schoenberg did marry Mathilde, but she left him for the painter Richard Gerstl, a Zemlinsky family friend. Mathilde returned to Schoenberg for the sake of their children in 1908, but the unhappy painter destroyed first his paintings and then his life. Zemlinsky felt personal responsibility.

Zemlinsky, like his Second Viennese School colleagues, believed in both the science of numerology and the importance of musical symbols. The son of a Catholic father and a Muslim mother, the passionately religious Zemlinsky converted to Judaism early in his life and later Protestantism. Patterns formed by his investigations into numerical relationships, many inspired by his broad theology, pervade his work; these function as both secret autobiographical revelations and structural organizers. All four of his string quartets, written over a forty-year span, are rich with extra-musical symbolism—yielding a layer of meaning that allies Zemlinsky most closely with the expressionist Alban Berg.

*String Quartet No. 1 in A Major, Opus 4 (1896)*

Allegro con fuoco
Allegretto
Breit und kräftig
Vivace e con fuoco

Early in his career Zemlinsky caught the attention of Johannes Brahms, who attended performances of his student works. Zemlinsky wrote that after delivering his customary frank criticism, "Brahms offered me a monthly grant, which would enable me to reduce my teaching schedule and spend more time composing." Zemlinsky devoted the summer of 1896 to his Opus 4 string quartet, a highly emotional late romantic statement. It was premiered at the Vienna Conservatory that fall.

The opening Allegro con fuoco (A major) develops restlessly with sudden dynamic changes, numerous changes of articulation from smooth to strongly marked, and ever-evolving rhythmic patterns. Passages marked *dolce* (sweet) and *con fuoco* (with fire) alternate throughout the movement. Two thematic areas, separated by rests, are developed in free sonata form. After an *espressivo* ritard the movement concludes with a brief coda.

13

The Allegretto second movement (A major) unfolds in ABA song form developed through brief repeated sections. The faster central area (F major) culminates in a passage marked *furioso* (furious). As a gesture of musical symbolism Zemlinsky had crafted from his birth date numbers a musical signature based on the notes C sharp, D sharp, F sharp—the second, third, and fifth steps of the B major scale. Intricately interpreted through Hebrew texts, Zemlinsky also derived the sentence "Logic is the mother of imagination and awareness," his dictum throughout his career. Heard in the first violin's opening two measures, this "self" motivic pattern recurs throughout his body of work.

As in the opening movement, the Breit und kräftig (broad and powerful) third movement develops with strong dynamic contrasts and expressive markings that alternate between gentle and forceful. A concluding phrase marked "Very sustained, with sentiment" leads to an Adagio conclusion.

Cast in sonata form, the vivacious Finale (A major) offers hints of Dvořák's *Slavonic Dances*. Near the end of the exposition, a brief passage recalls the finale of Brahms's Violin Concerto (1878). A passage marked "more motion" leads to a fortissimo conclusion.

*String Quartet No. 2, Opus 15 (1913–1915)*

Sehr mässig—Heftig und leidenschaftlich
Andante mosso—Allegretto—Adagio
Schnell
Andante—Allegro molto—Langsam—Andante

Subtitled his "Personal Inferno," Opus 15 is a strongly symbolic work inspired by Alban Berg's Expressionism. For its key Zemlinsky chose the visually significant F sharp minor, designated by three sharp signs arranged on the staff in a cross pattern. Although the quartet is primarily heard as centered on D major (two sharps),

Zemlinsky wrote to Schoenberg that he wanted the score to convey Christ's suffering on the cross at Golgotha.

Through its musical symbols Zemlinsky's turbulent Opus 15 quartet offers a veiled apology for the tragedy his sister Mathilde brought to Schoenberg. Many of the phrases are constructed in lengths of thirteen or fourteen bars, birthdate related numbers that held secret meanings for both composers. The third movement offers repetitions of the notes A and E flat, which are the musical initials for Arnold Schoenberg. Only briefly separated by rests, the quartet's movements connect to create a sense of emotional outpouring.

The large-scaled opening movement ("very moderate—violent and passionate") resembles in atmosphere Schoenberg's string sextet *Verklärte Nacht*. The lyric tradition of "Viennese espressivo" emerges in the lilting melodic lines of the Adagio (D major modulating to D minor), which suggests a Venetian barcarolle. Schnell, the third movement, is a metrically intricate burlesque that conjures dark satire (D minor). The finale begins calmly (C major) but becomes stormy at the direction "with energetic resolution" (F sharp major—six sharps forming two Golgotha crosses). The movement concludes in a mood suggesting quiet acceptance of fate.

## *String Quartet No. 3, Opus 19 (1924)*

Allegretto
Theme and Variations
Romanze: Sehr mässige Achtel
Burleske: Sehr lebhaft

Zemlinsky wrote his third string quartet rapidly as a response to the death of his sister Mathilde on October 18, 1923. Three numerical patterns, subtly insinuated into the structure, shape this autobiographical work: the number 22, which references

Mathilde's death on her twenty-second wedding anniversary; Zemlinsky's birthdate, the 14th of October; and his "self" motive, the second, third, and fifth scale degrees of the major scale. Opus 15 can also be heard as a bridge from late Romanticism into Modernism. Its expressive harmonies relate to traditional harmonic practice but move with new freedom, perhaps an influence of his German colleague Paul Hindemith.

The Allegretto derives thematic material from its opening quote of Alban Berg's *Lyric Suite*. As in Zemlinsky's earlier quartets, songful passages, initiated by motivic statements in the solo instruments, alternate with percussive, strongly rhythmic areas. The Allegretto's strident coda, articulated with strong unison bow stokes and concluding pizzicati, suggests Bartók.

The second movement develops seven variations ("mysteriously moving, not too fast") and a coda with symbolic allusions to Mathilde's death. Variations six and seven are both constructed in 22-bar lengths as reference to the twenty-two years of her marriage to Schoenberg. The variations unfold with a variety of sonorous effects: legato dialogues among the four instruments are accompanied by filmy tremolos, furious pizzicati, and strongly marked rhythms. As in the first movement, an assertive rhythmic section leads to a pizzicato concluding phrase.

The final two movements exploit Zemlinsky's "self" motif. A reflective autobiographical statement, Romanze is animated by wide leaps in its melodic lines, initially stated by the solo instruments. A lyrical viola solo brings the movement to an ethereal conclusion. The solo cello introduces the "very lively burlesque" rondo finale. The other instruments expand these motifs with vigorous passagework and piquant pizzicato interludes. The movement concludes with two emphatic chords.

## String Quartet No. 4, "Suite," Opus 25 (1936)

Präludium: Poco adagio
Burleske: Vivace
Adagietto: Adagio
Intermezzo: Allegretto
Thema mit Variationen (Barcarole): Poco adagio
Finale—Doppelfuge: Allegro molto, energico

Zemlinsky wrote his fourth and final string quartet as a tribute to Alban Berg, who died suddenly on Christmas Eve, 1935. When composing his *Lyric Suite* for string quartet, Berg had freely quoted from Zemlinsky's *Lyric Symphony*. To complete the circle of influence, Zemlinsky honors Berg's Suite through similar structure in his own string quartet, which is subtitled "Suite"—six movements grouped into three alternating slow-fast pairs. Within this framework the quartet develops with the heightened expressivity of Berg's individual language.

The darkly atmospheric opening Präludium, marked *senza espressione* (without expression) is based on the primary theme of Zemlinsky's second quartet, which is also his musical "self" signature. The abrasive Burleske is a rondo that resembles the closing movement of his Quartet No. 3. The lyrical third movement, the expressive heart of the quartet, is a brief Adagietto. As the focal center of the quartet, the energetic fourth movement develops with frenzied violin passages in their upper registers.

The contrasting Barcarole is a tranquil theme and variations movement that begins with an extended expressive cello solo. After an interlude, the viola solo following develops this motif. The vigorous finale brings the work to a stunning conclusion.

ARNOLD SCHOENBERG
B. SEPTEMBER 13, 1874 IN VIENNA,
D. JULY 13, 1951 IN LOS ANGELES

Arnold Schoenberg, together with his disciples Alban Berg and Anton Webern, formed the Second Viennese School, a term that placed them historically with the classical masters (Haydn, Mozart, and Beethoven) of the First Viennese School. Although revolutionary in its methods, which embraced atonality and the twelve-tone system, aesthetically the School held to the principal tenet of Romanticism—that music was the language of subjective emotion. Influenced by Freud's investigations into the human psyche, the group acknowledged the irrational forces that governed the ego, which led to the emotionally intense genre of Expressionism. Superstition about numbers was prevalent among the composers; Schoenberg himself had extreme fear of the number 13 (triskaidekaphobia), which coincidentally was both his birth and death day.

Early in his career Schoenberg had explored Wagner's late romantic chromatic techniques and exploited them in works such as his D major Quartet (1898), which his student Zemlinsky showed to an approving Johannes Brahms. Schoenberg continued to seek his own voice, and by the new century he had arrived at a freely chromatic, essentially atonal style. Lacking traditional formal organization, these imaginative early works are most often brief (as his Five Orchestral Pieces, Opus 16) or achieve coherence through their poetic settings (as *Pierrot Lunaire*, Opus 21). Realizing that he needed a new system to sustain long-range ideas, during the war years he relentlessly experimented with unifying schemes. By the 1920s, Schoenberg had refined his twelve-tone method, described by him as "composing with the twelve chromatic notes related only to one another." The vehicle for this system was the tone row, a scheme whereby the twelve tones of the scale (the black and white piano notes) were arranged in a unique fixed sequence with no note repeated until the conclusion of the phrase (although note repetition did occur in practice). The primary goal of the twelve-tone system was to achieve a new harmonic organization, but the creation of a note "row" also created motivic material. This melodic aspect of the row allowed for "developing variation" (*entwickelnde Variation*) manipulations—transposition, inversion, or retrograde (backwards), and upside-down backwards motion. As Schoenberg's student Anton Webern remarked of this regenerative challenge: "Once stated, the theme expresses everything it has to say. It must be followed by something new."

### *"Verklärte Nacht" for String Sextet, Opus 4 (1899)*
(Also arranged for Piano Trio by Edward Steuermann, 1932)

Sehr langsam
Breiter
Schwer betont
Sehr breit und langsam
Sehr ruhig

Schoenberg wrote his programmatic string sextet *Verklärte Nacht* (Transfigured Night) in the late summer of 1899. Its 1902 premiere in Vienna shocked an audience unaccustomed to strong stories told through chamber music (but fully acceptable through an orchestral setting). His first large-scale work, the sextet is an essentially tonal composition strongly influenced by Wagner's late nineteenth-century harmonic procedures. Perhaps Schoenberg's most accessible composition, *Verklärte Nacht* strives to express late Romanticism's highest ideal—that music can be the language of the most subtle human emotions.

Schoenberg based his Opus 4 on Richard Dehmel's poem *Transfigured Night* (1896). Cast in a single movement, the work falls into five sections that delineate and interpret the stanzas of the poem through intensely expressive motifs. The first and third sections portray the despair of the couple as they walk in the cold, moonlit night. The agitated second section suggests the woman's troubled story, and the fourth conveys the man's sustained answer. In the final section Schoenberg transforms the opening phrase of the work into a sublime statement heard in the upper register of the violin. By so doing, he creates the magical conclusion—the mystical transfiguration of the unborn child.

> Two people are walking through the bare, cold grove;
> The moon accompanies them, they gaze at it.
> The moon courses above the high oaks;
> Not a cloud obscures the light of heaven,
> Into which the black treetops reach.
> A woman's voice speaks:
> I am carrying a child, and not of yours,
> I walk in sin beside you.
> I have deeply transgressed against myself.
> I no longer believed in happiness
> And yet had a great yearning
> For purposeful life, for the happiness
> And responsibility of motherhood; so I dared
> And, shuddering, let my body
> Be embraced by a strange man,
> And have become pregnant from it.
> Now life has taken its revenge,
> Now that I have met you.
> She walks with awkward step.
> She looks up: the moon accompanies them.
> Her dark glance is inundated with light.
> A man's voice speaks:
> Let the child you have conceived
> Be no burden to your soul.
> O see, how brightly the universe gleams!
> There is a radiance on everything;
> You drift with me on a cold sea,
> But a special warmth flickers
> From you to me, from me to you.
> This will transfigure the other's child;
> You will bear it for me, from me;

You have brought radiance on me,
You have made me a child myself.
He clasps her round her strong hips.
Their breath mingles in the breeze.
Two people go through the tall, clear night.

*Translation by Lionel Salter*

## *String Quartet No. 1 in D Minor, Opus 7 (1905)*

Nicht zu rasch
Kräftig
Mässig
Mässig

Cast in one continuous movement with a duration of at least forty-five minutes, the densely written Opus 7 quartet suggests orchestral aspirations. Schoenberg himself admitted that the quartet was written in "too thick a style" for chamber music, and over the next decade he gradually worked toward more open textures. He did achieve his goal of thematic unity in Opus 7: the chromatic opening measures contain its motivic cells, and each ensuing figure is related to them. Schoenberg's own term for this process of deriving all material from the opening phrase was "developing variation" (*entwickelnde Variation*). He wrote: "Developing variation of the features of the basic unit produces all the thematic formulations which provide for fluency, contrasts, variety, logic, and unity on the one hand, and character, mood, expression, and every needed differentiation on the other hand—thus elaborating the *idea* of the piece." In practice, "developing variation" is a continuing process by which ideas generate successively through organic growth. Emotional contrast is as significant as thematic contrast in the highly romantic Opus 7, which contains numerous directives to play "with fullest expression." After ranging through the varied harmonic areas of G flat major, E major, D major, C major, B flat major, and back to D minor, this tightly constructed work closes on a serene D major chord.

## String Quartet No. 2, Opus 10 (1908)

Mässig (Moderato)
Sehr rasch
Litanei: Langsam
Entrückung: Sehr langsam

Schoenberg dedicated his Opus 10 quartet "to my wife," perhaps as a gesture of reconciliation since Mathilde had recently terminated her affair with the expressionist painter Richard Gerstl, their mutual friend and art teacher. Reflecting his heightened psychological state, the quartet begins with expressive chromatic harmonies that gradually become less tonally centered over the course of the work. Ostensibly written in the key of F sharp minor (which perhaps describes the cross of suffering), the final two movements carry no key signature; however, the work concludes on the chord of F sharp major as harmonic closure.

Opus 10 suggests the late romantic emotional world reflected in Gustav Mahler's early symphonies. Its second movement reveals affinities to the third movement of Mahler's First Symphony (1888–89): both are cast in D minor with the low string instrument establishing the key, and both reference popular folk tunes. In Mahler's work the bass intones the round "Brüder Jacob" in the minor key; in Schoenberg's second movement the second violin introduces the popular folk song "Ach, du lieber Augustin." In both works these tunes develop in dark emotional contexts far removed from their associations with childhood innocence.

Both composers score movements for soprano voice with tempos and dynamics sensitively fluctuating to reinforce the nuance of the words. The Opus 10's final two movements are settings of

German symbolist poems by Stefan George (1868–1933). Schoenberg wrote: "I was inspired by these poems to compose music to several, and surprisingly, without any expectation on my part, these songs showed a style quite different from everything I had written before." The poems are taken from George's collection *The Seventh Ring* (1907).

*Litany*
Deep is the sadness that comes over me,
Again I step, Lord, in your house.
Long was the journey, my limbs are weary,
The shrines are empty, Only anguish is full.
My thirsty tongue desires wine,
The battle was hard, my arm is stiff.
Grudge peace to my staggering steps,
For my hungry gums break your bread!
Weak is my breath, calling the dream,
My hands are hollow, my mouth fevers.
Lend your coolness, douse the fires,
Rub out hope, send the light!
Fires in my heart still glow, open,
Inside my heart a cry wakes.
Kill the longing, close the wound!
Take my love away, give me your joy!

*Rapture*
I feel air from another planet.
I faintly through the darkness see faces
Friendly even now, turning toward me.
And trees and paths that I loved fade
So I can scarcely know them, and you bright,
Beloved shadow—summoner of my anguish—
Are only extinguished completely in a deep glowing
In the frenzy of the fight
With a pious show of reason.
I lose myself in tones, circling, weaving,
With unfathomable thanks and unnamed praise,
Bereft of desire, I surrender myself to the great breath.

A violent wind passes over me
In the thrill of consecration where ardent cries
In dust flung by women on the ground:
Then I see a filmy mist rising
In a sun-filled, open expanse
That includes only the farthest mountain hatches,
The land looks white and smooth like whey,
I climb over enormous canyons,
I feel as if above the last cloud
Swimming in a sea of crystal radiance—
I am only a spark of the holy fire,
I am only a whisper of the holy voice.

## String Quartet No. 3, Opus 30 (1927)

Moderato
Adagio
Intermezzo: Allegro moderato
Rondo: Molto moderato

Inspired by the structure of Schubert's D. 804 A minor "Rosamunde" Quartet, Schoenberg cast his Opus 30 quartet in traditional sonata form. Now entering his clearer, more fluid "classical" phase, he had refined his twelve-tone system to accommodate note repetitions within statements of the row, and he freely used row fragments as motivic material. Opus 30 (approximately 30 minutes duration) carries no key signatures, although the primary cadences fall on C major.

The Moderato begins with a five-note ostinato (G-E-D sharp-A-C) repeated in a long phrase moving dynamically from loud to very soft; this figure pervades the movement through various permutations. Cast in free sonata form, the movement develops two contrasting ideas with emphatic fluctuations of tempo and register. The second theme, marked cantabile, features expressive duets between instrument pairs.

Adagio, five variations on a row characterized by wide intervals, begins as the instruments enter sequentially with expressive statements. Themes are developed with restless, aphoristic accompaniments, and the movement concludes in a calm atmosphere.

Intermezzo, cast in classical scherzo form (ABA), is designated scherzando, or rhythmically playful. A smoother central section provides contrast, and after the return of the opening material the movement ends with a *pesante* (heavy) cadence. Rondo (very moderate tempo) alternates duets with piquant *spiccato* (lightly bouncing) accompaniments and sustained passages marked *pesante*. Expressive tempo fluctuations articulate the structure. A calming tempo brings the work to a quiet conclusion.

## String Quartet No. 4, Opus 37 (1936)

Allegro molto, energico
Comodo
Largo
Allegro

Schoenberg wrote his Opus 37 Quartet soon after he had relocated to California, where he had accepted a professorship at the University of California at Los Angeles. Written within six weeks, the fourth quartet shows his command of classical principles. Schoenberg wrote: "I owe very, very much to Mozart. If one studies the way in which I write string quartets, one will see that I have learned much from him—and I am proud of it!" In Opus 37 Schoenberg uses twelve-tone technique with expressive freedom. Perhaps owing to his emulation of Mozart, the themes are now coherent, the rhythmic patterns move with suppleness, the homophonic and contrapuntal passages balance.

Cast in sonata form, the opening Allegro develops two contrasting themes, the first forceful (its row is heard in the first five bars) and the second marked *dolce* (sweet). After a development of ideas with new articulations such as tremolo and a restatement of ideas, the movement closes with full chords marked *pesante*.

Comodo (comfortable), marked slow and gentle, features motifs with wide intervals and strong dynamic contrasts (fortissimo to pianissimo within the measure). Constructed in ABA form, the central section is varied by contrasting colors created through *ponticello* and the use of mutes, as well as rhythmic alterations.

The Largo, cast in ABAB form, begins with a sustained, thinly textured statement that Schoenberg identifies as a recitative. In the alternate B section double stops create full, chordal harmonies. The A section returns in a condensed format, and the shorter B section returns with commentary by Schoenberg: "The first time the B section serves as lyrical contrast to the dramatic outbreak of the recitative, which it must overcome by the power of its inner warmth; the second time its purpose is to prepare for the conclusion."

The rondo finale, marked *agitato* (agitated), offers five variations of the theme, developed with piquancy through *spiccato* (bounced) bowing and colorful effects such as *col legno* (played with the wood of the bow) and *ponticello* (played at the bridge for a glassy sound). Three episodes intervene between statements. Schoenberg remarked of this movement: "This Allegro movement contains a wealth of thematic material because each repetition is extensively altered, introducing new formulations."

ALBAN BERG
B. FEBRUARY 9, 1885 IN VIENNA,
D. DECEMBER 24, 1935 IN VIENNA

Perhaps because of his deep human empathy and ongoing social activism, Alban Berg became the leading composer of the Expressionist movement, a late Romantic outgrowth that sought to convey the full range of man's psychological experience. In both his Expressionist operas *Wozzeck* (1914–1921) and *Lulu* (1928–1934), as well as his instrumental music, Berg conveyed various states of mind through intensely wrought melodies and heightened harmonic color. Essentially a lyricist, Berg favored elaborate songful lines, often based on number sequences, that develop through connected motivic webs. These lines are most often set to dense harmonies that are tonally ambiguous but still relate to late nineteenth-century practice. In part a traditionalist, Berg chose established forms such as sonata structure, romantic three-part song form, and the rondo as vehicles for his expressive style.

It is significant that Berg absorbed his mentor Schoenberg's twelve-tone concept but that he observed its technique with his individual voice and always with his characteristic warmth of affect. In works such as his *Lyric Suite*, Berg uses twelve-tone methods to create colorful background murmurs, and for the opera *Lulu*, a work of forceful dramatic symbolism, he derives its characters' motifs from permutations of a twelve-tone row. Berg's student Theodor Adorno states that he also learned the system of "developing variation" from Schoenberg and passed it along to his students: "The main principle he conveyed was that of variation. Everything is supposed to develop out of something else and yet be intrinsically different."

Of the three members of the Second Viennese School, Berg was the most obsessed with numerical patterns as well as the character of individual numbers. The number 23 held special fascination for Berg, possibly because he felt it related to a critical biorhythmic cycle. Works such as his Opus 3 String Quartet develop with reference to number sequences that carried for him mystical connections.

## *String Quartet, Opus 3 (1910)*

Langsam
Mässige Viertel

Written near the end of his tutelage with Schoenberg and premiered in 1911, Berg's Opus 3 was modeled in part on his mentor's first two string quartets. Berg's harmonic language especially resembles these prototypes because it hovers at the boundary between the expanded harmonic language of Wagner and atonality. Despite its high degree of chromaticism, the strong tonal resolutions at important structural points give Opus 3 harmonic clarity. The quartet has been identified as the first extended composition to be based throughout on symmetrical pitch relations.

After the quartet's immensely successful premiere, Berg described Opus 3 in a letter: "It is a work of solemn sweetness and ecstasy. It is full of wild and risky passages that ideally become pure euphony in a classic sense." Soon after, Berg sold personal belongings to finance the quartet's publication, which helped to establish his reputation.

Freely constructed in sonata form, the dense and introspective Langsam (slow) develops two songful themes. Both opening ideas, built on a modified twelve-tone scale, suggest the lyrical influence of Schoenberg's *Verklärte Nacht*. The development explores primarily the more delicate second theme. An energetic new motif is introduced in the recapitulation and reiterated at the coda, which also recalls the opening idea. Berg wrote that the movement should end "in an atmosphere of great exaltation."

The agitated second movement (moderate quarter note), which thematically references the "Love Duet" from Wagner's *Tristan und Isolde,* is structured as a rondo with five transformations of the primary motif separated by four contrasting ideas. Near the end of the movement the opening theme of the Langsam is recalled as unification for the work.

## *"Lyric Suite" (1926)*

Allegretto gioviale
Andante amoroso
Allegretto misterioso—Trio estatico
Adagio appassionato
Presto delirando—Tenebroso
Largo desolato

Obsessed with extra-musical associations, Berg frequently personalized his themes by deriving musical equivalents to names and events. From these resulting motifs he created a vast web of structural relationships. His philosopher friend Theodor Adorno identified Berg's *Lyric Suite* (1926) as "latent opera" because of its interconnected and emotional themes.

*Lyric Suite* has often been heard as an abstract work that achieves drama both through its progressively more contrasting tempos and through changes of character among its six movements. However, in 1977 Berg scholar George Perle discovered a new score with the composer's personal annotations. This revelation has led to a programmatic interpretation of the work as a depiction of the secret love affair between Hanna Fuchs-Robettin and Berg, both of whom were married at the time and living with their spouses.

On the opening page of the *Suite* Berg wrote: "I have secretly inserted our initials H. F. and A. B. into the music ... may it be a small monument to our great love." Since in the German context H is equivalent to the note B and the letter B becomes the note B flat, Berg easily weaves their initials into the musical pattern A-B flat-B-F. This theme is an important component of the Suite's tone row—Berg's arrangement of each of the twelve tones of the octave into "Hanna's motif."

After three introductory chords containing all twelve tones of the chromatic scale, the violin plays this row at the beginning of the Allegretto gioviale (cheerful and moderately fast). Berg states that this sonata form movement "gives no hint of the tragedy to follow."

At the top of the Andante amoroso (leisurely and lovingly) Berg writes a notation to Hanna: "To you and your children I have dedicated this rondo—a musical form in which the themes (specifically your theme), closing the charming circle, continually recur." Hanna's melody, again heard in the first violin, is twice interrupted by musical figures that represent her children. The repeated Cs in the viola—"do" in solfeggio terminology—represent her daughter's nickname, "Dodo."

In the Allegro misterioso (fast and mysterious) the twelve-tone row recurs as a murmuring coloristic device. Berg inscribes the beginning date of their relationship together with the statement that "Everything was still a mystery—a mystery to us." An agitated "trio estatico" section varies the movement's center.

As the climactic fourth movement, Adagio appassionato (slow and passionate), subsides, Berg writes widely spaced words: "And fading—into—the wholly, ethereal, spiritual, transcendental ..."

Berg's commentary for the Presto delirando (fast and delirious) fifth movement refers to "painful unrest" and "forebodings of pains and horrors to come." Largo desolato (very slow and desolate), the closing movement, includes a German translation of Baudelaire's poem "De Profundis clamavi" (I cry from the depths) from his collection *Les Fleurs du mal* (The Flowers of Evil) as well as the love motif from Wagner's *Tristan und Isolde*.

ANTON WEBERN
B. DECEMBER 3, 1883 IN VIENNA,
D. SEPTEMBER 15, 1945 IN MITTERSILL NEAR SALZBURG

The third member of the Second Viennese School, Anton Webern was a reserved idealist whose small body of works exerted a profound influence on twentieth-century composers as diverse as Messiaen, Stravinsky, and Stockhausen. Fond of intricate structures that convey hidden meanings, Webern wrote his doctoral dissertation on the Renaissance techniques of Heinrich Isaac (1450–1517) while simultaneously studying serial composition with Arnold Schoenberg. Since the Nazi government disliked his subtle, aphoristic works, Webern composed in obscurity, supporting himself primarily through proofreading. He was fatally shot by a soldier at the end of World War II when, disregarding military curfew, he strolled outside his home to smoke a cigar.

It is thought that Webern's study of Isaac's work, in which each note carries significance, influenced him to compose with extreme economy of means. The most radical of the Second Viennese group, Webern aimed to eliminate all extraneous gesture. He achieved the utmost compression of form through systematic organization of all parameters—pitch, rhythm, register, dynamics, and timbre. Like Isaac and his school, motifs are often developed through strict canons between voices. Carefully placed points of silence serve to define structure. Sparse textures and pointillistic melodic lines characterize Webern's work both before and after his adoption of Schoenberg's twelve-tone technique—an organizing system heard in his 1928 String Quartet. It has been observed that since emotion is a by-product of structure in his work, Webern paved the way for the mathematical and electronic procedures of the following generation.

## Rondo for String Quartet (1906)

Webern wrote his Rondo for String Quartet in 1906 but chose not to pursue publication. Accidentally discovered and subsequently published in 1965, the Rondo reflects Webern's early pre-atonal style, based on German late Romanticism. A single movement marked "Bewegt" (with motion), the Rondo shows Webern's command of the traditional quartet idiom. Yet there are indications of his growing interest in atonality, which at this time he experimented with in his piano works. The chromatic voice leading of this D minor work, which develops with the clear timbres and spare textures heard throughout Webern's oeuvre, leads to tantalizing oscillations between whole-tone and diatonic harmonies.

## *Six Bagatelles, Op. 9 (1913)*

Mässig
Leicht bewegt
Ziemlich fliessend
Sehr langsam
Äusserst langsam
Fliessend

The Opus 9 Bagatelles resulted from Webern's restructuring of two earlier efforts. He had intended for bagatelles two through five—marked "Gently moving," "Moderately flowing," "Very slow," and "Extremely slow"—to form a complete string quartet. Bagatelles one and six—"Moderate" and "Flowing"—were intended to be a new quartet's outer movements. Each bagatelle is a compressed statement that requires only a page of score and lasts the maximum of one minute. Meticulously constructed unities, the bagatelles cohere through tiny, interconnected gestures of pitch, dynamics, tone color, and register. Often called "the master of the pianissimo espressivo," Webern requires the utmost discipline from his performers to achieve his ethereal yet dramatic effects.

Schoenberg's preface to the Opus 9 publication offers important commentary: "Though the brevity of these pieces is a persuasive advocate for them, that very brevity requires an advocate. Consider what moderation is required to express oneself so briefly; to express a novel in a single gesture, joy in a single breath.... These pieces can be understood only by those who believe in the unique expressive power of music."

## String Quartet, Opus 28 (1938)

Mässig
Gemächlich
Sehr fliessend

Webern wrote his Opus 28 String Quartet after receiving a commission from the American patroness Elizabeth Sprague Coolidge. Like all of Webern's mature works, the quartet is based on a twelve-tone row, a specific arrangement of each of the chromatic tones of the scale. The first four notes outline a motive on the name BACH (B flat, A, C, B natural), the second four notes invert this segment, and the final four notes transpose the initial BACH motif a sixth higher. The opening movement (Moderately) is a set of six variations on this row, each unfolding as the melodic cells continuously mutate through inversions, expansions, and adjustments of position. Changes of tempo articulate a three-part fast-slow-fast structure in which each section develops two variations.

Webern called his two-minute long second movement (Leisurely) a "miniature scherzo that is a perpetual four-part canon." Entries in his sketchbook describe it as evocations of "seed, life, water (forest)." Its slower middle section provides a lyrical contrast. The third movement (Very flowing) develops in three-part form with fugal episodes heard in the outer sections. According to Webern's sketchbook, this movement was partially intended to recall Schwabegg, his mother's burial place.

By 1938 both Zemlinsky and Schoenberg had fled to the United States to escape the Nazis. Berg had already died, and Webern was not to survive the coming war. Despite all obstacles, their influences continued into the mid-century and beyond.

# THREE

# Revolutionary France

In 1879 Romanticist Camille Saint-Saëns spoke as France's oracle: "Tonality is in its death throes. There will be an eruption of the Oriental modes, whose variety is immense. Rhythm, scarcely exploited, will be developed. From all this will emerge a new art." Saint-Saëns's prescience was soon realized through Impressionism, the post-tonal movement launched by Claude Debussy, and later in the century by the exoticism of Olivier Messiaen, who blended ancient modes with sounds from the natural world. Early twentieth-century French composers, by tradition less committed to rigorous formal development than their Germanic counterparts, were receptive to all possibilities. Rhythms derived both from inflections of the French language and dance movements had already influenced a fluid national voice, heard especially in the sensitive works of Romanticist Gabriel Fauré. Poetry often guided composition, and composers such as Guillaume Lekeu even set their own texts (*Trois poèmes*, 1892).

A catalyst for change was the iconoclast Erik Satie (1866–1925), often characterized as "a composer of genius but little talent." Satie fascinated his generation with hypnotically repetitive works such as *Choses vues à droit et à gauche (sans lunettes)* (Things Seen from the Right and Left, Without Glasses) and *Gymnopédies* (Three Dances by Greek Athletes, numbers one and three orchestrated by his friend Claude Debussy). A revitalizing force that portended the irreverent Andy Warhol in the later twentieth century (who famously stated that "Art is whatever you can get away with"), Satie has earned recognition as the Godfather of Europe's avant-garde movement.

Paris after 1900 was widely renowned as Europe's most sophisticated intellectual and artistic center. The City of Light became the mecca for émigrés such as Prokofiev and Stravinsky, uncertain about Russia's artistic future, and young composers seeking educational opportunities, such as Villa-Lobos and Vaughan Williams. These visitors' unique concepts were exchanged among receptive French composers—especially those who perceived stagnation in the establishment's late Romanticism. A product of this mélange, the group *Les Six* (discussed below) stood on the edge of respectability with their bold experiments, particularly in the genre of chamber music. Their ideas influenced later French composers such as Jacques Ibert and pervaded Europe's mainstream and avant-garde circles.

CLAUDE DEBUSSY
B. AUGUST 22, 1862 AT SAINT-GERMAIN-EN-LAYE, FRANCE,
D. MARCH 25, 1918 IN PARIS

A generative force for twentieth-century music, Claude Debussy has been honored as the Father of Musical Impressionism. Classically trained at the Paris Conservatory, he infuriated his professors by flaunting its theoretic dogma (such as avoid parallel fifths and parallel counterpoint but do pursue orderly resolution of seventh chords and other dissonant structures). Awarded the Prix de Rome, a coveted prize granting three years of study in Italy, Debussy abandoned the honor after a year of mutual misunderstandings; he then relocated to Russia to serve as house musician and teacher for Tchaikovsky's patroness, Nadezhda von Meck. Impatient to begin a serious career, he left to join France's forward-looking arts community. He soon conceived his goal—a new musical art that would conjure the nuanced atmosphere that Monet and Cézanne conveyed through painting and that Stéphane Mallarmé achieved through his Symbolist poetry.

Debussy concluded that these "Impressionist" artists and writers, so labeled since the 1870s, owed their subtly evocative images to their liberation from rigid images and ideas. He observed that the short, pointillist brush strokes of painters such as Georges Seurat (1859–1891) cohered optically to form a full yet nuanced image. Perhaps most importantly, he perceived that the Symbolists' fragmentary word groupings came together to convey complete ideas. Returning to the roots of both language and music, Debussy began to consider linguistic sound patterns as building materials for his individual art. He gradually achieved his own Impressionism through five critical elements:

1. *Flexible rhythms*. Debussy's long phrases develop with varied rhythmic accents and quicksilver metrical shifts. Numerous tempo markings such as "gradually accelerate" and "a little slower" occur throughout.

2. *Fluent melodies*. Exploiting the sensuous possibilities of the French language, Debussy applied its rhythmic flexibility to his melodies, subtly woven into a sonorous tapestry with balance achieved through repetition of fragments.

3. *"Weightless" harmonies*. Debussy devised a tonal system that imparted a sense of weightlessness. He dispensed with the traditional "functional" strong-weak tonal hierarchy implicit in the major/minor Western scale system. He then constructed chords based on the whole-tone scale, a six-note framework with equidistant pitches (for example C-D-E-F sharp-G sharp-A sharp), imparting an atmosphere of ineffability. Ancient Greek scale patterns or scales of a limited note range (such as the pentatonic) provided alternate foundations.

4. *Luminous textures*. Bow effects such as tremolo and *sul ponticello* create shimmer, and the frequent use of mutes colors timbre. Varied left hand ostinato figuration throughout all instrumental ranges animates development. Subtle changes of dynamics are heard throughout.

5. *Bold ornamentation*. Colorful chains of intervals, often pungent dissonances such as the second or seventh, accompany the melody in parallel motion.

*String Quartet in G Minor, Opus 10 (1893)*

Animé et très décidé
Assez vif et bien rythmé
Andantino, doucement expressif
Très modéré

Debussy's Opus 10 string quartet brought the Impressionist movement, generated two decades earlier by the painter Claude Monet and the symbolist poet Stéphane Mallarmé, into the musical sphere. He imparted a similar atmosphere of the ineffable by emphasizing color and nuance rather than the systematic thematic and harmonic development of the Central European tradition. The quartet's flexible melodies, often based on whole tone or non-Western scales, are supported by shifting harmonies, subtle dynamics, and rapidly changing meters to create a uniquely sensitive and haunting style.

His first impressionist masterwork, the Quartet in G Minor reveals both established techniques and evidence of his revolutionary new language. Its movements conform to traditional sonata, scherzo, and three-part song form structures. The influence of his older contemporary César Franck can be heard in the quartet's cyclic form—a unifying device in which related thematic material permeates all movements. The quartet's evocative sonorities anticipate the impressionistic world that is further enhanced through literary associations in the orchestral work *Prélude à l'après-midi d'un faune* (Prelude to the Afternoon of a Faun, 1894).

The quartet opens with a strongly accented theme in the ancient Phrygian mode. Kaleidoscopic permutations of this motto idea recur throughout the entire quartet. A second idea, marked "expressive and sustained," leads to quiet restatements of the opening motif. Key centers change rapidly in the development area, expressively shaped through tempo adjustments and phrases contoured with a large dynamic range. The return to G minor and a forte statement of the opening motto signals the recapitulation. A coda marked "very animated" concludes the movement.

At the 1889 Paris Exposition, a Javanese gamelan orchestra had enchanted Debussy, and his contemporary critics heard similarly exotic effects in the scherzo (G major). Marked "rather fast and rhythmic" and animated by colorful pizzicato figures, this piquant movement inspired César Franck to observe that "Debussy creates music on needle points." (Franck's observation led critics to rename Debussy's style *pointilliste*, which Debussy preferred to the prevailing term Impressionist.) Cast in traditional three-part scherzo form with harmonic excursions at its quiet center, the movement concludes with intricate rhythmic variations on its opening idea.

The third movement, in three-part song form, is framed by a passionate song for muted strings. At its center a lyrical episode for viola and cello ensues without mutes. The tempo gradually accelerates, and a muted cello cadenza leads to the final statement.

The finale opens with a quiet introduction and accelerates with a fugato section based on the quartet's opening theme. An inventive synthesis of material from the preceding three movements, this agile movement concludes with a brilliant coda.

## "Danse sacrée et danse profane" (1903)

Debussy wrote his *Danse sacrée et danse profane* after a 1903 commission from Pleyel, the Parisian manufacturer of the new chromatic harp. Pleyel had patented this harp in 1897 and sought repertoire for diploma examinations at the Brussels Conservatory. However, performers remained loyal to the conventional harp, tuned according to the diatonic notes of the major scale and equipped with seven foot pedals, each of which controlled a scale degree and its chromatic alterations. Pleyel's new harp, constructed without pedals, provided a separate string for each chromatic note throughout its range. This unwieldy invention was soon abandoned primarily because of the amount of time needed to tune its many strings before each performance. Thus Debussy's *Danse sacrée et danse profane*, one of the few works composed for chromatic harp, has been performed on the traditional harp almost from the outset. It has become one of the most popular works in the harp literature.

Early listeners assumed that the main theme of *Danse sacrée* was taken from a well-known piano work by Portuguese composer Francisco de Lacerda. Another possible inspiration was Erik Satie's *Gymnopédies*, which Debussy greatly admired and even chose to orchestrate. Most probably Debussy intended for this slow and modally harmonized opening movement to evoke ancient music, an appropriate reference for Pleyel's new version of this most antique of instruments. The faster *Danse profane*, influenced by Spanish folk song, develops with rich passagework and colorful harmonic inflections.

## *Sonata for Flute, Viola, and Harp (1916)*

Pastorale: Lento dolce rubato
Interlude: Tempo di Minuetto
Final: Allegro moderato ma risoluto

The Sonata for Flute, Viola, and Harp was composed as France suffered through World War I. Debussy had projected a set of six sonatas for various combinations of instruments but completed only three before his death. Each of these works offers a different aspect of Debussy's style, but as a group they can be heard as statements of patriotism. His impressionistic gestures, now minimized, are replaced by a retrospective of classical seventeenth- and eighteenth-century French models emphasizing the older values of grace, formal balance, and logic. On the title page of each work he signed *Musicien Français* next to his name.

Debussy originally conceived the sonata to include the plaintive oboe timbre but decided that the viola would contribute a more sonorous balance. He described the work: "It is terribly melancholy, and I do not know if one should laugh or cry with it. Perhaps a little of both?"

The opening *Pastorale* explores two contrasting themes in sonata form. A faster episode replaces the central development section; the recapitulation reorders the opening material, and the movement reaches a quiet conclusion. The three-part *Interlude* offers a graceful minuet and an animated middle section; the minuet returns with the marking "sweetly and sadly," perhaps an allusion to Debussy's melancholy during wartime. Like the opening, the *Final* develops episodically, but its affect is more spirited. Near the end the first *Pastorale* theme reappears, and an animated coda concludes the work.

MAURICE RAVEL
B. MARCH 7, 1875 IN CIBOURE, FRANCE,
D. DECEMBER 28, 1937 IN PARIS

Debussy's younger contemporary, Ravel adopted his colleague's innovations but shaped them according to his individual voice. Despite the harmonic modernity of his musical language, Ravel was essentially a classicist. Compared to Debussy, his rhythmic patterns are more incisive, his melodic lines less decoratively blurred, his forms more clearly defined by cadence points. However, these two preeminent French composers enjoyed a mutually stimulating relationship. Since Ravel grew up near Spain's border, he was familiar with its dance rhythms, which Debussy borrowed for piano works such as *Estampes* (1903). The major beneficiary of Debussy's revolutionary techniques, Ravel consistently enriched his own tonal palette with colorfully expanded harmonies to create his desired atmosphere.

## String Quartet in F Major (1904)

Allegro moderato—Très doux
Assez vif—Très rythmé
Très lent
Vif et agité

Ravel composed his only string quartet during his affiliation as a student auditor at the Paris Conservatory. Two years previously he had been expelled from the formal program because of his unwillingness to write fugues: however, Gabriel Fauré continued to welcome Ravel to his composition class. Ravel dedicated his F Major Quartet to Fauré and with his encouragement submitted its first movement to the Prix de Rome jury. Three times previously the jury, comprised primarily of conservatory professors, had rejected Ravel's application for this important prize, which included three years of financial support. In his latest attempt he was eliminated in the first round—an outrage that touched off a scandal in the artistic community.

Controversy continued to surround the F Major Quartet after its official 1904 premiere. Critics heard striking parallels to Debussy's Quartet in G Minor (1893), which in fact had been a model, and comparisons were much discussed. The publicity upset Debussy and strained the composers' cordial friendship—but ironically it was Debussy who bestowed the highest praise on the new quartet. When Ravel asked for his opinion, Debussy replied: "In the name of the gods of music, and in mine, do not touch a single note of what you have written in your quartet."

Although Ravel's quartet was undeniably influenced by Debussy's opus, the new work essentially differs because of its clearer structure. Unlike Debussy, who strove to express the ineffable through a subtly nuanced mosaic of themes, Ravel grounds his quartet with clearly cadenced phrases. Yet Debussy's influence is heard in Ravel's free harmonic language and in his exploration of instrumental color. Like Debussy, Ravel was influenced by Far Eastern music, and one hears in his work a similar Javanese influence.

The Quartet in F Major is a cyclic work in which material from the opening movement recurs in the third and fourth movements to unify the structure. Classical poise is heard in the opening Allegro moderato, based on two lyrical themes. A long, rising F major scale in the cello's opening bars firmly grounds that key. As a parallel to Debussy's quartet, Ravel's "rather lively" second movement conjures the image of a Javanese gamelan orchestra. Its first theme is played pizzicato in the Aeolian mode (corresponding to an octave of piano white keys beginning on A); the serene second theme provides contrast. The colorful and rhapsodic third movement ("Very slow") interweaves themes from the Allegro moderato with new material. The vigorous finale, "Lively and agitated," alternates tremolo passages in quintuple meter with songful triple-meter passages derived from the first movement. A brief reprise of the movement's opening material and a passage of ascending thirds brings the work to a stunning conclusion.

*Sonatine, arranged for Flute, Viola, and Harp (1905)*

Modéré
Mouvement de Menuet
Animé

Ravel completed his *Sonatine* for piano solo in 1905 but had begun it two years earlier. Needing money, he entered its first movement in a magazine competition that offered a 100 franc prize for a piano sonatina of 75 bars or less. Ravel's contribution exceeded this limit, and he was disqualified—ironically, no winner was declared since the magazine went bankrupt. At its premiere the *Sonatine* was widely praised for its fine classical design, intriguing harmonic structures, and unique rhythmic patterns. However, Ravel worried about the difficulty of the rapid third movement, which even he did not dare perform publicly on his piano tours. He was pleased when harpist and composer Carlos Salzedo adapted the *Sonatine* for flute, cello, and harp, especially since its substantial technical problems could then be shared among three instruments. Ravel later transcribed the work for viola.

Modéré, in sonata form, offers two contrasting themes, the first animated and insouciant, the second more introspective. The central movement, in triple time, conjures a refined and elegant dance. The "perpetual motion" finale is a virtuoso tour de force revealing all the challenges of Ravel's original piano version. Its material is based on transformations of the Sonatine's opening ideas.

## Piano Trio in A Minor (1914)

Modéré
Pantoum: Assez vif
Passacaille: Très large
Final: Animé

In February 1914 Ravel left Paris to be near his mother in Saint-Jean-de-Luz, a small Basque fishing village near the Spanish border. He planned to work on two projects—a piano concerto incorporating Basque themes and a piano trio—but abandoned plans for the concerto and incorporated its themes, which he described as "Basque in color," into the trio's first movement. Composition proceeded well until the outbreak of World War I, which coincided with initial work on the finale. Ravel was eager to serve in the military, and in fact later became an ambulance driver for the French army. Yet he was reluctant to leave his aged mother. He wrote to a friend: "If you only knew how I am suffering. If I leave my poor old mother it will surely kill her. But so as not to think of this, I am working with the sureness and lucidity of a madman." Because of his feverish pace, the trio was soon completed. With its brilliant writing, wide range of instrumental color, and refined elegance, it is considered one of Ravel's finest works.

The first movement explores Spanish rhythms and melodies with French elegance. Its two themes are based on a popular Basque folk dance with a persistent 3-2-3 rhythm. After a brief development, the movement concludes as a fragment of the opening theme fades into a rhythmic outline tapped in the piano's low register.

Ravel entitled the scherzo movement "Pantoum," a Malay poetic form in which the second and fourth lines of one stanza become the first and third of the next. Its rapid rhythms, pizzicati, and harmonics create a dazzling effect. In the middle section the strings continue their brilliant passage work in a fast 3/4 meter while the piano articulates contrasting chorale-like phrases in 4/2 time.

The clear melodic contours, distinct rhythms, and lucid structure of the third movement, a *passacaglia*, suggest Ravel's classical orientation. Ten variations of its opening theme are arranged in arch form. The statements begin quietly and gradually gain fervor, then calm as the movement approaches its conclusion.

The energetic Animé, following without pause, opens with fortissimo repeated violin arpeggios. The primary theme, related to the principal theme of the first movement, is heard in the piano. Virtuosic trills, arpeggios, and tremolos propel the movement toward its exhilarating conclusion on a high A major chord.

*"Chansons madécasses" for Voice, Flute, Cello, and Piano (1926)*

Nahandove
Aoua!
Il est doux de se coucher

As did the poet Pushkin and the statesman Chateaubriand,

Ravel admired the *Poésies érotiques* of Évariste de Parny (1753–1814), a Creole who boldly translated original Madagascan texts into French. Ravel commented on the enhanced sensuality of these song settings: "I believe the *Chansons madécasses* introduce a dramatic—indeed erotic—element because of the subject matter of Parny's poems. The three songs are performed by a quartet group in which the voice plays the role of the principal instrument. Simplicity is all-important."

I. *Nahandove*, Andante quasi allegretto. In the opening song, the singer awaits a lover: "Nahandove, O beautiful Nahandove! The bird of night has begun its eerie calling, the half moon pours down upon my head, and the earliest dew moistens my hair. This is the hour, who can be detaining you, O beautiful Nahandove?"

II. *Aoua*, Andante. The second song celebrates a conquest averted: "Aoua! Beware of the white man, dwellers along our shores! In our fathers' time, white men set foot on this island ... a menacing fort arose, with thunder concealed in bronze mouths. The sky took up our battle and unleashed on them poisonous winds. Now they are dead and gone, and we live free!"

III. *Il est doux de se coucher*, Lento. In the third song the singer contemplates his leisure: "It is good to lie down in the heat of the day under a leafy tree, and to wait thus until the evening wind brings a cooling breath. Women, come to me. While I take my rest, delight my ear with your soothing voices."

## LES SIX

During the cultural ferment between the two World Wars, propinquity and common ideals created friendships among six Parisian composers: Georges Auric (1899–1983), Louis Durey (1888–1979), Arthur Honegger (1892–1955), Darius Milhaud (1892–1974), Francis Poulenc (1899–1963), and Germaine Tailleferre (1892–1983). Dubbed *Les Six*, a name inspired by the ruggedly independent "Russian Five" of the nineteenth century, the group aimed to rejuvenate a musical establishment they perceived as "stagnant and boring." Guided by two avant-garde gurus, the writer Jean Cocteau and his composer friend Erik Satie, the group *Les Six* was united in its aversion to Romanticism and Impressionism, its desire for clear and simple expression, and its disdain of pretense. An early member of *Les Six*, Darius Milhaud wrote about the group: "The six of us came together because we were pals and appeared on the same music programs, no matter if our temperaments and personalities weren't at all the same. Auric and Poulenc followed the ideas of Cocteau, Honegger followed German Romanticism, and myself, Mediterranean lyricism!"

Since the group had little access to large orchestral ensembles, its members created much chamber music for diverse combinations of instruments. Fond of free and daring experiments, the group also believed in "melody that comes from the heart," which spokesperson Darius Milhaud insisted was the basis of music. Much of the *Les Six* repertoire reveals a delicate lyricism that ironically indicates reverence for France's great melodists of the not-so-recent past (such as François Couperin, 1668–1733).

GERMAINE TAILLEFERRE
B. APRIL 19, 1982 IN SAINT-MAUR-DES-FOSSÉS,
VAL DE MARNE, FRANCE,
D. NOVEMBER 7, 1983 IN PARIS

*Piano Trio (1916, 1978)*

Allegro animato
Allegro vivace
Moderato
Très animé

The sole woman of the forward-looking *Les Six*, Germaine
Tailleferre was also one of the few early twentieth-century women
to study at the Paris Conservatory. Her promising works attracted
the attention of Francis Poulenc and Darius Milhaud, who invited
her to join their group *Les Nouveaux Jeunes* (the New Young Ones),
which after 1926 became known as *Les Six*. Tailleferre was soon
immersed in the rarified artist communities of Montmartre and
Montparnasse.

Tailleferre has been slow to gain recognition despite a career
that spanned six decades. Many of her works were published posthumously. She once stated with typical modesty: "I write music
because it amuses me. It's not great music, I know, but it's gay,
lighthearted music which is sometimes compared with the minor
masters of the eighteenth century. That makes me proud."

The first version of the Piano Trio was written during her student days. Tailleferre reworked it substantially in 1978, at which
time she added the second Allegro vivace movement and the finale,
"Very animated." More romantic in spirit than other *Les Six* works,
the gracefully nuanced trio suggests the lyric influence of Fauré
and the modernist harmonies of Ravel. Animated passagework
decorates its melodic lines, often propelled by fanciful arabesques
and piquant figuration. The richly romantic sonorities of the

Moderato movement provide moments of calm in this energetic and playful trio.

DARIUS MILHAUD
B. SEPTEMBER 4, 1892 IN AIX-EN-PROVENCE, FRANCE,
D. JUNE 22, 1974 IN GENEVA

*"Suite d'après Corrette" for Oboe, Clarinet, and Bassoon,
Opus 161 (1936)*

Entrée et Rondeau
Tambourin
Musette
Sérénade
Fanfare
Rondeau
Menuets
Le Coucou

A composer whose natural facility has resulted in an enormous output of impressive range, the classically-trained Darius Milhaud derived inspiration from diverse sources—jazz, native Brazilian music, Stravinsky's polytonal structures, and especially theater. Milhaud, who frequently wrote incidental music for various theatrical productions, describes his 1936 *Suite d'après Corrette* in his autobiography *My Happy Life*: "For the translation of *Romeo and Juliet* by Jouve and Pitoëff I wrote a suite based on themes by Corrette, a *petit-maître* of the eighteenth century, very freely handled as regards harmony and melodic line. It was very pleasant to work with Pitoëff. With the manuscript open before us we would pick out passages in which music was required and work out timing together. Then I composed my music, which corresponded exactly to the spoken text."

Milhaud conjures the gentle spirit of Michel Corrette (1707–1795), who wrote much theater music based on popular tunes of his day. Each of these brief movements displays a delicate lyricism and delightful harmonic reinvention.

## Suite for Violin, Clarinet, and Piano, Opus 157b (1936)

Ouverture
Divertissement
Jeu
Introduction et Final

Milhaud's Opus 157 Suite is his own arrangement of incidental music he had written for Jean Anouilh's play *Le voyageur sans bagage* (The Traveler without Luggage). The *Ouverture*, marked "lively and gay," develops with imitating themes. *Divertissement* explores the range of sonorities possible with differing pairs of instruments—violin and clarinet, clarinet and piano, violin and piano—and concludes in "quartet" style with one line each for violin and clarinet and two voices in the piano. After an animated opening section, the movement grows reflective. *Jeu* (Game), scored for violin playing double stops and clarinet, suggests a light-hearted jest. A dignified introduction leads to the *Final* (marked fast), which resembles a lively *gigue*.

FRANCIS POULENC
B. JANUARY 7, 1899 IN PARIS,
D. JANUARY 30, 1963 IN PARIS

*Trio for Oboe, Bassoon, and Piano (1926)*

Presto
Andante
Rondo: Très vif

Early in his career, the self-taught Poulenc gained notoriety as the most impudent member of the revolutionary *Les Six*. Influenced by the irreverence of Erik Satie and the energy of his Russian émigré friend, the *enfant terrible* Sergei Prokofiev, Poulenc cultivated a breezy, dissonant style enlivened by jazz (unfortunately much of his early work has been lost or destroyed). As his career progressed, Poulenc retained early tendencies described by a critic as "half monk, half naughty boy," but also composed lyrical works that ironically suggest the influence of classical French tradition.

Poulenc composed his first major chamber work, the brisk and tuneful Trio for Oboe, Bassoon, and Piano, during a sojourn on the French Riviera in April 1926. The first movement unfolds freely with the character of a recitative. After a slow introductory interlude, the Presto develops with wit and verve; melodic fragments exchanged among the voices suggest eighteenth-century Italian opera.

After a brief piano introduction, the lyrical Andante develops as a long-lined duet between the bassoon and oboe. In the scintillating Rondo ("very fast"), statements of the principal theme alternate with inventive interludes. The rapid coda enters as an abrupt surprise.

## *Sextet for Piano and Winds (1939)*

Allegro vivace
Divertissement: Andantino
Finale: Prestissimo

Poulenc's fellow Parisians once nicknamed him *le sportif de la musique* (the sporting musician) because of the frenetic physicality emanating from his compositions. As the self-taught Poulenc matured musically, his works gradually became more sophisticated and charmingly nostalgic. But he sought deeper sentiments. Poulenc stated his ideals in a letter: "Weary of Debussy, weary of Impressionism, I seek a musical style that is healthy, clear, and robust, a style that is plainly French.... I take as my models whatever pleases me, especially from every source."

When Poulenc began his Sextet in 1932 (completed in 1939) he was becoming known as a composer of sacred works; eventually he fully expressed this voice in the opera *Dialogues des Carmélites* (1956), a religious tragedy set against the background of the French Revolution. A professional pianist, Poulenc often included keyboard in his chamber works so that he could both premiere and perform them.

A composer who "adored wind instruments, vastly preferring them to strings," Poulenc integrates the diverse color of each wind into a sonorous whole in his Sextet. The Allegro vivace (A minor) radiates high spirits. After a bassoon cadenza, the piano plays a somber melody that is a slower version of the rapid opening theme. The bright first theme returns and the movement closes with a thematic echo of its beginning.

The three-part Divertissement (A minor) begins with a contemplative oboe melody marked "sweet and expressive." Its exuberant middle section, directed to be played "twice as fast," suggests a vivacious festival. Marked "very gay," emphatic rhythmic passages alternate with lyrical statements in the rapid Finale. The pensive coda, moving "suddenly very slow," relates melodically to the opening of the first movement.

## FRENCH SWITZERLAND

IGOR STRAVINSKY
B. JUNE 17, 1892 IN ORANIENBAUM, RUSSIA,
D. APRIL 6, 1971 IN NEW YORK

*Pastorale for Violin, Oboe, English Horn, and Bassoon (1907, rescored in 1924)*

A creation of his Russian phase, Stravinsky's original version of his Pastorale was a vocalise, a textless song for voice and piano. He remained fond of the work and rescored it for various combinations of instruments over the next twenty years. Most often heard in its 1924 version, Pastorale is notable for its calm, tonally centered melodic line, now scored for violin. The wind instruments execute clear linear writing; elegant and florid ornamentation enhances the work throughout. Pastorale reveals a poised and classical aspect of Stravinsky heard during the decade of the 1920s in Paris, where he adopted Satie's precept that "the largest measure of audacity lies in simplicity."

*Three Pieces for String Quartet (1914)*

Danse
Excentrique
Cantique

Stravinsky resided in Switzerland from 1914 to 1920 and became then a Swiss citizen. While summering near Lake Geneva after the sensation of his *Rite of Spring* (1913), Stravinsky completed his Three Pieces for String Quartet. Performed from the manuscript at its New York premiere, the work was originally entitled *Grotesques*. Stravinsky had arranged for a commentator, who introduced these fragmentary, potentially baffling movements as "contrasting studies in popular, fantastic, and liturgical moods." Poetess Amy Lowell was present at the performance, and, to Stravinsky's great delight, wrote a poem evoking her sensation of hearing the enigmatic Three Pieces (partially quoted below):

First Movement
Red, blue, yellow / Drunkedness steaming in colours; / Red, yellow, blue, colours and flesh weaving together, / In and out with the dance / Coarse stuffs and hot flesh weaving together...

Second Movement
Pale violin music whiffs across the moon, / A pale smoke of violin music blows over the moon, / Cherry petals fall and flutter, / And the white Pierrot, / Wreathed in the smoke of the violins, / Splashed with cherry petals falling, falling, / Claws a grave for himself in the fresh earth / With his fingernails.

Third Movement
An organ growls in the heavy roof-groins of a church, / It wheezes and coughs. / The nave is blue with incense, / Writhing, twisting, / Snaking over the heads of the chanting priests.

In 1928 Stravinsky included the Pieces in his Four Studies for Orchestra and at that time gave them titles. The chantlike *Danse*, based on four repeating notes, resembles popular Russian tunes. Stravinsky explained that *Excentrique* was inspired by the great performance of a spastic clown. He thought highly of the solemn, religious *Cantique*, saying it contained his best music of that time.

## *"L'Histoire du soldat," Suite for Violin, Clarinet, and Piano (1918)*

The Soldier's March
The Soldier's Violin
The Little Concert
Three Dances (Tango, Waltz, Ragtime)
The Devil's Dance

Following the Revolution of 1917 Stravinsky was a Swiss expatriate, cut off from both his Russian family estates and his music royalties. Needing income, he decided to create a touring work that required few characters and instrumentalists. He based the resulting *L'Histoire du soldat* (The Soldier's Tale) on the narratives of his Russian compatriot Alexander Afanasiev, who, appalled by the cruelly enforced recruitment for the Russo-Turkish wars under Nicholas I, wrote a cycle of stories describing the adventures of a deserter and his pact with the Devil. Stravinsky felt extreme sympathy for the common soldier; exiled in Switzerland, he had avoided service in World War I, but his brother Gury had died at the Russian front.

Stravinsky collaborated with Swiss poet Charles-Ferdinand Ramuz, who created a narration with acting and dance to convey his version of the Faust legend. As the story opens, the Soldier is returning home with his fiddle in his knapsack ("The Soldier's March"). The Devil approaches and offers to exchange his magic book for the Soldier's violin ("The Soldier's Violin"). The Soldier becomes wealthy through the book's devilish guidance, but he grows weary of his riches and misses his violin. He hears of a dying Princess and visits the King's castle to cure her and win her hand. The Devil, disguised as a virtuoso violinist, is waiting for him. Since the Soldier will gain control over the Devil only if he loses his devilishly gotten money, he willingly gambles it away. Now empowered, the Soldier seizes the violin from the Devil and begins to play ("The Little Concert"). The Princess is miraculously healed by this music and dances with joy ("Three Dances"). The Devil tries to interfere, but the Soldier defeats him with the violin, which compels him to dance to exhaustion ("The Devil's Dance"). The Devil vows that if the Soldier ever leaves the castle, he will become The Devil's Own. Eventually the Soldier decides to visit his mother, and the Devil, waiting at the forbidden frontier, claims his soul.

*L'Histoire* enjoyed a successful premiere in 1918. Soon afterwards most of the cast and musicians succumbed to the flu pandemic, and the tour had to be abandoned. Stravinsky then arranged *L'Histoire* as a suite for septet, and a year later he created a five-movement trio for his clarinetist friend Werner Reinhart, who funded the work's premiere.

Stravinsky wrote that jazz, although known to him only through sheet music, was an important influence for *L'Histoire*: "I borrowed the rhythmic style of jazz not as played but as written. Jazz meant a wholly new sound in my music, and *L'Histoire* marks a final break with the Russian orchestral school in which I had been fostered." Stravinsky also drew from a great variety of other musical sources for *L'Histoire*—Russian folksong, American ragtime, Argentine tango, Viennese waltz, Swiss brass band, and Bach chorale. All these heterogeneous elements are fused to create a remarkable homogeneity of style.

FRANK MARTIN
B. SEPTEMBER 15, 1890 IN GENEVA,
D. NOVEMBER 21, 1974 IN NAARDEN, NETHERLANDS

*"Trio sur des mélodies populaires irlandaises" for Piano, Violin, and Cello (1925)*

Allegro moderato
Adagio
Gigue: Allegro

The cosmopolitan Frank Martin lived in Paris during the 1920s and immersed himself in Ravel's music and the jazz style. He wrote his delightful Piano Trio on Irish Folksongs on commission—but to his client's disappointment he ignored the obviously popular melodies from Ireland and unearthed ancient airs from the Bibliothèque Nationale. A milestone in Martin's career, the Trio evolved into a technically difficult exploitation of metric possibilities inherent in these unknown songs, and the irate patron canceled his commission.

Martin comments about his Trio: "While exploring the rich musical resources of Irish folklore, I tried to submit to its idiosyncratic character. I avoided an abuse of the melodies chosen and never burdened them with falsifying harmonies. There is no trace of development in the classical sense in this trio. The principle of musical form was sought in rhythm and the rhythmic combinations.

"The first movement is based throughout on a rhythmic progression achieved by an accelerando at successive levels, each intervention of a new musical thought entailing a slight acceleration in tempo. In this movement the return of themes hardly plays a part; it is the rhythmic rapport of the various melodies which assures the unity.

"In the Adagio there is greater thematic unity because a melody attributed to the cello reappears; but this melody always returns in the same form, in the same register and tonality, merely alighting on a constantly changing melodic and rhythmic base. In the third movement, a jig, the metric independence of the various voices is apparent.

"Summarizing, the Trio hardly draws on harmony and the polyphonic principle of imitation. Everything is achieved through the rhythm and melody which constitute the basis of Irish song and dance."

# FRANCE SINCE WORLD WAR II

OLIVIER MESSIAEN
B. DECEMBER 10, 1908 IN AVIGNON, FRANCE,
D. APRIL 27, 1992 IN CLICHY, FRANCE

In 1936 Messiaen founded the group *La jeune France* with his colleagues André Jolivet, Jean-Yves Daniel-Lesur, and Yves Baudrier. Desiring to pursue a "human and spiritual" form of expression, the group's ideal was stated by Jolivet: "Music should be a sonorous manifestation related directly to the universal cosmic condition." To reach this goal, Messiaen stressed the creation of a mystical atmosphere through imaginative harmonies, melodies, and rhythms: "Mysticism is the best subject, for it encompasses all subjects. And the abundance of technical means allows it to open up freely." Messiaen became one of the twentieth century's most influential composers both because of his originality and his committed teaching of significant contemporaneous figures such as Pierre Boulez and Karlheinz Stockhausen. Messiaen is regarded as the father of Europe's mid-century avant-garde.

Originally a composer of contemplative organ works, Messiaen's later style incorporates medieval plainchant, harmonies based on Hindu modes, and intricate rhythmic patterns. Ornithology, his avocation, has strongly influenced his composition. Convinced that birds were "the greatest of all musicians," Messiaen carefully notated their individual songs and compiled them into a catalog. Works such as his colorful and rhythmically challenging *Le merle noir* for flute and piano (The Blackbird, 1952) were based on his stylized transcriptions of bird calls. The blackbird's song was perhaps Messiaen's favorite, and its distinctive sound emerges in the opening movement of his *Quartet for the End of Time.*

## "Quatour pour la fin du temps" for Clarinet, Violin, Cello, and Piano (1941)

Liturgie de cristal
Vocalise, pour l'Ange qui annonce la fin du Temps
Abîme des oiseaux
Intermède
Louange à l'Éternité de Jésus
Danse de la fureur, pour les sept trompettes
Fouillis d'arcs-en-ciel, pour l'Ange qui annonce la fin du Temps
Louange à l'Immortalité de Jésus

Messiaen's *Quartet for the End of Time* is perhaps the most significant musical work to emerge from personal experience with World War II. Incarcerated in a prisoner of war camp in Görlitz, Germany (now Zgorzelec, Poland) from 1940 to 1942, Messiaen wrote his quartet for himself and three other musician inmates. The premiere, performed on damaged instruments, took place on a cold January day in 1941 before 400 fellow prisoners and guards. He wrote: "Never was I listened to with such rapt attention and concentration." Messiaen drew his inspiration from the Biblical book of Revelation, chapter 10, verses 1 to 7: "Then I saw a mighty angel coming down from Heaven, wrapped in a cloud, with a rainbow over his head ... and he lifted up his right hand to Heaven and swore by Him who lives for ever and ever, saying 'TIME IS AT AN END'; but in the day of the trumpet call of the seventh angel, the mystery of God shall be fulfilled." Messiaen chose to focus not on the cataclysms and monsters of the Apocalypse, but rather on its "moments of silent adoration and marvelous visions of peace." He provides annotation:

I. "Crystalline liturgy." For full quartet: "Towards three or four in the morning, a solitary bird warbles, perhaps a blackbird or a nightingale, surrounded by a haze of sound, by a halo of harmony high up in the trees. Transfer that to a religious plane: you will have the harmonious silence of Heaven. The piano provides a rhythmic ostinato (juxtaposition of three Hindu rhythms). The clarinet unfurls the song of the bird."

II. "Vocalise, for the Angel who Announces the End of Time." For full quartet: "The first part and coda evoke the strength of that powerful angel. The background: the impalpable harmonies of Heaven. Gentle, multi-colored cascades of chords envelop the almost plainchantlike melody of violin and piano."

III. "The Abyss of the Birds." Clarinet alone: "The Abyss is Time, with its sadness, its lassitude. The birds serve as a contrast: they symbolize our desire for light, for stars, for rainbows and jubilant vocalise! The bird calls are written in the fantastic and gay style of the blackbird."

IV. "Interlude." Trio for violin, cello, and clarinet: "A little scherzo, more extroverted in character, but connected to the other movements by various melodic recalls."

V. "Praise to the Eternity of Jesus." A duet for cello and piano, marked "infinitely slow, ecstatic": "Here Jesus is considered as the Word. A broad phrase, extremely slow, in the cello, magnifies with love and reverence the eternity of the powerful and sweet Word, whose 'time never runs out.' "

VI. "Dance of Fury, for the Seven Trumpets." For full quartet: "The four instruments in unison evoke reverberations of the gongs and trumpets of the Apocalypse. Music of stone, formidable, granite sonority."

VII. "Tangles of Rainbows, for the Angel who Announces the End of Time." For full quartet. "Recurring here are passages from the second movement. Piece dedicated to the Angel, and above all the Rainbow which envelops him (symbol of peace, of wisdom, and of every luminous and sonorous vibration). In my colored dreams, I underwent a whirling intermingling of sounds and color."

VIII. "Praise to the Immortality of Jesus." Duet for violin and piano. "A broad solo for the violin, a counterpart to the cello solo of the fifth movement. Why this second hymn of praise? It is the second aspect of Jesus, Jesus the Man, the Word made flesh. It is all love. Its majesty builds to an intense climax, it is the ascent of man to his God, of the child of God to his Father, of the sanctified creature to Paradise."

"—And I repeat anew: all this is mere stammering if one compares it to the overwhelming grandeur of the subject!"


JACQUES IBERT
B. AUGUST 15, 1890 IN PARIS,
D. FEBRUARY 5, 1962 IN PARIS


*Deux Interludes for Flute, Violin, and Harpsichord or Harp (1946)*

Andante espressivo
Allegro vivo

Jacques Ibert is known for sophisticated and elegantly crafted works that demand the utmost virtuosity from their performers. At the Paris Conservatory, where he won the Prix de Rome and other coveted awards, Ibert studied with the poetically refined Gabriel Fauré. Perhaps because he held positions in both Paris and Rome, Ibert became a true eclectic. An admirer of Impressionism, he also drew inspiration from Hindemith and Stravinsky's Neoclassicism, which expressed eighteenth-century concepts in modern terms. Ibert combined these diverse elements to create his own somewhat mischievous style. "All systems are valid," he said, "provided that one derives music from them."

Ibert wrote *Deux Interludes* as incidental music for Suzanne Lilar's 1946 play *Le Burlador* (The Seducer) and he subsequently published movements as a trio for flute, violin, and harpsichord or harp. It has become one of Ibert's most popular works. The tuneful first interlude, Andante espressivo, develops as a gentle three-part song with rapid passages for harp at its center. The faster second interlude, Allegro vivo, explores a winsome theme made colorful with piquant harmonies, dashing chromatic runs, and decorative grace notes.

HENRI DUTILLEUX
B. JANUARY 22, 1916 IN ANGERS, FRANCE,
D. MAY 22, 2013 IN PARIS

*"Ainsi la nuit" for String Quartet (1976)*

Ainsi la nuit
Nocturne / Parenthèse 1
Miroir d'espace / Parenthèse 2
Litanies / Parenthèse 3
Litanies 2 / Parenthèse 4
Constellations
Nocturne 2
Temps suspendu

Celebrated as France's most significant composer of the millennium, Dutilleux continued to create well beyond his 90th year of age. Educated at the Paris Conservatory, Dutilleux won the prestigious Prix de Rome, which awarded him three years of study in Italy; but he left to become a medical orderly with the French army (and a member of the Resistance) during World War II. He later taught composition at both the École Normale de Musique in Paris and the Conservatory. Dutilleux's modernist works often reveal techniques of Debussy, Roussel, and particularly Bartók, who garnered his highest praise: "By resolving in one luminous synthesis the duality between folk music and learned music, has not Bartók been the herald for a new classical age?"

Dutilleux wrote his remarkable *Ainsi la nuit* (Thus the Night) in 1976 for the Juilliard String Quartet. The work began as a set of loosely related studies that he sent to the Juilliard for commentary. Over a six-year period, he gradually linked these preliminary sketches into a web of variations and cross-references that are worked out in minute detail but are intended to appear spontaneous. Connected by interludes called "parentheses," the seven movements bear titles that conjure poetic elements of the night: "Night Piece," "Mirror of Space," "Litany," "Constellations," "Suspended Time." Each of these movements exploits a specific sound effect: pizzicati, glissandi, harmonics, register contrast, and dynamics. Dutilleux himself described the work as "a sort of nocturnal vision ... a series of 'states' with a somewhat impressionistic side to them." The eight-note chord heard at the beginning of the short introduction permeates the entire work. Themes of both the first Nocturne and the first Litanies movement are based on this sequence of notes, as is the finale. Brief and atmospheric, the movements suggest the impressionist influence of Debussy.

# FOUR

# Czech Dialogues

A complex history predates the Czech Republic, a newly independent nation informally named "Czechia" in 2016. Various empires
had long imposed rule over this landlocked nation: Habsburg;
Nazi; Soviet. When the Habsburg Empire dissolved following
World War I, the Czech Lands of Bohemia, Moravia, and the
southern portion of Silesia joined with neighboring Slovakia to
form Czechoslovakia. For the following twenty years, this First
Republic was one of the most successfully industrialized nations
in the world; the Nazis during World War II, and then the Soviets
after 1948 were eager to claim its resources. The charismatic Czech
writer and former dissident Václav Havel, the last president of these
united countries, negotiated to restore democracy after decades of
Communist rule. This ended peacefully through the non-violent
Velvet Revolution (1989), and in 1993 the Czechs and Slovaks split
to affirm their national identities.

Throughout the years of anxiety, Czechia's café culture
encouraged and sustained modernist innovations in art, literature, and music. In the capital Prague, dozens of coffee houses
served as havens for the exchange of ideas among artists as well
as repositories of available foreign journals, freely distributed to
their loyal clientele. The influence of surrealist writer Franz Kafka
(*The Metamorphosis*, 1915) continued into the later twentieth century through works of acclaimed playwrights such as Czechia's
own leader, Václav Havel. Avant-garde theater flourished in an
atmosphere of ironic pessimism. Its aesthetic was articulated by

Theodor Adorno in his *Philosophie der neuen Musik* (Philosophy of New Music, 1949): "This art reflects without any concessions, and brings to the level of consciousness, what people would like to forget."

Conservatism and innovation were heard together in early twentieth-century Czech composition, variously shaped by both its native music and its progressive literary movements. Antonín Dvořák (d. 1904), in large part a folklorist, had left an indelible imprint on the Czech musical scene, and many composers such as the Moravian Leoš Janáček began their careers as his imitators. Once a provincial schoolteacher, Janáček's imagination was liberated by early experience with Prague's musical drama. Naturally a man of the theater, Janáček easily absorbed dramatic principles of direct simplicity, repetition, and contrast. He then shaped them intuitively according to his personal vision of music as flexible speech. Later composers such as Ervin Schulhoff, Jiři Gemrot, and Sylvie Bodorová have posed philosophical and artistic questions through their works, which can also be understood as miniature dramas.

LEOŠ JANÁČEK
B. JULY 3, 1854 IN HUKVALDY, MORAVIA,
D. AUGUST 12, 1928 IN OSTRAVA, CZECHOSLOVAKIA

The fiery younger colleague of Dvořák and Smetana, Leoš Janáček became renowned as Czechoslovakia's most outstanding figure after their deaths. Trained in the classic and romantic traditions, he renounced Western musical styles after 1890 and destroyed most of his early work. He then began to incorporate the rhythms and inflections of Moravian speech into his compositions to create "music of truth," an art that expressed heightened reality. Disdainful of the merely beautiful or interesting, Janáček crafted miniature dramas, each brought to life through specific techniques—continuously varied melodic and rhythmic material;

fluid modal harmonies that avoid the traditional tonic-dominant pull toward the cadence; strong dynamic contrasts. Although opera remained his favorite genre, he created numerous instrumental works that, he wrote, should sound "as if dipped in blood." He asserted that "every piece should contain both roses and thorns."

## String Quartet No. 1, "Kreutzer Sonata" (1923)

Adagio—Con moto
Con moto
Con moto—Vivo—Andante—Adagio
Con moto—Adagio

In 1923 the Bohemian Quartet, led by Dvořák's son-in-law Josef Suk, asked Janáček to compose two string quartets for them. The first, then titled *Quartet Based on the Kreutzer Sonata*, was written within eight days. "Note after note fell smoldering from my pen," wrote Janáček. This moody and emotional work was inspired by Leo Tolstoy's eponymous novella (1889), which references Beethoven's dramatic Opus 47 Violin Sonata ("Kreutzer"). Janáček explained: "I had in mind a miserable woman, suffering, beaten, wretched, like the great Russian author wrote about." Janáček sought to convey Tolstoy's narrative, a psychological profile of a failed marriage and a jealous murderer, through darkly expressive and subtly changing motifs.

Janáček states that in the first movement he depicts both "compassion for the miserable, prostrate woman" and her evolving character in the first movement, which corresponds to the exposition of the story. As in Janáček's operas, specific themes relate to corresponding emotional states.

The second movement actively develops the plot. The first violinist, portraying the seducer, suggests the fateful encounter in a furtive, trembling passage, followed by the first melodious admissions of love. Tension increases as the tempo accelerates. A soft but abrupt final chord forebodes the tragic end.

The crisis unfolds in the third movement. A brief quotation from Beethoven's "Kreutzer" Sonata conveys music's power to unleash varying passions—love in the woman, jealousy in the husband. Wild figuration is followed by sobs. A hymnlike passage portrays the woman seeking consolation with her lover.

A plaintive theme introduces the fourth movement. Agitated figuration portends the murder. The husband contemplates his dead wife and experiences a catharsis, conveyed musically through a majestic passage. Janáček wrote: "For the first time he saw a human being in her." The work concludes with human dignity restored to both the victim and the penitent.

## String Quartet No. 2, "Intimate Letters" (1928)

Andante
Adagio
Moderato
Allegro

Janáček's String Quartet No. 2 was inspired by his long association with Kamila Stösslová, a married woman thirty-eight years younger and his proclaimed muse. Developing with unpredictable shifts of texture, color, and rhythm, the quartet was intended to reflect the dynamic character of their relationship as revealed in exchanges of more than 600 letters. Janáček's estranged wife Zdenka, the mother of his two deceased children, wrote her own thoughts during her husband's passionate friendship. Published in 1998 as *My Life with Janáček*, Zdenka's memoirs detail the darker side of this brilliant and erratic composer.

The opening Andante portrays the lovers' fateful first meeting. As Kamila gradually becomes the composer's muse, the music grows faster and more rapturous. The viola, which assumes the persona of Kamila, maintains the dominant role. After a fortissimo trill in the cello and an introductory theme in the violins, the viola articulates an eerie theme *sul ponticello* (on the bridge). The cello, taking the persona of the composer, then shares this theme as the violins develop a melody alternately forceful and elegiac. The movement closes with a statement of the opening theme accompanied by high violin trills.

In the Adagio the composer contemplates Kamila giving birth to a son and considers his future life. (Janáček was devoted to Kamila's real-life son. Shortly after completing the quartet, the composer went on holiday with Kamila's family. Janáček caught a chill while hunting for the boy in the woods and quickly died of pneumonia.) The thematic material is based primarily on the viola theme heard in the first movement. A lively melody in 5/8 time provides a rhythmic contrast.

Strong contrasts of mood characterize the third movement. Two themes are explored through continuously varying tempos and textures. The Allegro finale portrays the composer's devotion to his muse: "You stand behind every note, you, living, forceful, loving. The fragrance of your body, the glow of your kisses—no, really of mine. Those notes of mine kiss all of you. They call for you passionately." An initial folklike melody is interrupted by a conflicting rhythmic pattern that gradually insinuates itself into the entire texture. The movement becomes a colorful amalgam of sounds: a cello line alternating pizzicato and bowed notes on successive beats; a rapidly accelerating theme; intrusions of the opening theme into the ongoing material. Near the end all four instruments play stridently at the bridge on a strong dissonance. The second violin trills a four-note theme, which leads to a re-exposition of the quartet's three primary motifs. The work closes on Janáček's favorite chord of D flat major with the added dissonance of E flat.

## *"Mládi" for Wind Sextet (1924)*

Allegro
Andante sostenuto
Vivace
Allegro animato

Janáček celebrated the month of his 70th birthday by writing a tribute to the joys of childhood, the wind sextet *Mládi* (Youth). Inspired by a contemporary wind concert in Salzburg, he decided to write a programmatic equivalent during conversations with his biographer Max Brod, who elicited reminiscences from Janáček's childhood. The resulting suite is a lighthearted depiction of Janáček's earliest school years and "the whistling little songsters," his playful friends. Janáček steadily revised the work during its rehearsals.

Janáček customarily drew his subtle motivic material from the melodious cadences of human speech. In his new composition he developed the Allegro's primary motif from the words of a wistful sigh, "Mládi, zlate mládi! (Youth, golden youth). The Slavic theme of the pensive Andante, which depicts the occasional loneliness Janáček experienced in his monastery school, is freely developed through four variations. The third movement is a lively scherzo with witty ornaments and imitative figures illustrating the pranks of his schoolboy friends. The main theme of the finale relates to the opening motif but is developed in a more serious guise—perhaps to convey that the passage of time has conveyed wisdom.

ERWIN SCHULHOFF
B. JUNE 8, 1894 IN PRAGUE,
D. AUGUST 18, 1942 NEAR WEISSENBURG, GERMANY

Erwin Schulhoff came from a prominent Prague family that encouraged his evident musical gifts. After Dvořák assured the young composer of his exceptional promise, Schulhoff sought and received the finest musical education possible throughout Europe, including studies with Janáček, Reger, and private tutelage from Debussy. Schulhoff developed into a virtuoso pianist and a versatile composer with a full command of the myriad "isms" of his day— German late Romanticism, Impressionism, Bartókian Folklorism.

After serving in the Austrian army during World War I, a grim experience that left a profound impression, Schulhoff moved to Berlin, where he befriended the artistic avant-garde. Cooperating with futurist visual artists, he organized a series of concerts to showcase experimental music. Jazz became an obsession after his return to Prague in the 1920s, and he joined the Prague Theater jazz orchestra as their pianist. Appalled by desperate postwar economic circumstances, the idealistic Schulhoff became a Marxist, which, together with his Jewish heritage, led to his imprisonment in a concentration camp. He died of typhus at Germany's Würzburg Camp in 1942.

Schulhoff's large body of works virtually disappeared from the concert scene after his death. He had completed eight symphonies, two piano concertos, an opera, and a setting for the complete German text of the *Communist Manifesto* by Marx and Engels (eventually premiered in Prague in 1962). Before 1930 Schulhoff wrote significant chamber compositions, including three for string quartet, many of which were premiered at the International Society for Contemporary Music Festivals. His surviving works are now undergoing a revival.

*Five Pieces for String Quartet (1923)*

Alla Valse Viennese
Alla Serenata
Alla Czeca
Alla Tango Milonga
Alla Tarantella

Schulhoff wrote the dance suite Five Pieces for String Quartet the year he returned to his native Prague from Berlin. Schulhoff's greatest pleasures then were jazz and dance, hints of which are heard throughout his body of work. He described his craving for dance in a letter to Alban Berg: "I have a tremendous passion for the fashionable dances, and at times I go dancing night after night with the dance hostesses, purely out of rhythmic enthusiasm and subconscious sensuality. This gives my creative work a phenomenal impulse, because in my subconscious I am incredibly earthy, even bestial."

Schulhoff admired the free harmonies and whimsical theatricality of French composer Darius Milhaud, to whom he dedicated the suite. The dances also suggest the modernist influence of Second Viennese School composers Berg and Schoenberg. The sardonic dissonances and spikey instrumental effects of Alla Valse and Alla Serenata create parodies of these traditionally elegant forms. Alla Czeca offers homage to his folk roots, and the suave Alla Tango develops from his love for popular modern dance. Alla Tarantella unfolds with the brilliant rhythmic vitality associated with this ferocious dance.

## String Quartet No. 1 (1924)

Presto con fuoco
Allegretto con moto e con malinconia grotesca
Allegro giocoso alla Slovacca
Andante molto sostenuto

Schulhoff's darkly mysterious String Quartet No. 1 projects his keen theatrical sensibilities. Strong contrasts of atmosphere occur throughout this episodic work, punctuated in its slower sections by dramatic pauses that lead to eerie declamatory passages. Schulhoff strived to emulate Bartók, and he treats the quartet's evident folk elements with similar devices—ostinato figures that underpin fragmentary Slavic melodies; rhythms of powerful drive; instrumental colors made brilliant through glissandi, *ponticello* passages, and pizzicato figures. Hints of Schulhoff's beloved jazz idiom are heard in the quartet's energetic syncopated rhythms. Essentially tonal, the work is centered on C major in its rapid movements, D minor in its slower.

Schulhoff breaks with tradition in his organization of movements. In normal placement a finale, the Presto con fuoco (very fast with fire) is a bold whirlwind. Unison bars with emphatic rhythms hammered "at the heel of the bow" frame the movement. The central section explores a more leisurely folklike theme.

The flowing and lyrical second movement, "somewhat fast with motion and grotesque melancholy," develops a complex scenario. Spectral effects abound: eerie passages marked quadruple piano (*pppp*) are played muted and on the bridge of the instrument to create a distant, glassy sound. The movement opens with *dolce* (sweet) and piquant passagework ornamented by appoggiaturas and glissandi, followed by a folklike theme in the viola and a cello recitative with high harmonics. A concluding Slavic theme is made sinister by glissandi and a scurrying accompaniment.

The Allegro giocoso is a wild folk dance with hammered notes that emphasize its unison theme. An ostinato figure in the cello underpins a colorful pizzicato effect that suggests primitive instruments. Three unison chords marked *secco* (dry) abruptly conclude the movement.

The slow finale develops its two themes through searching and passionate soliloquies, first a *dolce* cello solo in its upper register, then an emotional outpouring for violin. Pervasive ostinato figures provide accompanying support. At its conclusion, played with mutes, the main theme slowly fades to a hushed, dissonant chord in the two violins.

## *String Sextet (1924)*

Allegro risoluto
Tranquillo: Andante
Burlesca: Allegro molto con spirito
Molto adagio

Schulhoff's only string sextet enjoyed critical acclaim at its 1924 premiere (at which Hindemith played viola), but it remained unpublished until 1978. The first movement of this deeply serious, technically demanding sextet was written in Dresden in 1920. After moving to Prague, Schulhoff returned to the work and completed the remaining three movements in 1924. During his formative years in Germany, Schulhoff had closely studied the atonal works of Arnold Schoenberg. Grounded by a key center on C, the Sextet avoids atonality but develops with Schoenberg's expressive chromaticism. The dissonant chord and melodic unit based on the notes C-D flat-G provides much of the first movement's thematic material. This small cell also pervades the entire Sextet both as a supporting pedal ostinato, heard in the first movement coda and the opening of the second movement, and as the foundation for the Sextet's evolving melodic ideas. The eerily reflective second and fourth movements reveal lyrical moments suggesting the impressionistic influence of Debussy. The colorful Burlesca, propelled by a fiendishly rapid 5/8 meter, is a virtuoso showpiece.

BOHUSLAV MARTINŮ
B. DECEMBER 8, 1890 IN POLIČKA, BOHEMIA,
D. AUGUST 28, 1959 IN LIESTAL, SWITZERLAND

After early instruction in Prague with Dvořák's protégé Josef Suk, Martinů studied intermittently with Albert Roussel in Paris, where he lived after World War I. Roussel, a César Franck disciple with strong proclivities toward dissonance, steered Martinů away from descriptive program pieces and urged him to compose more abstract works with daring harmonies. Offended by the irreverent Satie and the flippancy of *Les Six*, Martinů began to emulate the disciplined neoclassical style of Stravinsky. By the mid-1920s Martinů's individual voice was defined by vividly pulsating rhythms, unexpected juxtapositions of tone color, and spontaneous folklike melodies. Martinů himself described the diverse elements of his style: "Rhythmic vitality plays an important part in Czech music, so I compose with vital rhythms. Sometimes I use Czech folk songs as themes, but more often I create thematic material colored by the style and spirit of the Czech folk idiom. I am attracted to the color and spirit of the music of Debussy, especially the Nocturnes. I am also attracted to English madrigals because of their freedom of polyphony and their affinity to Bohemian folk music."

## Quartet for Clarinet, Natural Horn, Cello, and Side/Snare Drum (1924)

Allegro moderato
Poco andante
Allegretto (ma non troppo)

This imaginative early quartet is a remarkable synthesis of widely divergent tone colors. A rare member of chamber ensembles, the side drum, also known as the snare drum, achieves its sharply staccato timbre from taut string wires vibrating against its back membrane. Also heard infrequently in small ensembles, the natural horn offers a contrasting round and sonorous timbre that pairs well with clarinet but in combination risks overweighting the cello. Martinů achieves a balanced whole by scoring individual solo passages with subtle support that does not intrude on thematic content. The influence of Stravinsky's chamber music is heard in the work's neoclassical structure as well as its bold instrumentation. Written for his Dutch cellist friend Maurits Frank, the Quartet showcases the string instrument's expressive range. It demands virtuosity from all its performers.

The solo drum's introductory tattoo, soon reinforced by the cello's marchlike rhythm, suggests an approaching military parade. The horn introduces the primary theme. An amiable atmosphere prevails until the parade ends with a concluding drum pattern and an ambiguous dissonant chord. An ethereal cello solo dominates the reflective Poco andante, a Slavic tinged, elegiac movement that suggests religious incantation. The clarinet joins to create a duet, then the horn. The drum offers short punctuations. The return of the theme in the cello quietly concludes the movement. The rhythmically complex finale offers echoes of Stravinsky's neoclassical *Suite italienne* (1920). Playful themes in the clarinet and horn are supported by drum flourishes and brisk scalar passages in the cello.

## *String Trio No. 2 (1934)*

Allegro
Poco moderato

While residing in Paris, Martinů wrote his String Trio No. 2 for his virtuoso friends in the Trio Pasquier. The technical possibilities of each instrument are fully exploited. The work develops with contrapuntal textures resulting from his recent studies of Corelli, Vivaldi, and Bach, but the trio's pulsing rhythms suggest Czech folk influence.

Often described as a "triple concerto without orchestra," the densely scored trio offers sonorous passages for each instrument. The neoclassical Allegro develops two contrasting subjects in sonata form; ethereal violin harmonics ornament the development. A cello cadenza creates a slow introduction to the Poco moderato. The main part of the movement, cast in sonata form, develops two contrasting subjects with energetic passagework.

## *String Quartet No. 5 (1938)*

Allegro non troppo
Adagio
Allegro vivo
Lento—Allegro

Martinů wrote his String Quartet No. 5 while he was profoundly distracted by increasing international tensions. Dedicated to the Belgian Pro Arte Quartet, which had planned to perform its premiere, the manuscript was left in Paris when Martinů fled to the United States. Assumed lost, the work was rediscovered and premiered in 1955. Critics at that time heard String Quartet No. 5 as a work that "evoked deeply felt personal experience and the composer's sense of urgency."

The work suggests the anxieties of Europe in the unsettled prewar era. Despite an ominous cast, its atmosphere is energized by Martinů's characteristic dynamic rhythms and vivid folklike melodies. The opening Allegro, written in sonata form, grows from a short motif that is extended into a broad melody marked "with great expression." After a turbulent development and brief recapitulation in a faster tempo, the movement ends with an eloquent passage for viola and cello supported by sustained violin lines.

Colorful effects—use of mutes, tremolos, and *col legno* (playing with the wood of the bow)—enhance the melancholy Adagio. The harmonically ambiguous closing passage is made sinister by intrusive knocks of the bow against the wood of the instrument.

Allegro vivo, the rapid third movement, is a grotesque scherzo varied by a section marked "sweetly" at its center. Frenzied note repetitions propel the line.

Introduced by a brief and meditative Lento, the finale develops an energetic theme played in unison at the opening bars. Structured in free sonata form, the movement is animated by rapid triple rhythms; slower contrasting sections and spontaneous tempo accelerations vary the texture. Fortissimo chords bring the work to a powerful conclusion.

## *String Quartet No. 7, "Concerto da camera" (1947)*

Poco allegro
Andante
Allegro vivo

Blacklisted by the Nazis after his widely broadcast *Field Mass*, a tribute to the Czech resistance, Martinů sought asylum in the United States in 1941. He longed to return to his homeland, and after the offer of a professorship at the Prague Conservatory, plans to relocate were underway by 1946. However, in July of that year Martinů suffered serious injuries when he accidentally walked off an ungated balcony at the Berkshire Summer Music School, where he briefly taught. During his year of recuperation, he composed while reclining on a board set at a 45-degree angle. Three chamber compositions emerged from this difficult period, the first of which was String Quartet No. 7; its amiability suggests that the recuperating Martinů was happy at least in his work. He completed the work quickly during the month of June.

Subtitled "Concerto da camera" as homage to similar three-movement forms of the late Baroque, the quartet launched Martinů's "classical period," a five-year interval during which he sought to emulate eighteenth-century masters. Compared to his densely scored earlier quartets, Quartet No. 7 develops with greater simplicity of form and harmony as well as increased textural transparency. The lyrical Andante, which offers echoes of Dvořák, suggests Martinů's pervasive nationalism. The finale exemplifies the melodic verve and rhythmic vigor characteristic of Martinů.

*Quartet in F Major for Oboe, Violin, Cello, and Piano (1947)*

Moderato poco allegro
Adagio—Andante (poco moderato)—Poco allegro

During the trying year of recuperation after his serious fall, Martinů completed three chamber works, the second of which was the brief and graceful Quartet in F Major for Oboe, Violin, Cello, and Piano. Almost Mozartean in effect, the Moderato poco allegro is structured in traditional sonata form. The oboe introduces the first theme, soon imitated by the violin and piano; the cello offers a lyrical second motif. After a development area with increasing chromaticism, the first theme returns sequentially in the oboe, violin, and piano.

Constructed in three sections with contrasting tempos, the second movement (C major) opens with forceful chords in the solo piano. A piquant dialogue between the violin and cello ensues, then free imitation among all instruments. Resonant and syncopated passages in the central section evoke the romanticism of Brahms. Ideas from the first movement return at the Poco allegro, and the scoring gradually grows denser. Emphatic C major chords conclude the movement.

*Musique de Chambre No. 1, "Les fêtes nocturnes" (1959)*

Allegro moderato
Andante moderato
Poco allegro

Martinů wrote his *Musique de Chambre No. 1*, "Night Festivities," while undergoing medical treatment in Switzerland. However, precarious health did not diminish his zest for composition—a festive atmosphere prevails in this work, which concludes with a suggestion of joyous fireworks. Scored for a diverse combination

of six instruments—violin, viola, cello, clarinet, harp, and piano—
*Musique de Chambre No. 1* offers a kaleidoscope of mysterious
and dazzling timbres. The work develops with vividly pulsating
rhythms and spontaneous melodies derived from both folk tradition and jazz. Eloquent solos punctuate the atmosphere, which is
often turbulent. This high-energy work demands both virtuosity
and intense focus from each of its performers.

ZDENĚK LUKÁŠ
B. AUGUST 21, 1928 IN PRAGUE,
D. JULY 13, 2007 IN PRAGUE

*Quintet for Harp and String Quartet, "Per tutte le corde,"*
*Opus 320 (2001)*

(Moderato)
(Molto allegro)

The prolific and versatile Zdeněk Lukáš composed over 320
works for various instrumental combinations. After graduation
from the Theater Institute in Prague, Lukáš became Director of
the Czechoslovak Radio Studio in Plzeň. During his residency, he
founded and directed the internationally acclaimed choir Česká
Píseň (Czech Song). He arranged numerous folk songs and gradually began to compose his own works.

Essentially self-taught, Lukáš benefited from spontaneous
family music sessions during his growing years. Tutorials with
Czech composer Miloslav Kabeláč inspired him to pursue full-time
composition. During the mid-1960s, Lukáš experimented with
electronic and avant-garde techniques. After the political chaos of
1968, Lukáš began to search for inspiration in his musical roots—
the Czech language, Czech folklore, and Czech pre-classic music.
Lukáš's later work synthesizes contemporary and folk influences.

Lukáš's Quintet for Harp and String Quartet develops with vivid rhythmic patterns, strong tonal color, and richly inventive melodies. Its clear modal harmonies hint of Czech folk influence.

JIŘÍ GEMROT
B. APRIL 15, 1957 IN PRAGUE

## Quintet for Two Violins, Viola, Cello, and Double Bass (2008)

Con impeto
Vivacissimo
Andante

Jiří Gemrot is known for a strong personal style that strives for direct communication with the listener. He states that his aim is "to fuse styles so that past and present are united." While appreciative of current compositional trends, Gemrot regards both nineteenth- and early twentieth-century composers as important models. His own works are permeated with their themes and structural details—the long phrases of his compatriots Dvořák and Janáček, the ironic melodies of Prokofiev, the original harmonies of Martinů. Primarily an instrumental composer, Gemrot believes that his inventive faculties are best suited to chamber groups. He is often inspired by the musicians who perform his works, as well as the great questions of philosophy.

Gemrot writes: "I composed the Quintet for Two Violins, Viola, Cello, and Double Bass between January and July 2008, and it was commissioned by the Arizona Friends of Chamber Music and premiered by the Pražák Quartet and double bassist Volkan Orhon on October 29, 2008. The first of its three movements (Con impeto, "with force") is in sonata form, and the second (Vivacissimo, "very lively") is a scherzo with an ABABA form. The last movement

(Andante) has two contrasting ideas. The ABABA form returns with a reminiscence of the motif from the opening introduction and then a synthesis of both themes from the finale. The coda is derived from the primary theme of the first movement."

SYLVIE BODOROVÁ
B. DECEMBER 31, 1954 IN ČESKÉ BUDĚJOVICE, CZECHOSLOVAKIA

Bodorová studied composition at the Janáček Academy of Music and Performing Arts in Brno and later at the Academy of Performing Arts in Prague. Her works have been performed on every continent, including the Antarctic (*Homage to Columbus*, 1997). She has been a member of Quattro, a group of Czech composers (including Zdeněk Lukáš) formed in 1996. A deep awareness of her cultural heritage is central to her musical aesthetic, and many of her works were inspired by the Czech Republic's haunting past. Ideally for Bodorová, the listener will bring an historic sense to support the performance experience. Both her 2003 *Mysterium Druidum* and 2013 Quartet for Clarinet and Strings were commissioned by the Arizona Friends of Chamber Music and premiered at the Tucson Winter Chamber Music Festival.

*"Mysterium Druidum": Quintet for Harp and Strings (2003)*

Fagus mysticus
Vindobona
Daemones igni

From the composer: "In the eighteenth century, a huge Celtic gold treasure was discovered at Podmokly, near Plzeň, in the Czech Republic. Today we can still easily discern the characteristic wrinkles in the beautiful landscape of the woods around the castle of Křivoklát, testifying to the remains of Celtic settlements, the *oppida*. My studio is near the place where the treasure was found, and during bicycle rides here I often wonder how much else has survived to the present from that ancient culture. The secrets of the places I know so well have led me to write *Mysterium Druidum* (Druid Mysteries). The choice of harp is not incidental—the Celts knew this instrument and used it, albeit in a different form.

"The first movement, 'Fagus mysticus' (Mystery beech), symbolizes the Celts' belief in the power of trees. These cult trees represented a source of knowledge and security, and the Celts used a tree ceremony to symbolize their enemies' defeat. The cradle of the Celts was found in Central Europe, one of the oldest settlements having been the *oppidum* 'Vindobona' (settlement), where Vienna lies today. Who knows if they were able to detect the scent and charm of the future city on the Danube, as we now know it centuries later. 'Daemones igni' (Demons of fire) relates to the Celts' close affinity with nature—their respect, reverence and interpretations of it."

## Quartet for Clarinet and Strings (2013)

Rotatio furosis (Rotation of wrath)
Rotatio doloris (Rotation of grief)
Rotatio temporis (Rotation of time)

The composer writes: "When delving into different historical epochs while composing my works, I have often come up against the fact that all the problems that we encounter 'rotate' with us—humans—for centuries. In some of the historical periods it is possible to trace them in a slightly different form, while in others they are sometimes the same, almost identical. I am always struck by how little we humans can learn from our mistakes. It is perhaps because everything happens over such long stretches of time so that human memory and experience are not able to embrace it, or perhaps it is simply because the young, not believing the old who remember a lot more, must gain their own experience. Or perhaps we are incorrigible.

"The principle of rotations is a musical principle, too, and the whole cycle is built upon it—upon a principle of construction in both the micro- and the macrostructure."

# FIVE

# Hungarian Quests

An intensely artistic nation that leads internationally in musical education, Hungary has contributed to world music through its outstanding pianist/composers such as Ernő Dohnányi and György Kurtág and its roster of acclaimed conductors and instrumentalists. Long under Habsburg cultural dominance, Hungary in the early twentieth century strived to encourage national consciousness of its musical traditions. Its efforts were realized only partially; tunefully westernized folk and gypsy elements, misleadingly identified as "peasant song," were freely insinuated into art music to cultivate nationalist sentiments in its audience.

Aware of the need for authentic material, Béla Bartók and Zoltán Kodály became pioneers of ethnomusicology—the systematic study of oral traditions launched in late nineteenth-century Central Europe. Beginning in 1905 the two colleagues packed their unwieldy recording equipment into a primitive truck and searched out songs from remote areas of Hungary and Romania. Their quest resulted in a vast archive of carefully catalogued melodies and rhythms that Bartók regarded as the inspirational starting point for his original compositions. He wrote: "It was not a question of taking unique melodies and incorporating them into our works. What we had to do was to divine the spirit of this unknown music and to make this spirit the basis for our own works." Bartók gradually assimilated the essences of these songs into his own musical thought processes. Much of the imaginative power of his writing stems from his fusion of art music with elements of deep folk origin.

Bartók wrote in his autobiography: "The study of peasant music was for me of decisive importance because it revealed the possibility of total emancipation from the hegemony of the major-minor system. The more valuable part of this treasure house of melodies lies in the old church modes, in ancient Greek modes, and certainly in the primitive scales (such as the pentatonic). The melodies also reveal free, varied rhythms and time changes. It was clear that the old scales, no longer heard in our art music, have not lost their vitality. Their application also enables novel harmonic combinations. These have led to a liberation from the petrified major-minor scale and to the completely free handling of each note of the chromatic twelve-tone system."

BÉLA BARTÓK
B. MARCH 25, 1881 IN NAGYSZENTMIKLÓS, HUNGARY
(NOW SÂNNICOLAU MARE IN ROMANIA),
D. SEPTEMBER 26, 1945 IN NEW YORK CITY

## STRING QUARTETS

Bartók wrote his monumental set of six string quartets during the years from 1909 to 1939, the core of his compositional career in Budapest before his emigration to the United States in 1940. Each quartet both marks the phases of his evolving creative development and serves as a diary of his emotional and intellectual life. These six string quartets, together with Shostakovich's fifteen string quartets, have been recognized as the most important contributions to the genre since the string quartets of Beethoven. Yet they remain demanding works for both listeners and interpreters, in part because of the high goal that Bartók set for their composition—to harness the instinctive, primitive forces inherent in his native music together with the intellectually sophisticated genre of the Western European string quartet. The quartets have five techniques in common:

1. *Expanded harmonies.* Bartók avoids a major-minor scale framework in favor of various modes, both ancient church modes and simplified folk types. One hears frequent parallel movement of dissonant intervals such as the second and seventh to destabilize tonality. His "wrong note bass" technique, whereby a sustained low tone of unexpected dissonance underpins the melodic line, adds further uncertainty to the tonality, which eventually resolves at important cadence points. Although harmonically complex and dissonant, his works are not atonal but center on a key.

2. *Folk-inspired melody.* Bartók explores two types of indigenous melody—freely shaped, improvisatory slow song; and dance song in strict rhythm. He rarely quotes a native melody directly, but brief fragments can be detected throughout. One hears their "essence" distilled by his thought process. His archived field melodies are most often thinly accompanied by a sustained modal voice; in his quartets, Bartók breaks melodies into discrete motifs and pairs them with rapidly repeating rhythmic units to achieve what has been described as "a strange feverish excitement."

3. *Folk-based rhythm.* "Dynamic percussiveness" characterizes Bartók's rhythmic language. He evokes the driving and complex rhythms of native dance through asymmetrical meters such as 3 beats plus 2 beats per measure. Frequent changes of meter punctuate and energize the flow. Ostinato figures, repeating units that underpin the melodic line, appear throughout.

4. *Inventive timbres.* Bartók pursues continuous variations of sound. Slow movements often feature impressionistic areas of "night music" that create shimmering atmosphere with suggestions of insect life. Rapid movements evoke the pungent, richly colored instrumental combinations he heard in the field—peasant flute and bagpipes, often paired with violin and guitar. Bartók selects

registers and articulations that best evoke native timbres.

5. *Ornamental sound effects.* Throughout the set of quartets, Bartók uses a vast range of expressive devices to enhance color. Left hand techniques such as trills, *acciaccaturas* (notes played quickly before the main note), glissandi (continuous slides along the fingerboard), and the "Bartók pizzicato" (an emphatic string pluck that percussively hits the fingerboard) are used for expressive punctuation. Bow techniques such as *ponticello* (bowing at the bridge to achieve a glassy sound), tremolo (rapid back and forth bow movements), *sul tasto* (playing at the fingerboard to achieve a wispy effect), and *col legno* (striking the string with the wood of the bow) appear in each quartet.

## String Quartet No. 1, Sz. 40 (1909)

Lento
Allegretto
Introduzione: Allegro—Allegro vivace

Stymied by an early disappointment in love, Bartók rebounded after his marriage to sixteen-year-old Márta Ziegler, and he soon completed his String Quartet No. 1. His friend Kodály called the quartet "an intimate drama, a return to life at the edge of nothing." Although influenced by the late Romanticism of Richard Strauss and Richard Wagner, Bartók in Quartet No. 1 forges a uniquely colorful style based on native folk elements underpinned by blocks of modal harmony and propelled by energetic rhythms.

Strong thematic connections unify the quartet, tonally centered on the key of A minor. The intensely chromatic Lento, ternary in form, begins with a double canon based on two motifs that reappear in different guises throughout the quartet. After an agitated development of themes, the opening ideas are briefly recapitulated. The Allegretto, a lively scherzo, proceeds without pause. Its thematic material references the Lento but is constantly reshaped and developed in a rustic, playful manner. The movement begins with chromatically rising thirds in the cello and viola. A gradual acceleration leads to a lyrical countertheme underpinned by a propulsive ostinato, a repeating accompaniment figure.

The finale, Allegro vivace, is introduced by a cello recitative that mimics the rhythms of Magyar speech—which typically emphasizes the first syllables of the words and falls into a short-long accent pattern. The main thematic area, derived from motives in the first two movements, conjures a vigorous folk dance. A slower section based on the famous Hungarian melody "The Peacock Flies" recalls the opening double canon of the Lento. Energy rebuilds and the movement concludes with a joyous spirit.

*String Quartet No. 2, Sz. 67 (1917)*

Moderato
Allegro molto capriccioso
Lento

Although he did not serve in World War l, Bartók suffered a psychological crisis at that time and withdrew from musical society. As a result, composition of Quartet No. 2 proceeded slowly over a two-year period. Intensely expressive and highly contrapuntal, the work suggests the chromatic influence of early Schoenberg but also reflects Berber elements that Bartók heard during his pre-war visit to North Africa. Bartók described its unusual structure: "I cannot undertake an analysis of the form—there is nothing special in the form. The first movement is a normal sonata form; the second is a kind of rondo with a development section in the middle. The last movement is difficult to define—mostly an augmented ABA form." Bartók's inversion of the traditional movement order creates an unorthodox framework for Quartet No. 2. The calm first movement is succeeded by a spirited Allegro, and the slow finale projects an atmosphere of brooding melancholy. Bartók's friend

Kodály observed that the quartet had an autobiographical basis and subtitled the work "Episodes: Peaceful life—Joy—Suffering."

The Moderato opens with a two-bar violin theme that provides the foundation for the entire movement. After its initial expansion, a three-note unit derived from an augmented triad and a tranquil third theme are developed with chromatic transitions. In the recapitulation, dissonant half-step intervals assume prominence. The closing section, with the theme heard in octaves in the first violin and viola accompanied by sliding parallel fifths in the cello, suggests the impressionist influence of Ravel. A coda combines the first and final themes, which can now be perceived as closely related.

Dominated by a barbaric ostinato inspired by drums heard in the Biskra region of Algeria, the Allegro evokes wild folk dance. Rapid changes from even to uneven meters build tension. The late romantic harmonic background of the first movement has vanished to be replaced by propelling percussive reiterations of dissonant intervals. A ghostly atmosphere prevails at the pianissimo coda.

The primary theme of the plaintive Lento suggests a folk dirge. Its melodic outline is an actual quote of the main theme of the first movement, soon reduced to short sighing figures. The mode changes from major to minor, and rising thirds in the violins, steadily increasing in dynamic level, convey tragic weight. Gravely quiet moments interrupt the flow. The work concludes in a subdued atmosphere with a cadence derived from Hungarian folksong.

*String Quartet No. 3, Sz. 85 (1927)*

Prima Parte: Moderato
Seconda Parte: Allegro
Ricapitulazione della prima parte: Moderato
Coda: Allegro molto

Concentrated and introspective, the third quartet coalesced after Bartók had closely studied the contrapuntal techniques of Bach. One hears passages of rigorous formal counterpoint as well as the continuous variation that is a leading characteristic of folk style. The briefest yet perhaps most concentrated of all Bartók's string quartets, Quartet No. 3 consists of a continuous flow divided into four sections to create a slow-fast-slow-fast format. The first and third sections are thematically related, as are the second and fourth. However, the connections between the first pair of sections are not immediately obvious since the recapitulation freely varies motivic units.

The basic element of the Prima Parte is a three-note cell composed of two intervals—a rising fourth and a descending third. This motif, derived from a Hungarian theme, is continuously developed so it is heard throughout the entire section. Especially remarkable is the area of "night music," subtle instrumental murmurs intended to evoke the rustling sounds of a mysterious forest.

The cello, playing pizzicato, introduces the pervasive motif of the rapid Seconda Parte—a simple scalar figure driven by a propulsive rhythm that evokes rural Hungarian dance. Harmonization in parallel thirds, percussive chords, and syncopations evoke a primitive atmosphere. Frequent metric changes and a rapid fugue intensify the rhythmic drive. Instrumental effects such as *col legno* (playing with the wood of the bow) and *ponticello* (bowing at the bridge to achieve a glassy sound) contribute expressive color.

The Ricapitulazione della prima parte (Recapitulation of the First Part) condenses and varies material heard in the first section. The three-note cell recurs persistently.

The coda is an altered reprise of the Seconda Parte. The tempo changes from Allegro to Allegro molto (fast to very fast) and the contrapuntal texture grows ever denser with canons and rapid inverted canons. Percussive repeated notes, glissandi, relentless *ostinati*, and rising and falling arpeggios create a wild atmosphere. The motion ceases with a chord of three superimposed fifths built on C sharp—the tonic note of the entire quartet, emphasized only at its conclusion.

## String Quartet No. 4, Sz. 91 (1928)

Allegro
Prestissimo, con sordino
Non troppo lento
Allegretto pizzicato
Allegro molto

During the time Bartók wrote his Quartet No. 4, he was absorbed by the subtle and complex interrelationships heard in the late quartets of Beethoven. Structural allusions to these masterworks permeate Quartet No. 4, particularly in the outer movements. Bartók succinctly described Quartet No. 4: "The work is in five movements; their character corresponds to classical sonata form. The slow movement is the kernel of the work; the other movements are, as it were, arranged around it." Strong architectural symmetry is evident throughout Quartet No. 4. Two thematically connected movements (I and V) form the work's outer pillars. The substantial third movement, divided into three parts, falls at the work's center. This movement, the keystone, is framed by two thematically connected scherzo-like movements.

Vivid tone colors create a kaleidoscopic atmosphere throughout Quartet No. 4. Bartók introduces innovative instrumental techniques such as the "pizzicato glissando" (plucking the string while simultaneously sliding the finger) and the "Bartók pizzicato," in which the strings are pulled so strongly that they slap the fingerboard. Contrasts abound: several large sections are directed to be played with mutes to achieve a mysterious atmosphere, and other areas derive energy from *col legno*, in which a passage is played sharply with the bow's wood.

The energetic Allegro, constructed in traditional sonata form, derives all its thematic content from a motif consisting of three rising scalar notes and three falling tones, first heard in the cello. This material, continuously expanded and developed, returns in the fifth movement. The shimmering second movement, muted throughout, departs significantly from traditional thematic structure. Rather than develop coherent melodic ideas, Bartók here explores fragmentary interval relationships, particularly the highly dissonant minor second.

The central movement opens with an extensive cello solo that suggests free improvisation. Its elegiac theme is based on a *táragató* melody—a slow moving, increasingly embellished line traditionally performed on an ancient Hungarian instrument related to the oboe. The first violin, followed by the solo second violin, continue this searching theme. The middle section, the focal point of the entire quartet, contains an area of "night music," evocations of bird calls and rustling forest sounds.

Bartók describes the Allegro pizzicato movement, which at moments suggests a relaxed guitar serenade: "Its theme is the same as the main theme of the second movement. There it moves in the narrow intervals of the chromatic scale, but here it broadens in accordance with the diatonic style." All instruments play pizzicato throughout, occasionally punctuated by chordal flourishes and the forceful snap of the "Bartók pizzicato."

The ferocious Allegro molto finale evokes the incipient wildness in native Hungarian dance. Rapidly hammered rhythms and densely chordal textures create an orchestral sonority. After a tumultuous coda, it cadences with an emphatic statement of the quartet's central theme—three rising and three falling notes.

## *String Quartet No. 5, Sz. 102 (1934)*

Allegro
Adagio molto
Scherzo: Alla bulgarese
Andante
Finale: Allegro vivace—Presto

String Quartet No. 5, dedicated to its American commissioner Elizabeth Sprague Coolidge, was written with uncharacteristic speed during the month of August 1934. A formal companion to String Quartet No. 4, written six years earlier, its five movements are arranged symmetrically in an arch form. The first and fifth sections, centered on B flat, are rapid sonata form movements that develop identical thematic material; the slow second and fourth movements are similar in their poetic effect; a rhythmically complex scherzo with a contrasting trio section forms the center of the work. Mirror imaging occurs in the opening Allegro's recapitulation as its three themes reappear inverted and in reverse order.

The opening chorale of the Adagio molto, accompanied by brief aphoristic statements, suggests homage to Beethoven's "Hymn of Thanksgiving" from his Opus 132 String Quartet. The following area of "night music," as in Quartet No. 4, is intended to evoke the murmur of a mysterious woods. Both ideas return with variations in the Andante fourth movement.

The central Scherzo moves in an irregular meter characteristic of Bulgarian folk song. Its measures, nine beats long, are divided so that accents fall at four, two, and three-beat units. The tempo accelerates in the trio section as the viola and cello sing a Hungarian folk melody over a ten-note ostinato pattern repeated fifty-nine times—a reference to the similarly repeating cello motif in Beethoven's Opus 135.

Serenity returns with the second slow movement's chorale restatement. Emphatic short-long rhythmic note pairs energize the folklike material that follows. Pizzicato passages suggest a guitar serenade.

The vitality of the opening Allegro returns in the presto finale, thematically based on the dissonant interval of the augmented fourth (B flat and E). A remarkable ethno-Western fugue features the two violins percussively playing *col legno* (striking the string with the wood of the bow) as the cello sustains a drone. A surprising shift occurs at the recapitulation—dissonance vanishes and the instruments are directed to play like a music box, *con indifferenza, meccanico* (with indifference, mechanically). Dissonance is reintroduced as the Presto resumes; a broadening of tempo leads to a Hungarian-inflected cadence (four rising notes and three falling) on B flat.

## *String Quartet No. 6, Sz. 114 (1939)*

Mesto—Più mosso, pesante—Vivace
Mesto—Marcia
Mesto—Burletta: Moderato
Mesto

Possibly his most accessible quartet, Bartók's Quartet No. 6 exemplifies his so-called late classic period, in which he wrote with less dissonance, increased formal simplicity, and clearer themes. Composed in Budapest between August and November 1939, the quartet reflects the sadness of his mother's final illness and his despair over the outbreak of World War II. The last work written in Hungary, the quartet premiered in 1941 after his emigration to the United States. The quartet's thematic content is based on a lament (Mesto, or mournful) that precedes each movement as a prologue. Individual instruments—the viola, cello, and violin—sequentially intone the lament, which grows in length and complexity in each movement. In the slow finale the lament becomes the central idea shared by all instruments.

The first statement of the recurring Mesto, heard in the viola, suggests a fusion of melodic Hungarian inflections with Western formal symmetry. A contrasting second theme evokes exuberant Hungarian folk dance. These two themes are developed and recapitulated in sonata form; a D major-minor tonality grounds the overall harmony of Quartet No. 6, which develops with less dissonance than its predecessors.

Perhaps reflecting wartime anxieties, the second movement opens with an aggressive march propelled by strident dotted rhythmic patterns. Its wildly free trio section, a passionate cello solo accompanied by violin tremolos and viola pizzicati, creates a rhapsodic contrast. The opening march returns in spectral guise.

Quartertone intervals between the two violins create a sardonic effect in the grotesque Burletta (Burlesque), a dark comedy relieved by its gentler, folklike trio section. The opening material returns with glissandi and fierce chords played "at the heel" of the bow.

Themes heard in the first movement return in the finale but are now directed to be played "without warmth" and "far away." The final pizzicato notes of the cello suggest a somber farewell.

## WORKS WITH VARIED SCORING

*Sonata for Two Pianos and Percussion, Sz. 110 (1937)*

Assai lento—Allegro molto
Lento, ma non troppo
Allegro non troppo

Bartók wrote his Sonata for Two Pianos and Percussion for himself and his pianist wife Ditta Pásztory (married in 1923), with whom he frequently concertized. Although he acknowledged the piano's lyric possibilities, Bartók regarded it as a percussion instrument, its official classification in orchestral scoring. The Sonata recalls his first two piano concertos, which exploit the sonorities of the piano in combination with a traditional percussion section; Bartók later transcribed the Sonata as a two-piano concerto with orchestra. A virtuoso work, the Sonata requires complex synchronicity between the pianos and percussion. To assure proper instrumental balance, Bartók wrote precise performance directions in the score and included drawings to indicate favorable instrumental placement. The percussion line frequently accompanies the pianos, which are treated as equal voices. In the final two movements the percussion, especially the xylophone, achieves a more prominent role.

The Sonata is a product of Bartók's "late classic period," during which he wrote with less dissonance and greater thematic clarity. Although complex harmonic relationships are heard within the sonata, a strong C major tonality prevails. Despite its rhythmic intricacies, much of the Sonata moves as a dance. The first movement, written in sonata form, develops four themes: a melodic line of half steps emerging from the piano's lower register and accelerating into the Allegro molto; forte piano chords with punctuations from the timpani; a slower theme based on rising and falling scales; a rising sixth in the second piano against sustained chords in the first piano. The four ideas coalesce in the brilliant fugal conclusion.

A tranquil melody frames the three-part Lento. Its central section, based on a five-note figure, includes an area of "night music," passages intended to evoke the mysterious nocturnal atmosphere of a deep forest. The finale is a rondo freely based on a theme first heard in the xylophone and then in canon with the piano. The music fades quietly with taps on the side drum and fingernail strokes on the suspended cymbal.

## "Contrasts" for Clarinet, Violin, and Piano, Sz. 111 (1940)

Verbunkos (Recruiting dance)
Pihenő (Relaxation)
Sebes (Fast Dance)

*Contrasts* was conceptualized in 1938 at a convivial dinner enjoyed by Joseph Szigeti, the eminent Hungarian violinist, and Benny Goodman, the legendary jazz clarinetist. The two musicians decided to perform together, but they realized that their unique chemistry required new repertoire. The obvious choice of composer for their collaboration was Szigeti's compatriot Béla Bartók, who could also perform with them as pianist during his projected 1940 visit to the United States. Szigeti wrote to Bartók, who was then on vacation in Switzerland: "Benny has offered to triple the commission you usually receive. Please write him a registered letter, in which you agree to write a six to seven-minute clarinet and violin duo with piano accompaniment, the ownership of which remains yours. It would be very good if the composition were to consist of two independent sections which could be performed separately, and of course we hope it will include a brilliant clarinet and violin cadenza! Benny brings out whatever the clarinet is physically able to perform at all—in regions much higher than in *Eulenspiegel* [Richard Strauss's virtuoso tone poem]!" Within a month Bartók mailed the new work to its commissioners. He subsequently added a central movement and apologized that he now "delivered a suit for an adult instead of the dress ordered for a two-year-old baby."

*Verbunkos* depicts a vigorous recruiting dance traditionally performed by Hungarian army officers dressed in full regalia. This marchlike dance was most often accompanied by the *tárogató*, the woodwind instrument most popular with Hungarian folk musicians.

*Pihenő*, Hungarian for "repose," was a late addition to the trio, which premiered as a two-movement work entitled Rhapsody in 1939. The expanded work was renamed *Contrasts* for its 1940 recording and Carnegie Hall performance with Bartók as pianist. Szigeti especially admired this slow interlude: "This 'night piece,' with its wonderful calm and free air, was highly necessary for balance."

For the *Sebes*, or Fast Dance, the violinist must prepare a second violin tuned to the notes G sharp, D, A, and E flat in order to create the effect of a *danse macabre*. Its slower middle section is based on the asymmetrical Bulgarian dance rhythm of 3+2+3+2+3. The movement concludes with a violin cadenza and a virtuoso passage for clarinet.

ZOLTÁN KODÁLY
B. DECEMBER 16, 1882 IN KECSKEMÉT, HUNGARY,
D. MARCH 6, 1967 IN BUDAPEST

Kodály today is revered by his compatriots as the embodiment of Hungary's spirit. A cellist, choral singer, and composer from a young age, Kodály was also an ethnomusicologist who wrote a Ph.D. thesis entitled "The Strophic Structure of Hungarian Folk Songs." During his lifetime, his fame as an educator who established important teaching principles rivaled his renown as a composer. Although studies in Paris gave him a wide perspective of modernist trends, as well as an impressionist cast to much of his early music, Kodály was convinced that the art music of a nation must develop from its indigenous material. Committed to a thorough investigation of Hungary's musical roots, Kodály and his close friend Béla Bartók devoted years to the scientific study of hundreds of folk songs collected in the field. The free melodies, supple rhythms, and modal harmonies of this trove pervade Kodály's work.

## String Quartet No. 1 in C Minor, Opus 2 (1909)

Andante poco rubato—Allegro
Lento assai, tranquillo
Presto
Allegro—Allegretto semplice

Kodály's Opus 2 quartet clearly reflects his deep immersion in native music. Although both he and Béla Bartók intended to use field studies as a basis for their own works, significant differences are heard in their resulting compositions. Kodály, the lyricist of the pair, projects folk elements more directly than the intellectually inclined Bartók, who fragments and alters material to create a high level of abstraction. Kodály's quartet does not achieve Bartók's modernist breakthroughs, but it does depart inventively from the prevalent German Romanticism. His attractive early opus develops with animated themes and expressively sustained lines, a reflection of his strong vocal interests; clear part writing, achieved through close studies of Palestrina; and vivid colors, a result of Debussy's impressionist influence.

The Andante introduction begins with a searching cello motif based on the Hungarian song "Lement a nap a maga járásán" (The Sun has Set in its Own True Course). An accelerando passage leads to the Allegro, cast in sonata form. Numerous metric changes shape its two themes, both derived from the opening song.

Cast in three-part song form, the Lento (F sharp minor) opens with an ethereal violin line accompanied by cello pizzicati. The central area (C sharp minor) is animated by pizzicati in the full ensemble. An extended viola soliloquy (F sharp minor), accompanied by shimmering figures in the other strings, reflects the opening material, related to the Hungarian song heard in the first movement.

The dancelike Presto in ABA form opens with a vivacious folk theme stated by the viola. A slower duo for viola and cello provides contrast. Declamatory areas vary the texture as the opening material returns.

The finale (C major) develops a Hungarian song, heard in the first violin, through eight variations of variety and verve. The fifth variation, a lively Allegretto cast in an asymmetrical 5/8 meter, was contributed by Kodály's wife Emma and credited to her in Kodály's footnote. A Presto coda with a cadence of Hungarian inflection concludes the movement.

## String Quartet No. 2, Opus 10 (1918)

Allegro
Andante, quasi recitativo—Allegro giocoso

During the interruption of his field research by the hostilities of World War I, which closed Hungary's borders and imposed a sense of isolation, Kodály wrote his String Quartet No. 2. Considered to be one of Hungary's most significant chamber works, this compact quartet is approximately half the length of its predecessor, written eight years earlier; because of its similar use of ethnic melody, the two quartets can be heard as companions. However, Quartet No. 2 does not develop with the traditional organization of the earlier work but rather as a free, multi-sectioned structure. Gradually shifting rhythms and subtly varied melodies mimic the improvisational quality of folk music.

The opening two movements reveal the impressionist influence of Debussy, whose 1893 G Minor Quartet provided a model. The Allegro, structured in an ABA pattern, explores three interwoven themes. Its solemn introduction returns near the end to form a bridge to the second movement. A rhapsodic violin solo begins the Andante, quasi recitativo, a condensation of the traditional slow movement that can be heard either as an introduction to the finale or as a brief separate movement. The dancelike Allegro giocoso follows without pause. A vigorous presto, alternately animated and rhapsodic, it is propelled by recurrent declamatory rhythmic figures. Six distinct themes, all based on Hungarian folk ideas, are introduced. Bagpipe effects and graceful ornamental notes create a folk atmosphere. Fine solo moments, especially for cello, vary the texture.

## Serenade for Two Violins and Viola, Opus 12 (1920)

Allegramente—Sostenuto, ma non troppo
Lento, ma non troppo
Vivo

Bartók described Kodály's Serenade: "In spite of its unusual chord combinations and surprising originality, the Serenade is firmly based on tonality, a system that has not been exhausted, despite the 'atonal' inclinations of modern music. Superbly rich in instrumental effects and extraordinarily rich in melodies, the work reveals a personality with something entirely new to say. Especially in the slow second movement, where the strangely floating passionate melodies of the viola alternate with spectral flashing motifs in the violin, we find ourselves in a fairy world not dreamed of before."

The energetic first movement develops two strongly-profiled subjects in sonata form. A movement with kaleidoscopic color shifts, the Lento unfolds as a dialogue between the first violin and viola over muted tremolo chords in the second violin. Its two themes create an AABA framework with the second theme (B) based on the main idea of the previous movement. The high-spirited and rhapsodic Vivo finale is a virtuosic set of variations that mimic the improvisatory quality of folk music.

Kodály's numerous affective markings in the Serenade's score (such as "hopelessly" at the end of the second movement) suggest a programmatic content. His Hungarian biographer, László Eősze, hears "three musicians playing a serenade beneath a woman's window, then a song by the lover, played by the viola. The second movement opens with a dialogue between the lover and his mistress, while the tremolos of the second violin suggest the atmosphere of night. To the lover's pleading the woman responds with laughter, her coyness gradually turning into passionate rejection. The lover dismisses the musicians, whereupon the woman relents and the man now laughs. The third movement portrays reconciliation, and the tale is brought to an end with an invigorating dance."

ANTAL DORÁTI
B. APRIL 9, 1906 IN BUDAPEST,
D. NOVEMBER 13, 1988 IN GERZENSEE, SWITZERLAND

## Notturno and Capriccio for Oboe and String Quartet (1926)

Notturno: Andante, rubato
Capriccio: Vivace, capriccioso

Trained in Hungary, Antal Doráti became an American citizen in 1947. He studied composition at Budapest's Franz Liszt Academy, where his important teachers were Zoltán Kodály, Leó Weiner, and Béla Bartók. Doráti is best known as a conductor who delivers "crisp, rhythmically alert" performances, and he has held important positions with the Philharmonia Hungarica, the Dallas Symphony Orchestra, and the Minneapolis Symphony Orchestra. His long career as a recording conductor is unprecedented. Sympathetic to the composers of Eastern Europe, he issued a comprehensive collection of Bartók's orchestral works on the Mercury label. In 1979 he published his autobiography, *Notes of Seven Decades.*

As a composer, Doráti shows the influence of his teachers, particularly Kodály, whose early work suggests French impressionism. Doráti wrote his *Notturno and Capriccio* while he was a twenty-year-old composition student. The opening *Notturno* (Nocturne) is an atmospheric tone poem intended to evoke the mysteriousness of the night. Its chromatic harmonies and flexible tempos impart a sense of restlessness. The whimsical *Capriccio*, "fast and capricious," reveals the impressionist influence of Debussy.

GYÖRGY LIGETI

B. MAY 28, 1923 IN DICIOSÂNMARTIN

(RENAMED TÂRNĂVENI), ROMANIA,

D. JUNE 12, 2006 IN VIENNA

### *String Quartet No. 1, "Métamorphoses nocturnes" (1954)*

Allegro grazioso
Vivace, capriccioso
Adagio, mesto
Presto
Prestissimo
Andante tranquillo
Tempo di Valse, moderato, con eleganza, un poco capriccioso
Subito prestissimo
Allegretto, un poco gioviale
Prestissimo
Ad libitum, senza misura
Lento

Ligeti describes his early String Quartet No.1: "'Transformations of the Night' was written in Budapest in 1953–54 but was intended only for my bottom drawer, since a public performance was out of the question. Life in Hungary at that time was in the grip of the Communist dictatorship, the country completely cut off from all information from abroad: outside contacts and foreign travel were impossible, Western radio broadcasts were jammed, and scores and books could neither be sent nor received. Even the Eastern bloc countries were isolated from each other. Instead, in Budapest there arose a culture of 'closed rooms,' in which the majority of artists opted for 'inner emigration.' The official art foisted on us was 'Socialist Realism,' a cheap kind of art aimed at the masses and designed to promote prescribed political propaganda. But the fact that everything 'modern' had been banned merely served to increase the attractiveness of the concept of modernity for non-conformist artists. All was done in secret. To work for one's bottom drawer was regarded as an honor.

"I was inspired to write String Quartet No. 1 by Bartók's two middle quartets, his Third and Fourth, although I knew them only from their scores since performances of them were banned. In the present instance, 'métamorphoses' signifies a set of character variations without an actual theme but developed out of a basic motivic cell (two major seconds, displaced by a minor second). Melodically and harmonically, the piece rests on total chromaticism, whereas, from a point of view of form, it follows the criteria of Viennese Classicism—that is, periodic structure, imitation, the spinning out of motivic material, the development section and the technique of phrases, which are then distributed among the different voices. Apart from Bartók, Beethoven's Diabelli Variations were my secret ideal. In short, the work is 'modern' in its melodic, harmonic, and rhythmic writing, but the articulation of the form—what I would call the 'discourse'—is traditional.

"Not until after I had fled Hungary in 1956 was this quartet performed, when the Ramor Quartet, which had similarly fled into exile, introduced it to Vienna in 1958."

GYÖRGY KURTÁG

B. FEBRUARY 19, 1926 IN LUGOJ, ROMANIA

### *"Officium Breve in Memoriam Andreae Szervánszky"*
### *for String Quartet, Opus 28 (1989)*

Largo

Più andante

Sostenuto, quasi giusto

Grave, molto sostenuto

Presto (Fantasie über die Harmonien des Webern-Kanons)

Molto agitato (Canon a 4)

Sehr fliessend: Canon a 2 (frei nach Op. 31/VI von Webern)

Lento

Largo

Sehr fliessend (Webern: Canon a 4, Op. 31/VI)

Sostenuto

Sostenuto, quasi giusto

Sostenuto, con slancio

Disperato, vivo

Larghetto: Arioso interrotto (di Endre Szervanszky)

Kurtág's profound *Officium Breve* is a memorial to his colleague Andreae Szervánszky (1911–1977) and also a set of brief statements that allude to works and persons meaningful to his own life and career. The title *Officium Breve* puns on the dual meaning of breve as a long musical note, common to early music and equal to two whole notes, and its legal definition as a writ issued by a court of law; officium is Latin for ceremony. A poised and reflective atmosphere prevails in this work, which develops with a wide range of sonorities and dynamics.

The Auryn Quartet, which premiered the work, writes: "Kurtág once described composition as a 'continual research' aimed at achieving 'a sort of unity with as little material as possible.' Like that of his model Anton Webern, Kurtág's aphoristic musical language and the forces he uses to express it are radically compressed. Yet despite the abundance of 'white space' in a typical Kurtág score, it would be misleading to characterize such densely packed and elusive music as 'minimalist.' Economical though he may be with notes, Kurtág has little in common with such composers as Philip Glass, John Adams, and Arvo Pärt. *Officium Breve* is a good example of the musical procedures that Kurtág has employed over his long career to create a richly evocative, delicately tinted, and highly personalized sound world. Three movements are based on material borrowed from the Serenade for String Orchestra by Kurtág's compatriot Andreae Szervánszky, while other movements pay tribute to four more friends and colleagues. But the musical and emotional centerpiece of *Officium Breve* is an arrangement of the four-part canon from Webern's Second Cantata, Opus 31. Kurtág notes that Szervánszky was also decisively influenced by Webern, which explains why an homage to Webern had to be included in a work composed in memoriam Szervánszky as well."

# SIX

# Forward Thinkers in Germany

Two cataclysmic World Wars and evolving political developments changed the trajectory of German music. Musical arts had long been an essential part of German life, necessary for entertainment, betterment of character, and contemplation of the Divine. The widely distributed and influential book *On the Beautiful in Music* (1854), written by critic Eduard Hanslick, held that the meaning of music was conveyed through its formal perfection, which to his circle constituted "beauty." He championed Romantic composers such as Robert Schumann, Felix Mendelssohn, and Johannes Brahms, all of whom pursued creation of the beautiful through songful, finely wrought works inspired by Beethoven's intrinsic Romanticism. Later composers such as Richard Wagner and Richard Strauss pursued the goal of beauty on their own terms as they created a "Music of the Future" that conveyed meanings beyond the music in their luxuriantly romantic works.

During the restless decade before World War l, German arts began a transition. Perhaps responding to cultural currents set in motion by philosopher Friedrich Nietzsche (1844–1900), who removed a lynchpin by denying the existence of a Christian God (although he condoned a mythic world view), artists began to create experimental works that presaged a break with the past. After the war's carnage, composers anxiously searched for a new ideal. Coinciding with the perception that the old forms were exhausted, profound new questions arose: was a quest for the sensuously beautiful relevant to a world that had suffered to such a brutal extreme? Should art serve a spiritual or social purpose? Should music emulate the functional forms of modernist architecture, which itself strived to incubate a new social order?

Creative solutions were warped or stifled by the Nazi regime in the difficult years before and during World War II. Visionary composers such as Hindemith sought freedom in the United States, and most who remained kept silent, if they survived. Stockhausen's handicapped mother, a gifted singer, was euthanized because she was deemed a "useless mouth." The old order also suffered; Mendelssohn's statue was toppled by Nazis in Leipzig, and the celebrated romanticist Richard Strauss was intimidated because he refused to join their party.

Energized by the postwar challenge to rebuild, composers experimented with new resources such as electronics as well as organization through the ostensibly "beautiful" and non-political system of mathematics. Remarkably, despite widely diverging results, both the ideals and methods of Beethoven—perhaps Germany's greatest genius in a nation of geniuses—remained present. Hindemith returned to Europe honored as the inventor of a new harmonic scheme—but he modestly identified his works as "crafts" much as Beethoven had termed his compositions "products of the human brain." Stockhausen departs radically from established language, but he emulates procedures of Beethoven as he creates large and intricate chamber works that begin with small "germ" cells. End of century works such as Wilhelm Killmayer's piano trio *Brahms-Bildnis* (Brahms Portrait) convey nostalgia for the old Germany, even as its future holds exceptional promise.

PAUL HINDEMITH
B. NOVEMBER 16, 1895 IN HANAU, GERMANY,
D. DECEMBER 28, 1963 IN FRANKFURT

One of the leading composers and theorists of the first half of the twentieth century, Paul Hindemith was also a virtuoso violist, outstanding conductor, and influential teacher. Because of his tremendous technical resources and creative energy, he became the spokesperson for post-World War I German composers who sought alternatives to the prevalent Romanticism. During the 1920s Hindemith participated in the *Neue Sachlichkeit* (New Objectivity movement), a practical reaction to enduring nineteenth-century sentimentality. He began to cultivate the genre of *Gebrauchsmusik* (music for use), functional and entertaining compositions of medium difficulty intended to encourage interest in contemporary music. Appointed head of the Berlin Hochschule für Musik in 1927, he soon caught the attention of the Nazis with his score (as well as his acting abilities) for the experimental film *Vormittagsspuk* (Ghosts Before Breakfast), copies of which they burned. Denounced by Goebbels as a "cultural Bolshevist" and "spiritual non-Aryan" after a Berlin performance of *Mathis der Maler* (Matthias the Painter), an opera based on the life of Matthias Grünewald as he struggled for freedom of expression in a repressive society, Hindemith fled Germany for Switzerland, then Turkey, and later the United States, where he became a citizen in 1946. He returned to Europe in 1953.

A neoclassicist who advocated clear and concise expression, Hindemith regarded the composer as a skilled craftsperson who must create solid musical edifices, tonally and formally lucid constructions in sound. Seeking rapport with both performers and audiences, he sought to produce coherent musical speech that was also an individual and contemporary tonal language. To this end, Hindemith gradually formulated a new tonal system based on psychological and acoustical principles. Mirroring characteristics of the physical world, he established key centers through melodic and harmonic progressions moving gravitationally toward the tonic triad. Despite this tonal grounding, Hindemith's music is freely dissonant in that it equally develops all twelve tones of the octave and avoids distinct major-minor scale patterns. An admirer of

Bach, Hindemith is renowned for the artful lines of counterpoint heard in many of his works.

## String Quartet No. 3, Opus 22 (1921)

Fugato: Sehr langsame Viertel
Schnelle Achtel, sehr energisch
Ruhige Viertel, stets fliessend
Mässig schnelle Viertel
Rondo: Gemächlich und mit Grazie

Hindemith wrote his Third String Quartet at a time of extreme social and economic upheaval in Germany. The overall logical structure of this turbulent quartet reflects Hindemith's esthetics, linked to an extent with his contemporary, the figurative painter Max Beckmann (1884–1950). Although Beckmann was perceived as an Expressionist, a conveyer of heightened emotional experience through colorful abstractions, he rejected that term and allied himself with the unsentimental realists of the New Objectivity movement. Although often disturbing, Beckmann's highly symbolic canvases reveal an underlying order that suggests his fundamental belief in a rational universe.

Hindemith opens his quartet with a neoclassical fugue (Fugato: very slow quarter notes) in which a lyrical melody is passed among the four instruments. Savagely hammered rhythms heard in the second movement (Fast eighth notes, very energetic) offer an abrupt contrast; after a quiet interlude, the opening material returns. The second violin, accompanied by pizzicati in the viola and cello, sings the gentle theme of the extensive third movement (Calm quarter notes, always flowing). Polytonality is heard as the violin plays its melody in C against the lower strings in A.

The fourth movement (Moderately fast quarter notes) can be heard as a brief introduction to the finale. It opens as a cadenza for cello, joined by the viola, and leads without pause to the fifth movement (Rondo: leisurely and with grace). An homage to Bach, this movement is a two-part invention with a contrasting middle section and a calm conclusion, a condensed restatement of the opening material.

## *Kleine Kammermusik for Wind Quintet, Opus 24 No. 2 (1922)*

Lustig. Mässig schnell Viertel
Walzer: durchweg sehr leise
Ruhig und einfach
Schnelle Viertel
Sehr lebhaft

Between 1921 and 1927 Hindemith wrote eight works entitled *Kammermusik* (Chamber Music), each scored for a different combination of instruments. This *Kammermusik* series, often written for unconventional scoring, is admired for its exuberance and astringent wit. Opus 24 No. 2 (1922) is the second of the pair entitled *Kleine Kammermusik* (Little Chamber Music); both its harmonic style and standard quintet scoring reflect a more conservative approach than its predecessor, a polytonal work that included an accordion and siren. Opus 24 No. 2 suggests not only the modernist influence of Stravinsky but also the historic reference of the entertaining eighteenth-century wind divertimento.

The clarinet introduces the three important motifs that are expanded and developed in the first movement, "Joyous with a moderately fast quarter note." A propulsive three-note figure becomes a recurring ostinato with driving energy. The oboe introduces a calmer second theme; the bassoon echoes this motif at the gentle, whimsical conclusion. The ironic waltz ("Always very light") that follows leads into the somber third movement, "Quiet and simple." Moving with a "Rapid quarter note" tempo, the fourth section is a bridge that leads to the finale, "Very lively." The three-note ostinato heard at the opening returns in this syncopated and vigorous movement; near the conclusion each instrument plays a brief cadenza.

### *"Minimax: Repertorium für Militärmusik" for String Quartet (1923)*

Armeemarsch 606 (Der Hohenfürstenberger)
Overtüre zu "Wasserdichter und Vogelbauer"
Ein abend an der Donauquelle: Intermezzo für zwei
    entfernte Trompeten
Löwenzähnchen an Baches Rand: Konzertwalzer
Die beiden lustigen Mistfinken: Charakterstuck, Solo für
    zwei Pikkoloflöten)
Alte Karbonaden: Marsch

In his early years, Hindemith created much irrepressibly buoyant music that expressed both his keen sense of irony and his good-natured but irreverent sense of fun. His penchant for jokes is apparent in *Minimax* (1923), a parody on military music named for a popular brand of fire extinguisher. The seven-minute work also offers homage to his music patron Prince von Fürstenberg since Hindemith combines the nicknames of the Prince and Princess, Max and Minzi. In a photo taken at the premiere the musicians, wearing paper helmets, salute with their bows. Although the work was rarely performed in Hindemith's later years, it was the first chamber work of a living composer to be broadcast by the new Frankfurt station in 1924.

The titles of the movements translate as: Army March, Overture to The Water Poet and the Birdcage, An Evening at the Source of the Danube (Intermezzo for Two Distant Trumpets), Dandelions at the Edge of the Brook, Two Cheerful but Filthy Persons, and The Old Carbonade Soldier.

## *Quartet for Clarinet, Violin, Cello, and Piano (1938)*

Mässig bewegt
Sehr langsam
Mässig bewegt

Hindemith wrote his clarinet quartet from April to June 1938, shortly after he had left Hitler's Berlin for Switzerland. A tonal work with occasionally dissonant departures, the quartet is centered on the key of F major. In the first movement, "moderately animated," the piano presents the main theme, followed by a lyrical second subject shared by all instruments. The three-part second movement, "very slow," opens with a leisurely melody that develops to a fortissimo climax in its turbulent middle section. A calm transition passage leads to a return of the opening material. The final movement, also in three sections, begins with a moderately paced section followed by an exuberant, rhythmically complex dance. The tempo slows as the piano articulates staccato figuration in its upper registers. A coda, introduced by barbaric rhythms in the piano, brings the work to a brilliant conclusion.

RICHARD STRAUSS
B. JUNE 11, 1864 IN MUNICH,
D. SEPTEMBER 8, 1949 IN GARMISCH-PARTENKIRCHEN,
WEST GERMANY

## *Sextet from "Capriccio," Opus 85 (1941)*

Richard Strauss composed his Sextet as the *Einleitung* (Introduction) to his final opera, *Capriccio*, premiered in Munich in October 1942. A neoclassical work set in eighteenth-century France, the opera provided relief from the difficult circumstances of wartime Germany. Strauss, who had endured harassment from the Nazis, including the bullying of Goebbels, bravely described it as "an agreeable evening for respectable people," despite the premiere's attendance of Rudolph Hess in uniform.

In the opera's context, the Sextet has been recently composed by the musician Flamand, and the actual introduction functions thematically as its rehearsal. Near the conclusion of the Sextet the curtain rises on the garden of a rococo chateau, and one hears the final strains as if it were played in an adjacent room. The Sextet's polished phrasing and refined workmanship evoke aristocratic grace and elegance. Structurally, it falls symmetrically into three sections. The outer areas develop calm and poised themes with graceful counterpoint, and the more turbulent and chromatic middle section provides contrast.

Strauss, who wrote that his opera was "a conversation piece for music," used *Capriccio* as a vehicle for exploring a philosophical question that had long absorbed both him and his eighteenth-century predecessors: which is more important to opera, the music or the words? *Capriccio* is set during the time when the French composer Gluck was urging composers to streamline the music in opera so that the words might be clearly discerned. The main characters of *Capriccio*—the young, widowed Countess and her two suitors—explore this issue through extended conversations about theater and opera. The Countess must decide over the course of one evening which of the two suitors she will marry, the poet Olivier or the composer Flamand. At the end she faces the mirror and realizes that her indecision will remain—a symbolic gesture implying the perfect equality of text and music.

WILHELM KILLMAYER
B. AUGUST 21, 1927 IN MUNICH,
D. AUGUST 20, 2017 IN STARNBERG, GERMANY

## *"Brahms-Bildnis" for Piano Trio (1976)*

Although Wilhelm Killmayer was influenced initially by the direct simplicity of his mentor Carl Orff, his music evolved through a serialist phase to a neo-romantic mode of expression. Killmayer was essentially an instrumental chamber musician who avoided both avant-garde techniques and the electronic technology available to him, occasionally to the detriment of his reputation within Germany. Killmayer's strong literary consciousness is evident in the poetic quality of his works, which proceed with the subjective character of human speech. His motivic treatment is fragmentary and distinctly tonal, with free use of dissonant chords. One hears solo lines set against chordal punctuations from the rest of the ensemble. Large sections often appear rhythmically static because of their slow tempos; yet their incessant note repetition creates forward momentum.

*Brahms-Bildnis* (Brahms Portrait) explores Killmayer's spiritual relationship to both Brahms and to German Romanticism. The work demands the focused attention of its listener; as Orff commented, it is music that "ideally should be listened to in a darkened room."

Killmayer writes: "My piano trio is a one-movement composition and is approximately fifteen minutes in length. It begins with an almost concerto-like solo violin passage and builds to a catastrophic outburst. This is reinforced in the use of the piano's upper register with the shrill sound of the hammers prevailing. After a short and resigning cantilena, the piece comes to an abrupt close. One can see this work as a portrait of Johannes Brahms. The contrasts between life's chaotic nature and its reconciliations are thematically expressed in the piece."

KARLHEINZ STOCKHAUSEN
B. AUGUST 22, 1928 IN MÖDRATH, GERMANY,
D. DECEMBER 5, 2007 IN KÜRTEN, GERMANY

Acclaimed as one of the great visionaries of the twentieth century, Stockhausen is known for his groundbreaking work in electronic music, his significant refinements of serial technique, and his bold explorations of spatial effects. Trained at Cologne and Paris, where he was taught by Olivier Messiaen and absorbed the style of Anton Webern, Stockhausen became a leading figure of the Darmstadt School, an international contemporary music center. His wide range of non-traditional compositions, created over a career of six decades, encompass solo and chamber works, choral and orchestral music, and seven full-length operas. Stockhausen produced seventeen volumes of theoretical writings containing valuable commentary about his compositional process; they also offer guideposts to compositional theory of the postwar era.

In creating his works, Stockhausen considered the personality of performers and their instrumental techniques as critical elements of composition. He appreciated the controlled improvisatory elements that can result from performers' interactions during rehearsals. Often his performances suggest the group approach of jazz as one performer indexes off the next—but now realized with avant-garde techniques. The acoustics of the performing venue are also of utmost importance. Stockhausen describes his ideal hall as "a spherical space which is fitted all around with loudspeakers. In the middle of this spherical space a sound-permeable, transparent platform would be suspended for the listeners. They could hear music composed for such standardized spaces coming from above, from below, and from all points of the compass."

Stockhausen's influence is far reaching. Stravinsky discussed Stockhausen's music in his conversation books with Robert Craft, and Stravinsky's later music draws from Stockhausen's work. Pierre

Boulez commented: "Stockhausen is the greatest living composer, and the only one I recognize as my peer." British composer Brian Ferneyhough observed: "I doubt that there has been a single composer of the intervening generation who, even if for a short time, did not see the world of music differently thanks to the work of Stockhausen." Jazz musicians such as Miles Davis also cite Stockhausen as an influence, as does the world of pop and rock. Stockhausen's image was included on the album cover of The Beatles' *Sgt. Pepper's Lonely Hearts Band*, and their song "A Day in the Life" drew from Stockhausen's electronic techniques. International stars such as Björk and Frank Zappa, as well as members of Pink Floyd and the Grateful Dead, also acknowledge his influence. Perhaps his highest written tribute came from New Zealand composer Robin Maconie: "If a genius is someone whose ideas survive all attempts at explanation, then by definition Stockhausen is the nearest thing to Beethoven this century has produced. Reason? His music lasts."

Ideally, one should listen to a Stockhausen composition while following its score. Each work has unique intricacies, and the score will illuminate the more elusive, as well as heightening intellectual enjoyment. A composer with a strong visual imagination, Stockhausen created scores, occasionally color coded, that in themselves are works of art. *Refrain* is especially remarkable for its inclusion of a rotatable repeated section (the refrain) on a transparent plastic strip.

*"Kreuzspiel" for Oboe, Bass Clarinet, Piano (with woodblocks), Three Percussionists, Cat. No. 1/7 (1951). Duration ca. 11 minutes 30 seconds.*

Perhaps the cars moving in opposing lanes of a German highway sparked a visual epiphany for Stockhausen, who in a flash translated it to a sound image as he sat at a rest stop in August 1951. After assimilating this moment of insight, he organized its elements into the outlines for *Kreuzspiel* (Crossplay), his first critically acclaimed work. Influenced by the serialism of his teacher Olivier Messiaen, Stockhausen crafted two series of six tones, one comprised of high notes and the other low. He positioned these groups into opposing sets that start at the high and low ends of the piano and gradually meet at the middle (with articulation by oboe and bass clarinet). The voices then cross over to the side opposite to their starting register; their total range is six octaves. At the point of convergence between the two rows, there occurs a mysterious songlike phrase within the interval of an octave.

Several types of "crossings" occur as permutations of the original twelve note (2 times 6) pitch row sequence. Most of these permutations, however, are not readily audible, unlike the simple scheme of points meeting and parting. Players comment that the work has meticulous construction but nevertheless produces a subconscious effect of continuous unpredictability.

Considered to be his first mature work, *Kreuzspiel* was Stockhausen's first composition to be guided by processes other than thematic melodic motifs. Here he treats notes as "points" rather than groups of themes, a technical advance at a time when composers created serial music that verged on late Romanticism but with liberated harmony. Stockhausen revised the score both during rehearsals and after the first performance. He comments on the pivotal nature of *Kreuzspiel*: "From this time forward I planned the structure of all my works, from the number of movements to the evolution of single parameters to the analysis of the particles of sound or groups of sound to be used."

---

*"Kontra-Punkte" for Flute, Clarinet in A, Bass Clarinet, Bassoon, Trumpet, Trombone, Piano, Harp, Violin, and Cello, Cat. No. 1 (1953). Duration ca. 14 minutes 13 seconds.*

---

A serial composition for ten diverse instruments, *Kontra-Punkte* (Counter-Points) explores contrasts among both six instrumental timbres and their extremes of dynamic levels and note durations. At the conclusion, the contrasts are resolved into a soft and homogeneous texture. Stockhausen comments: "Counter-Points is a series of the most concealed and also the most conspicuous transformations and renewals—with no predictable end. The same thing is never heard twice. Yet there is a distinct feeling of never falling out of an unmistakable construction of the utmost homogeneity. An underlying force that holds things together—related proportions: a structure. These are not the same *Gestalten* (shapes) in a changing light, but rather various *Gestalten* in the same light, which permeates everything." The current version, completed in 1953, is a reworking of the 1951 original.

The title's hyphenation signifies a "counter-action" against the stylistic pointillism in vogue during the 1950s. Here Stockhausen gathers disassociated points into cohesive groups. Importantly, the hyphen differentiates this chamber work from an earlier orchestral score originally entitled *Kontrapunkte* but after reworking named simply *Punkte*.

The ensemble is divided into six compatible sound groups (flute-bassoon, clarinet-bass clarinet, trumpet-trombone, piano-harp, violin-cello). Stockhausen states that the work is "transformed irregularly but steadily into a soloistic style articulated by 'groups' that gradually focus on the piano part." Long notes are replaced by short, rapid groups to erode the initially sparse texture. Simultaneously, the contrasting timbres are reduced to the piano's monochrome. Fluctuating note values are reduced to notes of similar value, and the extreme dynamics are reduced to a soft level. A parallel to Haydn's "Farewell" Symphony finale, in which performers gradually depart to leave a pair of violins as the sole players, has often been observed.

*"Zeitmasse" for Flute, Oboe, English Horn, Clarinet, and Bassoon, Cat. No. 5 (1956). Duration ca. 15 minutes.*

*Zeitmasse* (Time Measures) began in 1955 as a brief tribute to a friend before his honorary dinner. Stockhausen comments on its origin: "I had to write something quickly, by that evening. Suddenly, I heard this little four-minute piece for voice and wind quintet. Later I replaced the vocal part with an English horn, and the resulting 'piece' is the first four minutes of *Zeitmasse*, based on these French lyrics: 'We are seeking to find something. But we do not know quite what for.'" Stockhausen later increased its length and mass by adding five cadenzas. The work was premiered in Paris by his colleague Pierre Boulez, who later took it on tour to London and engineered its first recording.

*Zeitmasse* literally means "tempo" in German, and Arnold Schoenberg famously used the term to indicate restoration of the earlier established tempo in his string quartet scores. In Stockhausen's terminology the title refers to differing ways of treating time as a "mass" quantity. Stockhausen explained the concept of *Zeitmasse* in his article "How Time Passes" (1956). Essentially he organizes rhythm in a twelve-step process that mirrors the serial organization of pitches, a secondary aspect of this work. He outlines these categories of "Time Measures": the twelve degrees of metronomic tempos; alternation of controlled and flexible sections in which areas are to be played "as fast as possible" or "as slow as possible"; fast tempos with drastic slowing and slow tempos with rapid speeding.

The work is divided into three sections. The first corresponds to the original song; five sets of number values control time duration, and a twelve-tone row provides the pitch set. The longer second section is built on permutations of seven note groups and individual chords that recur four times. Four complex cadenzas (regulated by a 9 times 9 number grid) are interspersed. The third section is the most rhythmically complex since it is based on five duration sets. Cadenzas occur as perceivable interruptions but are integrated into the flow. The result is an interlaced pattern of eleven continuous sections.

*"Refrain," Trio for Piano with Woodblocks, Vibraphone with Alpine Cowbells, Amplified Celesta with Antique Cymbals, Cat. No. 11 (1959). Duration ca. 12 minutes.*

Stockhausen writes: "The title refers to a short refrain, recurring six times, that disturbs a placid and widely arcing sound texture. These refrains are notated on a rotatable plastic strip, superimposed on curved staves which allow the refrain to be repositioned in order to introduce these disturbances in different places. Each of the three performers plays an accessory instrument, creating six distinct timbres reflecting the pitch structure, which divides the twelve-tone row into two symmetrical six-note cells. The three performers are also required to vocalize tongue clicks on five approximate pitches and short, sharp phonetic syllables to be pitched near the sounds they play, in a manner reminiscent of Japanese theatre. The background layer of the piece consists of a series of chords derived from an all-interval twelve-tone row used in a number of other works. The work concludes with a coda in which the elements are merged into a single complex sound."

*"Examen" from "Michaels Jugend," Scene 3 from Donnerstag aus Licht, for Tenor Voice, Trumpet, Dancer, Piano, and Bassett Horn, Cat. No. 49 ¾ (1979). Duration ca. 22 minutes.*

*Donnerstag aus Licht* (Thursday from Light) is the first of seven operas composed for Stockhausen's monumental cycle *Licht: die sieben Tage der Woche* (Light: The Seven Days of the Week), written over a period of twenty-six years and scored for vocal, instrumental, and electronic forces. Its libretto is by the composer. The seven operas together constitute an epic drama centered on the evolving relationships of the archetypal characters Michael, Eve, and Lucifer, who over the course of the operas endure conflict, face temptations, and finally achieve union. These highly symbolic, multimedia works are structured so that acts and scenes can be performed separately or even paired successfully with non-*Licht* works. The cycle was premiered at Milan's La Scala in 1981 and later that year given the Premio Critica Musicale Award for "Best New Work of Contemporary Music."

The twenty-nine hour long cycle is controlled by a "super-formula," a three-layered melodic/thematic "backbone" that coalesced while Stockhausen visited Japan and absorbed its theatrical tradition in 1977. Permutations of this one-minute-long pattern, most barely perceptible, are insinuated throughout the entire cycle in various guises. Stockhausen states the importance of the melodies derived from the formula: "The characters and the stage action are essentially a visual and physical manifestation of the musical elements."

First portrayed as a human, Michael is the cosmic protagonist of the opera, and the work celebrates his growth from child to man as he journeys around Earth, finds his soulmate Eve, and eventually rejoins the stars. "Examination," scene three from "Michael's Youth," is written for tenor voice, trumpet, dancer, piano, and basset horn. The "jury" (ad libitum) consists of soprano, bass, and two dancer-mimes.

Stockhausen writes: "'Examination' is about life—my life, and I believe, the life of every person on this planet. You must assess yourself and learn. 'Examination' is a scene from the first opera of the Light cycle. Why Thursday? Thursday is the day of learning. A person learns from an examination, and as I see it, learns most of all from music, as it is the most Beautiful of all the Arts, the most subtle form of communication and of vibrations."

"Examination" consists of three recitals that Michael performs to depict the different aspects of his character; after each is successfully completed, he "graduates" to the next state. Each recital is accompanied by a pianist to suggest a conservatory setting. At the first examination, Michael is a singer performing for a jury that consists of two father figures and two mother figures. At this first performance he gradually assumes the gentle character of his mother Eve; his speech becomes confused as he mingles the characters Eve, Lucifer, and himself. After a description of his childhood, he moves to the second examination, an instrumental section portraying the difficult life of his father. The trumpet now depicts the father and the basset horn the mother, who appears as a guardian angel. After a vigorous section Michael moves into another dimension, and the third examination begins. Michael floats spirit-like and his childhood is conjured from the child's perspective. Stockhausen states this is "more in the realm of fantasy and the beyond and of the here and now, where there exists no barrier at all."

*"Tierkreis" (Trio version) for Clarinet, Flute and Piccolo, Trumpet, and Piano, Cat. No. 41 9/10 (1983). Duration ca. 29 minutes.*

Perhaps Stockhausen's most popular composition, *Tierkreis* (Zodiac) has been honored by the City Council of Cologne with the decree that his melodies corresponding to current Zodiac signs be played daily at noon by the 48-bell carillon of the Town Hall. The composer writes: "*Tierkreis* is a cycle of musical formulas for the twelve months of the year and the twelve human types. These formulae lend themselves to innumerable versions. A trio version was made during rehearsals with its dedicatees."

In performance, the three musicians change position at each new section to clarify the instrumentation and structure. All movements are carefully described in the score and documented by photographs. Each of the twelve movements is a character piece representing the signs of the zodiac. Based on a tone row of twelve to fourteen notes, the melodies are centered on an individual pitch that rises by half steps over the duration of the work. Each has its own distinctive tempo and rhythms, also organized serially, to achieve maximum contrast between sections. In the trio version, the varied effects of the four seasons are conveyed through tone colors and instrumental timbre.

*"Rotary Wind Quintet" for Flute, Oboe, Clarinet in B flat, Bassoon, and Horn, Cat. No. 70 ½ (1997). Duration ca. 8 minutes.*

The *Rotary Wind Quintet* was composed as a commission to celebrate the Cologne-Römerturm Rotary Club's 25th anniversary. The work was premiered as a surprise for its captive audience of 200, who had gathered for a banquet. Although many present normally would have avoided a Stockhausen concert, its members gave the work a standing ovation. After Stockhausen outlined its earthy humor, which would have delighted Mozart in his uninhibited moments, the quintet was immediately repeated with similar acclaim.

A component of the opera *Mittwoch aus Licht* (Wednesday from Light, completed 1998), *Rotary Wind Quintet* is an adaptation of the concluding "carousel" section of scene 4, "Michaelion," a vocal "spatial sextet" titled "Menschen, hört" (Mankind, hear). In this scene delegates from several stars meet to elect a new president. A camel (Lucicamel) enters and sings an ode to the planetary angel while simultaneously defecating seven new planets. Delegates then carry these fertile deposits to distant corners of the universe. Stockhausen reconceives the voices as pungently sonorous instruments for his wind quintet.

Clarinettist Suzanne Stephens writes: "*Rotary Wind Quintet* is based on a module of three melodic strands in the fabric of the 'carousel' section. These strands consist of the three-layered superformula of *Licht* and are rotated vertically four times. At each change of the layers, the musicians also rotate positions in the performance space." Stephens describes the rotations among the five instruments within the four divisions of the work: "The four phases are connected by sustained chords during which the performers change position. Each phase presents a different vertical disposition of the three strands of the *Licht* superformula. In phase 1 the Michael formula is in the upper voice, the Lucifer formula in the lowest voice, and the Eve formula in between. In phase 2, the Lucifer formula moves to the top, Michael is in the middle, and Eve below. In phase 3 the Eve formula is uppermost, Lucifer in the middle, and Michael below. In phase 4 the three formulas return to their starting positions. Each phase is a longer more elaborate version of the formula than its predecessor."

*"Schönheit, Sixth Hour" from "Klang," for Flute, Bass Clarinet, and Trumpet, Cat. No. 86 (2006). Duration ca. 30 minutes.*

Stockhausen worked on *Klang—Die 24 Stunden des Tages* (Sound—the 24 Hours of the Day) from 2004 until his death in 2007. His intention was to create 24 chamber compositions, each representing a separate hour of the day. A specific color is systematically assigned to each hour according to Wilhelm Ostwald's color theories (1917); Stockhausen explained: "I start with the darkest color at one o'clock in the night, then I progressively turn the circle in order to coincide with a clock." For consistency, he suggests that the players wear the section's color during its performance. Although the last three hours are incomplete, the existing works (catalog numbers 81-101, which include solos, duets, trios, and a septet) constitute an invaluable addition to chamber repertoire. All are based on a 24-note series that relates to a two-octave chromatic scale.

A companion to his opera cycle *Licht*, the title "Klang" signi-
fied for him acoustic vibrations. He wrote: "Above all, the inner ear
knows the divine Klang, the mystic sound of the beyond with the
voice of the conscience—in German: die *Stimme des Gewissens*....
It seems that I am listening again more for moments, atmospheres,
rather than formulas with their limbs ... a special concentration
and freedom must be trained for listening to the soul's vibrations."

The specified color for *Schönheit* (Beauty), the Sixth Hour, is
turquoise blue. The work's five sections are all based on the material
of the preceding hour, *Harmonien* (Harmonies), and each section
contains the three consecutive groups from the *Harmonien* cycle.
*Schönheit's* numerous permutations and simultaneous combinations of tempos create complex relationships that belie the work's
deceptive simplicity; as Marco Blaauw writes, "It is a work of synthesis that requires a great intellectual effort on the part of the
listener." The work progresses with increasing intricacy as Stockhausen rotates segments of the row among the three instruments
to create a "homophonic canon."

WOLFGANG RIHM
B. MARCH 13, 1952 IN KARLSRUHE, GERMANY

*String Quartet No. 11 (2010)*

One of Stockhausen's most celebrated students at Darmstadt
in the 1970s, Wolfgang Rihm is a highly prolific composer in virtually every genre. He has written thirteen string quartets over the
course of his career as well as three imaginative piano trios (*Fremde
Szenen*, Distant Scenes) that reference the idiom of Robert
Schumann. Rihm's style, while thoroughly contemporary in idiom,
incorporates elements of Expressionism and the New Simplicity
movement, with which his name was particularly associated in the

early 1980s.

Violist Geraldine Walther from the Takács Quartet describes String Quartet No. 11: "The work is composed as one movement, with slight pauses between sections in order to change moods. The piece shows the composer's grasp of string colors and transparencies of textures, as well as turbulent and violent textures and rhythms. We start out quietly, the two pairs of instruments conversing calmly, with small introductions of individual rhythms. It builds to a cadenza-like outburst by the viola, which is joined by the others. The violins then change the mood with embroidery of sweet legato exchanges and the excitement returns. Calm returns for a moment then another short explosion until everyone tires. A chorale, almost religious in purity, follows.

"A cello solo leads the group to a strong abrupt stop and leaves the first violin playing a quiet held note, as if it were a question mark. Then we are off again into a very exciting, fast rhythmic section. At the climax of the piece the instruments are almost shooting short sounds back and forth at each other. We then tumble down scales and come to rest on a double stop in the viola. Suddenly a very simple motive, almost like a fragment of a forgotten children's song, comes into play from the first violin, and gradually the instruments pass this motive back and forth, developing it, playing with it in a pizzicato section and leading the group to further loud discussion.

"Finally, after much turbulence, the instruments start to calm down and want to cooperate, and after hearing the simple tune a few more times, the four players leave with quiet chords and a final hushed unison pizzicato."

# SEVEN

# Poland Ascending

Poland, a Catholic nation, has long been encircled by politically and religiously diverse groups—Protestant Germany to the west; Orthodox Russia to the east; the former Ottoman Empire, assimilated by the Habsburg Empire, to the south. Their disparate artistic influences have been heard over the centuries in Poland's music, which often reveals the pull between the Oriental and the European. Ancient and modern forces persistently strive for dominance.

The Polish National Foundation comments on Poland's cultural heritage and the history that has influenced its national philosophy: "Reaching into our past, learning lessons from the lives of our ancestors, and unearthing our vital springs are essential means for our survival and development. Poland, poised between East and West, is located at the 'crush zone' between the great powers. In the historical and existential sense, Poles live in a country that has been repeatedly threatened with complete annihilation, being wiped off the world maps. That actually did occur for 123 years during the crucial time of the industrial revolution and progress of the Western world. There are people among us who remember the destroyed Warsaw and the horrific effects of World War II. Poland in the twenty-first century is governed by awareness and memory of that past. It takes a reflective search for solutions in the new world order."

Karol Szymanowski, Poland's leading musical figure in the early twentieth century, envisioned a national school that incorporated his country's folk culture with broadly European trends (see below). During the Stalinist era (1922–1953), dogmatic "social realism" prevailed in the arts, and innovative composers went underground. After Stalin's death and the resulting political détente, new artistic standards were quickly adopted. In October 1956 musicians celebrated the first "Warsaw Autumn" Festival of Contemporary Music, a venue that inspired the establishment of the Polish Composers' School. Initially centered on twelve-tone composition, its aesthetic tendencies gradually evolved toward Sonorism, a technique that prioritizes tonal qualities above other elements of a composition (e.g., melody and rhythm). Leading proponents of this technique, Witold Lutosławski, Krzysztof Penderecki, Henryk Górecki, and Grażyna Bacewitz created significant chamber works that are important contributions to the repertoire.

During the last decade of the twentieth century, Polish composers began to explore a "golden middle" of proportions between the contemporary and the traditional. Composers such as Stanisław Krupowicz (b. 1952), Paweł Szymański (b. 1954), and his student Paweł Mykietyn (b. 1971) acknowledge historical tradition in disciplined, contemporarily structured compositions of hypnotic beauty. Composers born after avant-garde influences have now assumed an important role, and each will express important ideas in the twenty-first century.

KAROL SZYMANOWSKI
B. OCTOBER 3, 1882 IN TYMOSZÓWKA, KIEV GOVERNORATE
(NOW UKRAINE),
D. MARCH 29, 1937 IN LAUSANNE, SWITZERLAND

Composer and pianist Karol Szymanowski, born into Poland's landed gentry, was trained in Warsaw and travelled extensively throughout Europe to absorb international styles. Avoiding recruitment into the Russian army because of health, during the early years of World War I Szymanowski settled into his family home and forged an individual style, an idiom that combined post-Wagnerian Romanticism, the Impressionism of Debussy, and mystical elements of late Scriabin. This idyllic interlude came to a brutal end in 1917 when the Bolsheviks destroyed his home and gratuitously hauled his grand piano into the lake of the estate. He then devoted himself to literature for a healing interval and wrote the two-volume novel *Efebos* (Youths), but the manuscript was tragically destroyed in the 1939 Warsaw fires.

After the war Szymanowski was appointed Director of the Warsaw Conservatory, his forum for the re-invigoration of Polish musical education and the establishment of new models for training future generations of composers. Returning to composition, he became fascinated by the culture of the Gorals, Poland's Highlanders of the Tatra Mountains. Szymanowski conceived a Polish national style that merged these authentic folk elements with European late Romanticism exemplified by Richard Strauss. Hoping that other Polish composers might seek a similar synthesis, Szymanowski vigorously promoted awareness of Poland's native folk idiom. Its uninhibited rhythms and harshly dissonant harmonies became a strong influence for composers of the decades following.

## *String Quartet No. 1 in C Major, Opus 37 (1917)*

Lento assai—Allegro moderato
Andantino semplice: In modo d'una canzone
Vivace—Scherzando alla burlesca: Vivace ma non troppo

Although he professed indifference to the string quartet form, Szymanowski composed two highly expressive examples as competition entries. The Opus 37 won the lucrative top honor at the 1917 event sponsored by the Polish Ministry of Culture. Eventually premiered in 1924, the work was frequently performed by Europe's leading ensembles for the following decade. An overall calm and serene work, the quartet reveals the gentle melancholy characteristic of his music during the early years of World War I. Broad, lyrical melodies and tonally related harmonies in the opening two movements convey poise and serenity.

The first movement is cast in traditional sonata form. Its introduction begins with a calm thematic statement in the solo violin (Lento assai, rather slow) that is developed imitatively by the other instruments. The tempo is then metrically doubled, and the movement connects without pause to its central ideas—an animated opening theme that alternates with a tranquilly lyrical second motif.

Andantino semplice is subtitled "in modo d'una canzone" (in the style of a song). Cast in three-part form (ABA), it unfolds with flexible themes and contrapuntal inventiveness. The opening idea is varied at its return.

An early example of polyphonic writing, the Scherzando alla burlesca (playful and mocking) finale simultaneously scores the lines for each instrument in different keys throughout: violin 1, A major; violin 2, F sharp major; viola, E flat major; cello, C major. Structured in sonata form, this vivacious movement develops with wittily inventive contrapuntal writing.

### String Quartet No. 2, Opus 56 (1927)

Moderato
Vivace, scherzando
Lento—Doppio movimento

Szymanowski composed his second quartet as an entry for the Musical Fund of Philadelphia's lucrative 1927 contest. Although it lost to Béla Bartók's String Quartet No. 3, the committee praised Opus 56 for its "richness of timbral effects." Ironically, Opus 56 suggests the influence of Bartók because of its wide range of sonorities and its forceful, driving rhythms. Varied bowing articulations contribute color—*sul tasto* (on the fingerboard), *sul ponticello* (bowed very close to the bridge), passages played at the point of the bow. Left hand techniques such as trills and passages indicated *molto vibrato* (wide and fast vibrato) emphasize and color the melodic lines. Like Bartók, Szymanowski throughout synthesizes his native folk elements with classical structures.

The opening Moderato, cast in sonata form, begins with a statement of the principal theme in the muted violin and cello (heard two octaves apart) supported by tremolo accompaniment in the other instruments. The ensuing rhapsodic flow (*dolce e tranquillo,* sweet and calm) is interspersed with harsh *ponticello* passages. Intensely expressive late romantic harmonies suggestive of Richard Strauss are heard throughout. Frequent double stopping (two notes played simultaneously) in all instruments contributes to an orchestral effect.

The solo cello leads into the second movement, which unfolds with strongly profiled rhythms (*marcatissimo,* very marked) and wildly free melodies inspired by Tatra folk music. Subtle gradations of dynamics and tempo create drama.

Based on themes of Tatra origin, the finale opens with a calm thematic statement (*dolce espressivo*) in the second violin; the other instruments answer imitatively as they enter in succession. The individual lines grow increasingly chromatic and the tempo accelerates dramatically. Fervent bowing repetitions create dense texture. Interjections of pizzicato passages together with strong contrasts of tempo, dynamics, and articulation conjure a restless atmosphere. Marked *strepitoso* (clamorous), the conclusion evokes chords characteristic of Polish folk bands.

GRAŻYNA BACEWICZ
B. FEBRUARY 5, 1909 IN ŁÓDŹ, POLAND,
D. JANUARY 17, 1969 IN WARSAW

Grażyna Bacewicz, Poland's most honored 20th-century woman composer, is acknowledged in Warsaw with public statues and streets that bear her name. A child prodigy who forged a first career as virtuoso violinist and pianist, Bacewicz pursued composition exclusively after sustaining serious injuries in a 1954 car accident. Although early studies in Paris with Nadia Boulanger had shaped her as a neoclassicist, Bacewicz in the mid-fifties embraced the avant-garde techniques of her compatriot Lutosławski. She gradually evolved a personal style of composing in tone color that has been identified as Sonorism. Although she continued to value the clarity of Neoclassicism, the works of her last years develop as kaleidoscopic progressions of sound images. Bacewicz writes about her music: "For me, the work of composition is like sculpting a stone, not like transmitting the sounds of imagination or inspiration. I stand alone and work out my own system."

Bacewicz composed in a wide variety of genres. Although she perhaps achieved her greatest international success with her early Concerto for String Orchestra (1950), which was performed in Washington, D.C., by the National Symphony Orchestra, chamber music remained her favored medium.

## *Piano Quintet No. 2 (1965)*

Moderato—Allegro
Larghetto
Allegro giocoso

Bacewicz's Piano Quintet No. 2 imaginatively explores a wide range of tone colors and instrumental textures. Dissonant but not fully atonal, the work is punctuated by pungent note clusters. Constructed like a mosaic, the Quintet develops through an architectural buildup of short, intense motifs. Rhythmically free and strict passages alternate.

The opening Moderato plunges the listener into a mysterious, somewhat ominous, sound world. Instrumental effects such as *ponticello*—phrases played at the bridge to achieve a thin, ominous sound—as well as percussive pizzicati and prominent glissandi create strong color. Varying tempos and textures delineate the structure.

The Larghetto, sonorous and dramatic, opens with phrases in the strings then the piano. Tremolos and glissandi enliven the reflective atmosphere. The Allegro giocoso (fast and playful) follows directly. The strings and piano engage in playful dialogue, and congeniality prevails.

### WITOLD LUTOSŁAWSKI
### B. JANUARY 25, 1913 IN WARSAW,
### D. FEBRUARY 7, 1994 IN WARSAW

Trained at the Warsaw Conservatory by Witold Maliszewski, a disciple of the Russian colorist Rimsky-Korsakov, Polish composer Witold Lutosławski initially hoped to continue studies in Paris but was drafted into the ill-fated Kraków Army during World War II. After a narrow escape from a Nazi prison camp, he played in cafes and composed resistance songs; during the repressive Stalinist era that followed the war, he composed politically correct "functional" music to earn a living. When Stalin died (1953), Lutosławski came into his own artistically. He soon secured his reputation as a significant composer with a penchant for formal and harmonic experimentation. Beginning in the 1980s he developed his principle of "chain technique," which allows layers of sound to overlap between sections. Although selected works employ limited elements of chance and avant-garde techniques, as well as the twelve-tone system, Lutosławski remains grounded by the lyricism of Mozart and Chopin. Critics have praised Lutosławski as a "contemporary classic ... who finds the amazing point where tradition transforms itself into the future."

## "Dance Preludes" for Clarinet and Piano (1954)

Allegro molto
Andantino
Allegro giocoso
Andante
Allegro molto

Early in his career Lutosławski was a fervent nationalist strongly influenced by tonally-centered Polish folk music. He originally wrote his *Dance Preludes* in 1954 as a commission for the publisher Polskie Wydawnictwo Muzyczne, who wanted an accessible work for skilled amateur performers. The composer described the *Preludes* as his "farewell to folklore," for soon after their composition he adopted the adventuresome techniques of the European avant-garde. However, he remained fond of this folk-based work, and revisited the *Preludes* twice with rescorings: a version for clarinet, harp, piano, percussion, and string orchestra (1955), which was premiered at the 1963 Aldeburgh Festival with Benjamin Britten conducting; and a nonet for flute, clarinet, oboe, bassoon, horn, violin, viola, cello, and double bass (1959).

Lutosławski greatly admired Bartók, who captured the essence of his native Hungarian music in his compositions. Perhaps under this influence, Lutosławski based his *Dance Preludes* on the spirited folk songs of northern Poland but avoided direct quotations. These ingratiating works unfold with rhythmic vitality and mildly pungent dissonance. They alternate in tempo and mood, with Preludes 1, 3, and 5 rapid and lively, and Preludes 2 and 4 slower and reflective.

## String Quartet (1964)

Introductory Movement
Main Movement

Lutosławski's only string quartet was commissioned by Swedish Radio to celebrate the tenth anniversary of its new music program "Nutida Musik." The composer provided commentary:

"My string quartet lasts approximately twenty-four minutes. The introduction opens with a violin recitative followed by several separate episodes, and the movement ends in a kind of suspense. The main movement starts with a 'furioso,' its violent character dominating until a 'crisis' occurs in the highest registers of all four instruments. A soft chorale follows, then a longer section marked *funèbre* (funereal). The final episodes constitute a commentary on what went on before.

"In this Quartet I have sought to develop and enlarge the technique employed in two preceding works, *Jeux venetiens* and *Trois Poèmes d'Henri Michaux*, the technique of what I call 'controlled aleatorism.' It employs the element of chance for the purpose of rhythmic and expressive enrichment of the music without limiting in the least the full ability of the composer to determine the definitive form of the work."

After the introductory section, the main movement begins with driving ferocity that is leavened by whimsical pizzicato figures. The performers begin at set points and are allowed individual metrical freedom, resulting in "rhythmically elastic polyphony." Lutosławski did not provide a set of notated individual parts for the finale of his quartet because he did not want to imply synchronization. He stated: "If I did write a normal score, superimposing the parts normally, it would be false, misleading, and would represent a different work." However, when the work was premiered in 1965 by the LaSalle Quartet, they requested that the parts be at least bound together, and Lutosławski complied.

One of the most widely performed and recorded twentieth-century quartets, the work has been critically lauded. As Graham Rickson wrote in *The Arts Desk*, "The music's complexities do not detract from its vivid, communicative power. Lutosławski's masterful ability to create beguiling sounds is just as potent in his chamber writing. The quartet's spectral ending remains astonishing."

KRZYSZTOF PENDERECKI
B. NOVEMBER 23, 1933 IN DĘBICA, POLAND,
D. MARCH 29, 2020 IN KRAKÓW

After Penderecki graduated from the Kraków Academy of Music with degrees in violin and composition, he began his career as composer during the 1959 Warsaw Autumn Festival, Poland's arts celebration of the end of Stalinism. During that same year he captured international attention when three of his works won prestigious competitions. A prolific composer, he has created a distinguished body of colorful orchestral, chamber, and choral works that incorporate a wide range of contemporary techniques to achieve compelling effects. Penderecki is best known for large-scale explorations of grand themes—the place of Man in the Universe (*Kosmogoniai*), the mystery of human salvation (*St. Luke Passion* and *Utrenia*)—dynamic work that is considered a summary of achievements made by his contemporaries Stockhausen, Boulez, and Xenakis. While his early compositions develop with serial and avant-garde techniques, he always maintained a broad perspective of music history. In later years his style evolved to incorporate traditional harmonic language.

*String Trio for Violin, Viola, and Cello (1990–91)*

Allegro molto
Vivace

Reflecting his belief that "a composer must absorb all that has already existed," Penderecki freely structured his String Trio in an eighteenth-century format. After its premiere in Metz, Germany, Penderecki decided to recast the trio as his Sinfonietta for String Orchestra.

At the trio's introduction rapid, emphatic chords (marked *feroce*) in all instruments alternate with successive cadenza passages in the violin, viola, and cello. The element of strong contrast—initially between dissonant vertical chords and the unmetered, quasi-improvisational lyricism of the solo instruments—is continued throughout the movement. Subsequent sections create a vivo-adagio-vivo-adagio pattern.

The Vivace opens with an extended viola solo; the violin joins at the interval of the fifth to create a canon. This simple theme, borrowed from Penderecki's opera *Ubu Rex* (1990–91), recurs throughout to unify the form. Freely structured in sonata form, the movement continuously exploits contrasts between chord blocks and chromatic melodic units heard in the opening movement.

*String Quartet No. 3, "Blätter aus einem nicht geschriebenen Tagebuch" (2008)*

Penderecki wrote his String Quartet No. 3 for the Shanghai Quartet as a request from Peak Performances of Montclair State University and the Modlin Center for the Arts on the occasion of his 75th birthday.

Penderecki writes of his quartet, a partly autobiographical work which he subtitled "Leaves from an Unwritten Diary": "While composing the quartet, I remembered a Hutsul folk melody which I had frequently heard played by my father. I made use of this theme, which grew in successive variations and almost took over my whole composition."

The Shanghai Quartet discusses the structure of the work: "The Quartet is roughly sixteen minutes in length and is composed in a single movement with strongly defined subsections. Starting with an almost grave introduction, a dark, screaming melody in the viola leads directly into a driven, brilliant vivace in G minor which recurs throughout the piece. Soon a beautiful waltz emerges, followed by a poignant and sweetly singing notturno, then back to the vivace pattern, which Penderecki insisted we play 'faster, faster.' By the end of our work with the composer in November we could barely play all the notes in this furious tempo. As we increased the tempo, however, the excitement and intensity were slowly revealed.

"Towards the end of the work, a spectacular gypsy melody appears, a theme that hasn't been heard in any of the composer's previous works. We asked Maestro Penderecki about this theme, and he told us that it is a melody his father used to play on the violin when he was a child, perhaps a Romanian melody. Soon after comes the climax of this masterpiece, where all the previously heard themes collide in a powerful moment that is full of intensity and drama. The end follows shortly after this: soft and introspective, almost walking off into the distance, with stopped harmonics played by the second violin, echoing the gypsy melody as the work draws to a close."

# EIGHT

# Soviet Utopia

The cataclysm of October 1917 altered Russia's artistic course profoundly. Both fear and economic uncertainty led to the departures of significant composers: the prescient Stravinsky had relocated to Paris before the Revolution, and Rachmaninoff and Prokofiev emigrated soon after. A cluster of deaths (Scriabin, Taneyev, Liadov, and Cui) underscored the rupture with Russia's past. Miraculously, a degree of continuity was maintained by the determined guidance of Alexander Glazunov (1865–1936), a musical traditionalist who remained head of the Petrograd Conservatory despite opposition. Colleagues such as Reinhold Glière (1875–1956) also stayed to sustain musical life in the new system's early days.

*Proletkult*, the first experiment in proletarian culture, guided the training of workers and peasants in the rudiments of the arts. Vladimir Lenin issued a dictum in 1918: "Art belongs to the people. It must penetrate with its deepest roots into the very thick of the broad working masses. It must be understandable by these masses and loved by them. It must unite the feeling, thought, and will of these masses, inspire them." Two polarized bodies were responsible for the oversight of artistic production: the Russian Association of Proletarian Musicians (RAPM), which denounced the classics as "bourgeois"; and the Association for Contemporary Music (ACM), which supported the autonomy of the creative musician and continuously argued with the other branch. The ACM's liberal views prevailed in the early years of the new government, and modernist works could be heard, particularly in Leningrad. After fierce disputes, the ACM collapsed in 1931. Under the proletarian control of the surviving RAPM, the Moscow Conservatory drastically lowered its standards; composition students needed to produce only two or three mass-songs celebratory of the Red Army to earn its degree.

Joseph Stalin, who had been appointed as the Communist Party's General Secretary of the Central Committee in 1922, observed these musical power struggles and decided that he did not like either faction. Weary of the RAPM's crudities and suspicious of the ACM's "art for art's sake," in 1932 his Central Committee established the Union of Soviet Composers "to safeguard 'socialist realism' in music." The RAPM and ACM were now minor history, and under Stalin, Socialist Realism became the true creed. As ruthlessly as his politics, Stalin plotted Soviet Russia's artistic path until his death in 1953.

"Socialist Realism" is a concept critical for the understanding of music composed during Stalin's regime and beyond, as it lingered until the breakup of the Soviet Union in 1991. After Maxim Gorky published his defining article "Socialist Realism" (1933), it became the mantra for Soviet writers and artists. Its ideal has been defined by Gerald Abraham: "Soviet art must be understandable and loved by the masses, but it must be worthy of its ancestry in classic Russian and world art; and by its strength and optimism it must help to build socialism." Stalin termed socialist realist artists "engineers of souls" who would instill party values through glorified depictions of a utopian state. As the state's handmaiden, music must inspire positive energy conducive to work. Depictions of tragedy or melancholy were inimical to music's function as propaganda, and, more dangerously for composers, were viewed as implicit criticisms of the Communist state.

After World War II, socialist realism entered an era of rigorous interpretation that lasted until the rise of Nikita Khrushchev following Stalin's death. Composers chafed under the repressive Zhdanov Doctrine of 1948, the cultural manifesto of Central

Committee Secretary Andrei Zhdanov. In its musical sphere, the doctrine rejected "formalism," defined by the Soviets as "elitist catering to purely individual experiences of a small clique of aesthetes while rejecting the classical heritage." The doctrine discouraged chamber music as art for "a handful of connoisseurs" and advocated "program music on concrete subjects of Soviet life." Yet flashes of aesthetic insight did happen: for Stalin, the greatest socialist realist composer was Beethoven, whom he much admired but imperfectly understood.

DMITRI SHOSTAKOVICH
B. SEPTEMBER 25, 1906 IN ST. PETERSBURG,
D. AUGUST 9, 1975 IN MOSCOW

## STRING QUARTETS

Shostakovich's fifteen string quartets had their genesis in a brush with disaster. Stalin had angrily left an early performance of Shostakovich's expressionist opera *Lady Macbeth of the Mtsensk District* (1934)—a "tragic satire" portraying the murderess Katerina and her seamy interactions with the bourgeoisie—and immediately banned the work from the repertory because of its amoral content and dissonant setting. After reading its devastating review in *Pravda*, Shostakovich wrote: "I was completely destroyed. It was a blow that wiped out my past. And my future."

Shostakovich knew that out-of-favor artists often disappeared permanently during Stalin's dangerous regime. To survive he needed to win Stalin's favor by adhering to his doctrine of socialist realism (see above). Shostakovich was advised about a suitable model—Ivan Dzerzhinsky's *Quiet Flows the Don*, an innocuous opera premiered the year after *Lady Macbeth*; ironically, Shostakovich had given substantial musical assistance to its composer, who dedicated the work to him. Aware that the operatic genre was a minefield, Shostakovich began to create large scale instrumental works with "official" messages embedded in them; but he also wrote intimate chamber works that could escape Party oversight. Since his impressive series of quartets—only one fewer than Beethoven, as he was aware—began to emerge in censorious times, they are often regarded as expressions of Shostakovich's most private thoughts. Although this view is a simplification that minimizes the personal importance of his symphonies, it is undeniable that Shostakovich's most daring innovations of form, harmony, and textural range are heard in his string quartets. Perhaps more importantly, these quartets provided an outlet for his strongly theatrical sensibilities. Because of their dramatic scope, these intensely expressive quartets are best understood as moments of revealing theater—or latent operas.

*String Quartet No. 1 in C Major, Opus 49 (1938)*

Moderato
Moderato
Allegro molto
Allegro

After *Pravda* in 1936 denounced Shostakovich for "modernist formalism of the worst kind," he realized that more than just his career was at stake. Promising the authorities "a Soviet artist's practical creative reply to rightful criticism," Shostakovich revised his compositional style toward the harmonious and uplifting. He publicly wrote about his Quartet No. 1: "In composing my First Quartet, I visualized childhood scenes and somewhat naïve and bright moods associated with spring."

A pleasant work of overt simplicity, the quartet is written in a clear, transparent style. The work opens with a tranquil melody heard in the first violin; a songlike second theme is introduced by a glissando figure in the cello. After brief development, a varied restatement of themes concludes the movement. The Moderato offers three variations on a widely arcing theme that is remarkably both marchlike and soulful. The solo viola introduces the soaring melody, which suggests the character of Russian folk music. As the theme is developed by other instruments, it grows alternately fervent and pensive.

Shostakovich once claimed that the Allegro molto was his favorite scherzo movement of all the quartets. Emotionally ambiguous, this rapid movement is played throughout with mutes to achieve the illusion of shadow; a lyrical central section varies the flow. The two themes of the joyous finale move through various changes of meter toward a virtuosic conclusion.

## String Quartet No. 2 in A Major, Opus 68 (1944)

Overture: Moderato con moto
Recitative and Romance: Adagio
Valse: Allegro
Theme and Variations

At the insistence of Soviet officials, Shostakovich in September 1944 relocated to Ivanovo, a government retreat for artists and writers a safe distance from war zones. Energized by his conviction that victory over Nazi Germany was imminent, Shostakovich wrote with white heat. Within three weeks he simultaneously produced his Quartet No. 2 and his substantial Piano Trio No. 2; both works were premiered together that November. Shostakovich wrote to his composer friend Shebalin: "It is exactly twenty years since I first met you, and to commemorate the anniversary I would like to dedicate the quartet to you. I worry about the lightning speed with which I compose. Undoubtedly this is bad. It is exhausting, somewhat unpleasant, and at the end of the day you lack any confidence in the result. But I cannot rid myself of the bad habit." The most epic of his fifteen-quartet cycle, the work does not suggest overtly the duress of war; however, its quotations of Russian folk music illustrate his patriotism.

Shostakovich described the Overture as "a promise of things to come." This theatrical and quasi-symphonic movement (A major) develops two spirited ideas in sonata form. The mood becomes ambiguous as the tonality shifts to minor, but the movement concludes joyously in the major key.

Recitative and Romance (B flat major) opens with an extended violin cantilena accompanied by simple chords in the other instruments. Initially a pensive statement, the Romance develops with fervor as other voices join. The violin soliloquy returns to suggest a lone voice in the crowd—perhaps a reminder that individuals exist within the immense collective event of the war.

Shostakovich states that the darkly-keyed third movement (E flat minor) "is a valse macabre. And if it were to be compared to the classics, it should be compared to the Waltz from the Third Suite by Tchaikovsky." Played with mutes throughout, this rapid and sinister movement is based on the second subject of the first movement.

As a thematic connection to the waltz, the finale opens with a brief Adagio section in E flat minor. The ensuing variations movement (A minor) is based on the Russian folk theme also heard in his Piano Trio No. 2. Its thirteen variations begin in a tranquil atmosphere, but their mood gradually grows intense and fervent. After an agitated climax, the calm mood returns with a chorale-like section in B major. A reflective reprise leads to a clear statement of the theme in the first violin. An Adagio section (A minor) brings the work to a powerful conclusion.

## String Quartet No. 3 in F Major, Opus 73 (1946)

Allegretto
Moderato con moto
Allegro non troppo
Adagio
Moderato—Adagio

Guided by the musical preferences of Joseph Stalin, Soviet authorities urged composers to create heroic works that drew from folk tradition. Shostakovich indicated that his projected Symphony No. 9 (1945) would offer the desired uplifting statement. However, at its premiere the symphony was heard as mere entertainment, and Shostakovich was denounced for "formalism"—defined by the Soviets as "elitist catering to purely individual experiences of a small clique of aesthetes while rejecting the classical heritage." Much shaken, Shostakovich did not undertake another symphony until Stalin's death in 1953; private composition of his quartet series offered a refuge. Soon after the debacle of his Ninth Symphony, Shostakovich began his Quartet No. 3.

Conceived as a war statement, Opus 73 was originally given programmatic subtitles for its five movements:

I.   Calm awareness of the future cataclysm
II.  Rumblings of unrest and anticipation
III. The forces of war unleashed
IV.  Homage to the dead
V.   The eternal question: Why? And for what?

Shostakovich suppressed these subtitles as too programmatic, but many groups such as the Borodin Quartet insist on their inclusion as historically significant.

The musical progression of Opus 73 generally follows the emotional effect of its subtitles. The sonata form Movement I begins in a lighthearted atmosphere, but ever more frenzied development (a double fugue with fast-moving harmonies) and a final acceleration of tempo conjures agitation.

Movement II is a sardonic waltz. Passagework grows lugubrious near the end as the instruments descend into their lower registers.

Movement III (F minor), perhaps an echo of the sinister Scherzo movement from Symphony No. 5, is a ferocious and martial statement. Its two themes, heard in the violin and cello, are accompanied by strident chords in the other instruments. The movement ends abruptly.

Movement IV is a *passacaglia* (a stately seventeenth-century form built on a repeating bass line) that opens with all instruments in unison. A violin soliloquy leads to a somber cello lament, accompanied by pizzicati in the viola; the viola assumes the lament, now accompanied by cello pizzicati. After fugal development, the movement ends quietly.

Movement V can be heard as an operatic act with the four players as its wordless personae. It opens with a cello theme whose foreboding dissonance belies its relaxed and limber rhythm. As the tempo grows faster, the atmosphere becomes anguished. Sustained notes halt the momentum; it then resumes with a folklike theme, then a passionate phrase in the cello's upper register. The violin sings a poignant theme, perhaps of Jewish origin, that moves ever higher as it poses its question: Why? What is it for? The movement closes *morendo* (dying) on a sustained low F in the cello.

*String Quartet No. 4 in D Major, Opus 83 (1949)*

Allegretto
Andantino
Allegretto
Allegretto

Shostakovich reached artistic maturity at the midpoint of the century, a time when USSR intellectual and cultural stagnation was so extreme that reportedly even the Stalinist authorities who created it were uncomfortable with what they had wrought. Especially between the years 1946 and 1952 it was customary for Shostakovich to premiere works assured of state approval, such as the 1952 cantata *Song of the Motherland*, but to hide potentially controversial works in his bottom drawer and hope for better times. One such protected work was his Quartet No. 4, written in 1949 but premiered in 1953 after Stalin's death. This quartet risked censure because of its Jewish themes, politically unpopular among the Stalinists. Shostakovich, who composed several works based on Jewish material during these years, wrote: "By setting these themes I might be able to tell the fate of the Jewish people. It is an important thing to do because I can see anti-Semitism growing all around me." The work is now one of the most frequently performed of Shostakovich's quartets in Russia.

Quartet No. 4 opens in a popular vein as the violins play folklike themes of Jewish origin while the viola and cello imitate a hurdy-gurdy with sustained pedal notes. Emerging dissonances gradually create pandemonium, but the movement ends quietly with a return of the violin theme over supporting pedal tones. The lyrical Andantino is an unorthodox waltz that alternates between triple and duple meter. The quartet's emotional center, this F minor movement develops with a variety of affecting harmonies.

The third movement, muted throughout, is a scherzo that develops with subtle instrumental colors. A recurring dotted rhythmic figure underpins the melodic material, which echoes the Jewish themes of the opening movement. The richly inventive finale, full of colorful pizzicati and glissandi, often suggests a grotesque dance. After an impassioned section that moves through various meters, the gentler mood of the Andantino returns. The movement ends quietly with hushed pizzicati under a sustained high note in the cello.

## *String Quartet No. 5 in B flat Major, Opus 92 (1952)*

Allegro non troppo
Andante—Andantino—Andante—Andantino—Andante
Moderato—Allegretto—Andante

Shostakovich wrote his Quartet No. 5 in the fall of 1952 and dedicated the work to the Beethoven Quartet, who premiered the work after Stalin's death the following year. Its three movements are performed without pause, a new formal development for Shostakovich and one that he would continue in subsequent works. The quartet reveals the composer's fluent counterpoint, a favorite technique that he continued to develop after he had participated as judge for J.S. Bach's 1950 bicentenary competitions in Leipzig. Shortly before composing his Quartet No. 5, Shostakovich wrote his 24 Preludes and Fugues for Piano as homage to Bach.

Two highly personal motifs organize the quartet. The primary motif is based on the musical spelling of his signature DSCH (D-E flat-C-B), with S corresponding to the note E flat and H the German equivalent to the note B. (This motif is heard as permutations in the following three quartets and becomes structurally significant in Quartet No. 8.) The viola introduces this motif at the beginning of the Allegro non troppo. The second personal motif consists of several bars quoted from the Clarinet Trio in B flat Major written by his student, Galina Ustvolskaya. Following the recent death of his first wife, Shostakovich had proposed marriage to Galina, but to his acute disappointment she refused him. Agitated counterpoint between these two personal themes creates an atmosphere of frenzied longing. The closing section grows calmer as Galina's theme is played by the first violin and Shostakovich's motif follows in the viola. The first violin plays a sustained high F, which leads directly into the next movement.

The second movement quotes themes from earlier Shostakovich works that had remained unpublished until Stalin's death. Ideas from the second and final movements of Quartet No. 3, as well as his violin concerto, are developed with spare, sustained lines that conjure deep stillness.

The finale opens in a sanguine atmosphere (Moderato), but the agitated mood of the opening movement returns (Allegretto). The tempo slows at the Andante section, and the violin plays a reflective soliloquy that suggests the austerity of the second movement. The cello assumes the melody, which becomes a nostalgic waltz that conjures the old Europe. An extended cello reverie follows, then a violin statement accompanied by sustained chords. The movement concludes on a quiet B flat major chord with the directive *morendo* (dying).

*String Quartet No. 6 in G Major, Opus 101 (1956)*

Allegretto
Moderato con moto
Lento
Lento—Allegretto—Andante—Lento

In the summer of 1956 Shostakovich, then a widower with two children, decided to remarry. The attractive Margarita Kainova caught his eye, and to contrive an introduction he purchased a pair of opera tickets and sent her one anonymously. However, Margarita was not a music lover, and she gave away the ticket. Arriving at the opera he was distressed to discover her seat occupied by a stranger. Undaunted, he then asked a colleague to set up a meeting. The shy composer shocked friends and family by proposing to Margarita that same afternoon. Shostakovich explained: "She is a good woman, and I hope she will be a good wife to me and a good mother for my children." However, he should have realized when the opera ticket stratagem failed that he had little in common with Margarita, and after three years Shostakovich filed for divorce. But that August Shostakovich was a relaxed man on his honeymoon, during which he undertook composition of his Quartet No. 6. He completed the quartet within days and reported that for the first time in years he was satisfied with a new work. Although Opus 101 cannot be described as one of the composer's grander quartets, its genial affect attests to the range and diversity of Shostakovich's formidable contribution to the genre.

The harmonies of Quartet No. 6 are basically diatonic. However, before each movement reaches its final cadence, it articulates the pungent chord D-E flat-C-B—a musical spelling of DSCH, Shostakovich's characteristic signature. The carefree opening Allegretto leads into the dancelike Moderato movement (E flat major), which is varied by a chromatic section at its center. The reflective Lento (B flat minor) is a *passacaglia*, a set of eloquent variations over a ten-bar theme intoned by the cello. The complex finale, in sonata-rondo form, proceeds without pause. As its two themes build to an exuberant peak, themes from the earlier movements are recalled, now varied in tempo. The movement ends quietly with all instruments muted.

*String Quartet No. 7 in F sharp Minor, Opus 108 (1960)*

Allegretto
Lento
Allegro—Allegretto

Shostakovich's Quartet No. 7 is a birthday remembrance for his adored first wife, Nina Varzar, who had died from cancer six years earlier but would have celebrated her fiftieth had she lived. Critics consider Opus 108 to be the first of his final group of quartets, works through which he sought to offer thoughts on life, death, and immortality. Many listeners have attributed the increasingly melancholy atmosphere in these later works to Nina's early demise.

Written with the utmost economy of texture, Quartet No. 7 develops its ideas primarily through extended solo, duo, or trio passages rather than full quartet voicing. This deliberate sparseness especially enhances the sense of desolation in the austere central movement (Lento), the cool heart of the quartet. The opening Allegretto explores two chromatic themes made whimsical by frequent meter changes. At its recapitulation the first theme, played pizzicato in triple meter, is transformed into a bizarre waltz, which reappears in the closing section of the finale.

After a brief introduction, played with mutes in all instruments, the Allegro finale restates the chromatic viola motif heard at the end of the Lento and develops it as a spectral waltz. The movement concludes with a quiet coda.

## String Quartet No. 8 in C Minor, Opus 110 (1960)

Largo
Allegro molto
Allegretto
Largo
Largo

In the summer of 1960 Shostakovich travelled to Dresden to compose the score for a commemorative Russian war film, *Five Days, Five Nights*. Surrounded by evidence of this once glorious city's destruction, Shostakovich recalled his own horrific experiences as a volunteer firefighter during the Siege of Leningrad (1941–1944). While intensely focused on these vivid memories, Shostakovich created his eighth string quartet, written feverishly within the period of three days. Dedicated "in memory of victims of fascism and war," the quartet develops with a fervor that sets it among the most compelling of Shostakovich's string quartets.

An autobiographical statement, Opus 110 develops with a recurring motto based on the musical spelling of Shostakovich's own name: the notes D-E flat-C-B represent the initials "D.Sch" (Sch is the German transliteration of the single Russian character that begins his surname). The quartet's five movements are performed without pause. The cello introduces the composer's personal motto in the opening Largo, formally a rondo that includes quotations from Shostakovich's first and fifth symphonies. Shostakovich portrays the war's brutality most vividly in the frenzied second movement, which evokes the relentless bombing of Dresden. A quotation of the "Jewish theme" heard in his second piano trio recalls the horrific discovery of the death camps, specifically that of Majdanek, Poland, among the first to be liberated by the Red Army. The Allegretto is a sardonic waltz based on a theme from Shostakovich's first cello concerto, a motif that returns in the fourth movement.

The fourth movement begins with insistent fortissimo chords that suggest the dreaded police knocks at the door; its second theme recalls the Russian revolutionary song "Languishing in Prison." At its climax the cello sings an aria from Shostakovich's 1934 opera *Lady Macbeth of the Mtsensk District*, which Stalin condemned. The final Largo, which recalls the opening movement, is a slow fugato based on the motif DSCH. Shostakovich intended for this closing movement to stand as an epitaph for all who fell in the fight against Nazism.

*String Quartet No. 9 in E flat Major, Opus 117 (1964)*

Moderato con moto
Adagio
Allegretto
Adagio
Allegro

Shostakovich completed his austere and dramatic ninth quartet four years after he had written his powerful Quartet No. 8. An earlier version of Quartet No. 9, based on favorite themes from his childhood, was discarded. He wrote: "In an attack of self-criticism I burned it in the stove. This is the second such case in my creative practice. The new quartet is completely different."

The quartet's five movements contain no ostensible literary program but reveal personal motifs such as his musical signature D-S-C-H, played as D-E flat-C-B natural. Unified by common thematic and textural elements, the movements are performed without pause. The dark emotional atmosphere of Quartet No. 9— conveyed through biting *sforzandi*, glissandi, and passages of eerily thin texture—anticipates Shostakovich's late style.

Written in classical sonata form, the opening Moderato (E flat major) develops three subjects that recur throughout the quartet. The following Adagio (F sharp minor) is a poignant dialogue between the first violin and viola. The Allegretto third movement (F sharp minor alternating with F major) is a three-part scherzo with a songful middle section contrasting with dissonant and menacing outer sections. Starkly expressive, the Adagio fourth movement (E flat minor-major) explores two themes that were foreshadowed at the quartet's opening.

Cast in five sections, the substantial Allegro finale at moments evokes a wild central Asian folk dance that Shostakovich heard while visiting Tashkent shortly before he wrote the quartet's second version. Its development section, which begins softly and gradually reaches fortissimo, culminates in a brilliant fugue built on variants of the principal subject. The intense closing section builds contrapuntally to a forceful climax as themes from previous movements are recapitulated.

*String Quartet No. 10 in A flat Major, Opus 118 (1964)*

Andante
Allegretto furioso
Adagio
Allegretto—Andante

The appealing Quartet No. 10 was written during the spring and summer of 1964 for Shostakovich's friend, the prolific but little-known composer Moishe Vainberg (also known as Mieczyslaw Weinberg). Except for the densely scored second movement, the quartet develops with new simplicity. The lyrical Opus 118 has become one of Shostakovich's most popular chamber compositions.

The solo violin introduces the gentle thematic material of the opening Andante, and the other instruments respond with a passage of restrained three-part polyphony. The material is recapitulated in a muted *ponticello* passage (instruments played "at the bridge" to produce a glassy sound).

A scherzo with relentless fortissimo dynamics, the Allegretto furioso (E minor) is a strident contrast to the opening movement. The first violin introduces the aggressive main theme, and the cello articulates the agitated second theme in its upper register. A variation of the opening idea returns as a violin duet. Because of its savagely dissonant harmonies, demanding octave lines in the violins, and rapid accents, this movement requires the utmost stamina and virtuosity.

The ethereal Adagio is cast as a strict *passacaglia*, a baroque form in which variations are built over a repeated "ground" in the bass line. Heard primarily in the cello, this ground pattern recurs nine times as the other instruments explore the theme, which is richly harmonized and ornamented with countermelodies. The movement closes with a suspended A flat major chord as the viola initiates the finale, which proceeds without pause.

The finale's Allegretto was inspired by the *trepak*, a dance of the Russian Steppes. The viola presents two subjects: the first theme, animated by a repeating rhythmic figure, revolves around a single note, and the second idea reiterates a simple motif against a continuous drone in the other instruments. A transformation of the second movement's main theme accompanied by pizzicati creates a contrasting third idea. The Adagio's *passacaglia* motif is restated fortissimo by the cello; momentum slows into the Andante as themes from earlier movements return. The work concludes in the calm spirit of its opening.

*String Quartet No. 11 in F Minor, Opus 122 (1966)*

Introduction: Andantino
Scherzo: Allegretto
Recitative: Adagio
Etude: Allegro
Humoresque: Allegro
Elegy: Adagio
Finale: Moderato

Quartet No. 11 is a memorial tribute to Vasily Petrovich Shirinsky (1901–1965), a friend, composer, and longtime second violinist with the Beethoven Quartet—the premiering group for most of Shostakovich's string quartets. Ostensibly the celebration of a musical life, Quartet No. 11 develops with the spare texture and lean harmonies often heard in his late quartets. Alan George, violist with the Shostakovich Quartet and an esteemed colleague of the composer, describes the work: "The Quartet inhabits a strangely withdrawn region which in the end is deeply touching. The casting of the work into seven highly contrasting movements, rather like a suite of character pieces, might seem to have run a risk of diffuseness; but at this stage of his career Shostakovich was firmly committed to continuity and cogency in his quartets. He achieves a disarmingly simple unity through stringent economy of means; the work is constructed on only two motifs, both subjected to Shostakovich's highly developed technique for exploiting all latent possibilities. So all the characters are in reality the same one: the same clown with different faces, be it tender, whimsical, severe, mercurial, droll, elegiac, or the simple *yurodivy* (the traditional Russian 'Holy Fool').

"Up to the end of the fourth movement all the violin solos have been taken by the first violin. The irony is that the quartet is dedicated to the memory of a second violinist. But he can play only two notes, and he manages to keep them up throughout the entire Humoresque—which doesn't even get its own tempo, there being no change of pulse from the preceding Etude. All this represents a wry comment on the role of the second violin and also reflects Shirinsky's droll sense of humor.

"Eventually we come to the real purpose of this piece: an elegy that begins with great seriousness and intensity. Its dominant rhythm perhaps recalls the *Eroica* Symphony for the Beethoven Quartet, and is grimly prophetic of the Funeral March in Quartet No. 15—composed after the death of Shirinsky's brother, the cellist in the quartet."

## *String Quartet No. 12 in D flat Major, Opus 133 (1968)*

Moderato—Allegretto
Allegretto—Adagio—Moderato—Allegretto

As appreciation for his long association with the Beethoven Quartet, Shostakovich dedicated string quartets to each of its members. With Quartet No. 12 he honored first violinist Dmitri Tsyganov, a player known for his darkly expressive "Russian" sound, and also expanded his previous quartet's tribute to the recently deceased second violinist Vasily Shirinsky. Shostakovich wrote Quartet No. 12 in a self-described "non-conformist" two movement format. The composer himself provided a brief explanation: "The first movement portrays the world of high ideals. The second movement stands in sharp contrast to it. Its first (as well as third) section presents a disturbing 'Scherzo,' an agony, which is unable to cope with the contradictions of life."

The opening Moderato sets up a harmonic duality between modernist atonality and traditional tonality. Introduced by the solo cello, the work opens atonally with a twelve-tone row as pioneered by Schoenberg—all notes of the chromatic scale arranged in a specific sequence without repeats. This harmonically unsettled statement is followed by a singing passage in a clear D flat major tonality. The ensuing sections are connected by recurrences of the twelve-note row in the solo instruments.

Alert to the significance of numbers, Shostakovich contrives an extra-musical statement by delaying the entrance of the second violin until measure 34. The Beethoven Quartet had played for 34 years with violinist Vasily Shirinsky, who had recently died. As a tribute, the new violinist must wait that many measures before entering.

The finale combines elements of traditional movement forms into one continuous section. Its rapid, atonal opening area ends with a mysterious *ponticello* (on the bridge) passage—a section that has been described as perhaps most unusual and sinister in all of Shostakovich's quartets. The following Adagio consists of an extended cello solo accompanied by chords in the other instruments. The movement closes with a dramatic synthesis of themes developed throughout the work.

### *String Quartet No. 13 in B flat Minor, Opus 138 (1970)*

Adagio—Doppio movimento—Tempo primo

Quartet No. 13 was described by *Pravda* following its premiere: "It is a meditation upon the brevity of man's life, and a passionate glorification of the beauty and majesty of the human spirit which asserts itself despite the inexorable fatefulness of nature."

Shostakovich dedicated the quartet to Vadim Borisovsky, a founding member of the Beethoven Quartet and its continuing violist for forty years. The viola line is prominent throughout the quartet, and its technical and expressive possibilities are explored to a degree rare in chamber literature. Quartet No. 13 is cast as three extended sections played without pause. The unaccompanied viola introduces the Adagio's elegiac opening theme, constructed on the twelve notes of the chromatic scale, and it concludes the movement with a solo recitative in its upper register. Three strongly dissonant chords lead to the Doppio movimento, which moves at twice the speed of the opening Adagio. A scherzo with an aura of fantasy, the section begins with a sinister idea in the first violin accompanied by percussive bow taps on the wood of the instruments. In the mysterious final Tempo primo, the opening Adagio idea returns as the viola and cello engage in solemn dialogue. The viola reprises the main themes in an extended solo, accompanied by percussive bow tapping. The viola line rises to its upper register then abruptly ends with a sustained crescendo on its highest B flat.

*String Quartet No. 14 in F sharp Minor, Opus 142 (1973)*

Allegretto
Adagio
Allegretto—Adagio

When Shostakovich's health began to deteriorate near the end of his life, he attempted to summarize his thoughts on life, death, and immortality through his chamber works. Among other conditions, he suffered nerve impairment of his right hand, a possible reason for the leaner scoring in these late quartets.

Shostakovich began Quartet No. 14 while he was visiting Benjamin Britten at his home in England in 1972. Shostakovich's violinist colleague Christopher Rowland conveyed the composer's ideas about the quartet in an interview: "The existence of a fourteenth quartet was casually mentioned in a letter written to me from Copenhagen on May 4, 1973. The following March the music arrived with a covering letter apologizing for the delay and explaining that he had been very ill and therefore unable to write it out.

"Because of its spare texture, it is very easy to underestimate the Fourteenth Quartet. Yet few people underestimate Mahler's Tenth, despite its incompleteness, and the two works say strikingly similar things to us—as well as being rooted in the same key, F sharp minor. These two works leave us in similar emotional states—a recognition of a painful longing for life which is slipping away, and a passionate love and desire to be alive. The Fourteenth Quartet shares with the other late works an atmosphere of private contemplation—yet this quartet is unique because of its impassioned radiance."

The Allegretto opens with a viola statement that introduces the lyrical main idea, treated fugally by the first violin and cello. This delicate theme combines with chromatic interludes to create a poignant atmosphere. The emotional center of the work is the sparely written Adagio (D minor), which offers soliloquies between the first violin and the cello—homage to the quartet's dedicatee, cellist Sergei Shirinsky. The impetuous Allegretto finale (F sharp minor) alludes thematically to the earlier movements; the mood grows serene at its Adagio conclusion.

*String Quartet No. 15 in E flat Minor, Opus 144 (1974)*

Elegy: Adagio
Serenade: Adagio
Intermezzo: Adagio
Nocturne: Adagio
Funeral March: Adagio molto
Epilogue

The year before his death from heart disease Shostakovich wrote his final string quartet. Many listeners have heard this work as his own requiem. Quartet No. 15 consists of six profoundly moving adagios, played without pause. The work opens with a quiet fugal lament, an elegy that recalls the Russian Orthodox style. In the second movement each instrument in turn articulates a poignant cry through a single sustained note that begins in a soft dynamic but grows ever stronger. The following serenade conjures a macabre atmosphere; it ends with a pianissimo pedal note in the cello that leads into the brief but furious Intermezzo. The Nocturne moves with undulating figuration in the second violin and cello that underpins a plaintive melody sung by the viola. Near its conclusion an ominous pizzicato figure in the violins foreshadows the Funeral March, emphatically announced by all instruments in unison. Solo passages for the first violin, viola, and cello form the basis of the movement; the march is interjected as a refrain. The spectral finale quotes themes from the earlier movements before it concludes quietly with a somber chant.

Shostakovich had intended to write sixteen string quartets to equal Beethoven's oeuvre. Although his death deprived him from reaching that goal, the fifteen quartets that exist are the most priceless gems of the modern Russian chamber repertory.

## WORKS WITH VARIED SCORING

*Two Pieces for String Octet, Opus 11 (1925)*

Prelude: Adagio
Scherzo: Allegro molto

Shostakovich wrote his brief Opus 11 during his experimental early period, the post-student years when he wavered between the "revolutionary Romanticism" of 1920s Russia and an astringent classicism. The Octet, his first important chamber work, emerged soon after his delicately transparent First Symphony (Opus 10).

The emotionally intense D minor Prelude explores its chromatic themes with rhythmic freedom. The movement falls into three sections: a declamatory opening section is followed by a presto with numerous points of imitation; in the final area, a violin cadenza leads to a recapitulation of the opening material.

Zestful movements came easily to Shostakovich, and the G minor Scherzo was written within a month. Satirical and dissonant, the Scherzo reflects his attraction to the more avant-garde idioms in European music. Propelled by ever more rapid canons, decorated by numerous glissandi, this Scherzo has been called the wildest movement in all the literature for eight instruments.

### Piano Trio No. 1 in C Minor, Opus 8 (1923)

Shostakovich wrote the first of his two piano trios while he was a sixteen-year-old student at the Petrograd Conservatory. His life circumstances at that time were particularly harrowing. His father had recently died from pneumonia, most probably contracted because of cold and malnutrition, common sufferings in post-Revolutionary Russia. Since the Petrograd Conservatory had no heat, professors often failed to show for class; but the determined Shostakovich simply sought them at their homes. However, Shostakovich developed a dangerous throat condition, for which he received an operation. He was sent to a sanatorium in the Crimea to recuperate, and in that healing environment he wrote his Opus 8 Piano Trio.

He subtitled this trio "Poème" and dedicated it to his erstwhile love and lifelong friend Tatyana Glivenko, whom he met during his convalescence. Shostakovich performed as pianist at its 1923 premiere, which also served as his audition for the Moscow Conservatory. He wrote: "I played the Trio with the violinist Vlasov and the cellist Klevensky. They played appallingly, but the result was completely unexpected. The committee decided to regard the

Trio as my sonata-form piece, and immediately I was accepted on the free composition course." The Opus 8 predates all work that Shostakovich considered significant. Although he considered repurposing the trio as cinema accompaniment, after its premiere he never performed it again. Missing its final twenty-two bars, the work remained in rough manuscript until it was reconstructed by his pupil Boris Tishchenko. Opus 8 was published posthumously in 1983 as part of a collected edition.

Despite its uncharacteristic romanticism, the work reveals gestures that recur throughout Shostakovich's career—a sparse but colorful linear texture, dissonances interspersed within an essentially tonal harmonic framework, elegiac passages alternating with displays of manic energy. Played without pause, the trio's five sections develop two ideas derived from its opening motive, a lengthy theme that unfolds with expressive chromaticism; the ethereal second idea is related to an earlier piano sonata. Freely constructed in sonata form, the trio's motives recur in different guises throughout to create a highly unified composition.

*Piano Trio No. 2 in E Minor, Opus 67 (1944)*

Andante—Moderato
Allegro con brio
Largo
Allegretto

Shostakovich wrote his second piano trio as a tribute to his recently deceased friend, the musicologist Ivan Sollertinsky. Earlier that year, Sollertinsky, although a young man, had died of a heart attack incurred while evacuating the war zone in Leningrad. Shostakovich described his jovial and eccentric friend: "He was a brilliant scholar who spoke dozens of languages and kept his diary in ancient Portuguese to keep it safe from prying eyes. He found great pleasure in a merry and liberated life, even though he worked very hard. Sadly, people will probably only remember that his tie was askew and that a new suit on him looked old in five minutes."

Sollertinsky introduced Shostakovich to music of the eastern European Jews, and it affected him profoundly. He stated: "This music can appear to be happy when it is tragic. It is multifaceted ... laughter through tears." Throughout his memorial trio, Shostakovich incorporates themes suggestive of both Russian folk song and ethnic Jewish dance music. At the time he composed the trio, Shostakovich had just received grim reports about the massacres of Jewish concentration camp inmates at the hands of the Nazis. Although he never professed programmatic intentions, many listeners at the work's premiere heard depictions of doomed persons dancing at the edges of their graves in the work's finale.

The elegiac Andante begins with a remarkable sonority— a wistful theme played in high harmonics by the cello accompanied by the violin in its lowest register. After this introduction, the movement develops folklike themes in a calm atmosphere. The following scherzo movement, propelled by energetic dance rhythms, conveys turbulent joie de vivre.

The Largo is an elegiac *chaconne* (a slow triple-time form built on a repeating bass theme) with eight chords reiterated by the piano as the violin and cello sing a continuously varied, sorrowful duet. This powerful movement serves as the introduction to the finale, the dramatic center of the trio. Tension builds as ever more frenzied themes suggest macabre dances of death. Fragments of the earlier themes return. The closing notes, a quiet recollection of the movement's beginning, suggest serene resolution.

## *Piano Quintet in G Minor, Opus 57 (1940)*

Prelude: Lento
Fugue: Adagio
Scherzo: Allegretto
Intermezzo: Lento
Finale: Allegretto

Shostakovich wrote his Opus 57 Piano Quintet during a year of calm between storms in Soviet Russia. The Great Terror, during which hundreds of artists and writers were arrested and often killed, had mostly subsided, and Germany did not yet threaten to invade. Stalin, the author of the Terror, viewed Shostakovich with suspicion ever since he had angrily left a 1936 performance of the composer's expressionist opera *Lady Macbeth of the Mtsensk District*. Soon after, both Stalin and *Pravda* vehemently denounced Shostakovich for writing decadent music that lacked correct moral and social values, and the composer's career was temporarily stalled. However, Stalin did admire the Piano Quintet and awarded it his 1940 "Stalin Prize." This immense cash award of 100,000 rubles was perhaps justified by the enthusiastic public response—at its premiere the ensemble repeated the Scherzo and Finale to satisfy the cheering crowd. But Western critics were skeptical of a work so strongly endorsed by the Soviet government. Despite its conservative formal structure, the Quintet eventually won wide critical acceptance because of its fine themes and superb craftsmanship.

Shostakovich had written his Opus 57 at the request of the Soviet Union's Beethoven Quartet, which asked him to perform as their pianist. Prominent throughout the Quintet, the piano introduces and develops many of the work's thematic ideas. The contemplative three-part Prelude leads without pause to the Fugue, influenced by J.S. Bach. Scored initially for strings, this contrapuntal movement opens with a somber theme that suggests Russian folk origin. Momentum gradually builds to an impassioned thematic statement then slowly subsides to a hush.

Brilliantly colorful string effects—glissandi, pizzicati, upper register passages—give vibrancy to the explosive Scherzo. This hard-driving movement careens to a stunning conclusion.

The broadly melodic Intermezzo opens with a lyrical passage in the first violin; drama increases as other instruments enter. The rhapsodic Finale follows without pause. The piano introduces its two themes, first a subdued motif then an angular second idea, famed as the clowns' entrance music in the Russian circus. The work concludes quietly with a gentle statement derived from the movement's first theme.

SERGEI PROKOFIEV
B. APRIL 27, 1891 IN SONTSOVKA, UKRAINE,
D. MARCH 5, 1953 IN MOSCOW

Renowned as a pianist with athletic virtuosity, Prokofiev was trained in composition at the St. Petersburg Conservatory by Glazunov and Rimsky-Korsakov, significant links to Russia's great nineteenth-century tradition. He established his early reputation with two piano concertos and the "barbaric" *Scythian Suite*, which created a scandal at its premiere. Seeking a more modernist artistic environment, Prokofiev left Russia in 1918 and spent years abroad in the United States and Paris before his permanent return to his homeland in 1934.

Although cultural homesickness was his primary motivation, Soviet Russia's assurance that the state would provide all material needs did influence his decision. Married to a fashionable singer and the father of two young sons, Prokofiev suffered incessant worries about his finances. (The decision proved to be disastrous for the beautiful Lina, whom he divorced after their arrival. As were many expatriates, she was accused of spying activities and sent to a labor camp in the Gulag. She survived to be released in 1955.) His colleague Shostakovich commented on this repatriation: "For some fifteen years Prokofiev sat between two stools—in the West he was considered a Soviet and in Russia they welcomed him as a Western guest. The final impetus came from his hopes to straighten out his financial affairs in the USSR. But once there, there was a period when he was frightened out of his wits. Two of his cantatas had been rejected by the authorities, a close colleague had been arrested, and he had injured a pedestrian in a traffic accident. He survived, and he was overjoyed when he received his first Stalin Prize."

During his twenty years in the USSR, Prokofiev was internationally praised for his synthesis of traditional techniques with twentieth-century innovations in his numerous large-scale compositions. But life in Soviet Russia was continuously dangerous. Like Shostakovich, Prokofiev endured the sweeping 1948 composers' censure by the Central Committee of the All-Union Communist Party and was forced to issue a public apology for artistic errors—"infatuation with western formalism and folk melodies arranged in an overly complex and decadent manner alien to folk art," among others. He wrote: "No matter how painful, I welcome the just criticism, which demonstrates that the formalist movement is alien to the Soviet people, that it leads to the impoverishment and decline of music. Evidently I caught the infection from contact with some Western ideas, but I have concluded that such a method of composition is faulty." Prokofiev's music was banned in the USSR until 1950. When he died suddenly in 1953 (on the same day as Joseph Stalin), he left on his desk a large amount of unpublished work in progress, of which Shostakovich wistfully commented: "A new period began in his work just before his death. Perhaps this music would have been profound, but we don't know the continuation."

*Quintet in G Minor for Oboe, Clarinet, Violin, Viola, and Double Bass, Opus 39 (1924)*

Tema con variazioni
Andante energico
Allegro sostenuto, ma con brio
Adagio pesante
Allegro precipitato, ma non troppo presto
Andantino

Anticipating a difficult artistic climate in post-revolutionary Russia, Prokofiev left his homeland in 1918 for an extended period. Like many of his fellow Russian expatriates, he went to Paris, where he befriended his fellow enfant terrible, Francis Poulenc, and absorbed the ideas of *Les Six*. Soon he joined the creative group contributing to Serge Diaghilev's *Ballets Russes*. Surrounded by this modernist set, Prokofiev experimented with polytonality and strongly dissonant harmonies to establish himself with sophisticated European audiences. However, his energetic, astringent works found only muted reception.

In 1924 Prokofiev received a ballet score commission from fellow expatriate and impresario Boris Romanov, who planned a circus-themed work for his touring company. Since Romanov could afford only a limited number of players and a small commission, Prokofiev maximized his use of the score by arranging it for a chamber group. Prokofiev describes the genesis of Opus 39, which incorporates his ballet score *Trapèze*: "I proposed a quintet consisting of oboe, clarinet, violin, viola, and double bass. The simple plot from circus life served me as a pretext for composing a chamber piece that could be performed as pure music. This explains the impractical rhythms, like the numbers written in 5/4 (3+4+3), which gave the choreographers a great deal of trouble. Nevertheless, the ballet ran in several cities in Germany and Italy with some success."

Movements of Opus 39 correspond to sections of Prokofiev's original ballet: the first and second "The Ballerina," the third through fifth "Dance of the Tumblers," and the sixth "Mourning the Ballerina." Both the choice of instruments and the harmonic and rhythmic style of Opus 39 suggest the influence of Stravinsky, particularly his *L'Histoire du soldat*. Because of its numerous points of polytonal scoring, the quintet emerges as one of Prokofiev's most dissonant works. The complex third movement, written in 5/4 meter with frequent changes of rhythmic pattern, recalls Stravinsky's Octet for Wind Instruments. Despite its similarities to works of this Russian contemporary, the Opus 39 score, written "in a spirit of quest," contains the energy, subtle wit, and inventively scored lyrical lines that are unmistakably Prokofiev.

*String Quartet No. 1 in B Minor, Opus 50 (1931)*

Allegro
Andante molto—Vivace
Andante

Prokofiev wrote the first of his two string quartets during the Great Depression in the United States, then his country of residence. For much of 1931 Prokofiev concertized throughout the United States, Canada, and Cuba. The Library of Congress had asked him to compose a string quartet, and Prokofiev began its composition as he travelled on a train. He wrote: "Before starting work on the quartet, I studied Beethoven's quartets, chiefly in railway carriages on my way from one concert to another. In this way I came to understand and greatly admire his quartet technique. Perhaps this explains the somewhat 'classical' idiom of the first movement of my quartet. It has, however, two distinctive features: firstly, the finale is the slow movement and, secondly, the key of B minor is one rarely chosen for quartets. I ended the quartet with a slow movement because the material happened to be the most significant in the whole piece."

Serious and introspective, the quartet suggests Prokofiev's growing inclination toward a more typically "Russian" melodic style with rhapsodic sweeping lines. The opening movement develops three ideas in sonata form. Brilliant passages in this movement as well as the second movement's Vivace reveal his characteristic driving energy and subtle wit. Prokofiev thought highly of his poetic Andante and transcribed it as the fifth of his Six Pieces for Piano, Opus 52.

## *String Quartet No. 2 in F Major, Opus 92 (1941)*

Allegro sostenuto
Adagio
Allegro—Andante molto—Quasi Allegro I,
    ma un poco più tranquillo—Allegro I

In 1941, with Moscow under constant bombardment from the Nazis, the Soviet Committee on Artistic Affairs decided to evacuate leading artists to distant Nalchik, the provincial capital of the North Caucasus. Somewhat relieved, Prokofiev settled into a cramped room in the Hotel Nalchik, where he composed his Opus 92 string quartet and pondered ideas for his later opera *War and Peace*. Government officials had introduced Prokofiev to the local Kabardian folk music, and he decided to incorporate these themes into his quartet. He wrote: "Bringing new and untouched Eastern folklore together with the most classical of all classical forms—the string quartet—could yield interesting and unexpected results."

In his treatment of the folk material, Prokofiev rejected the "oriental salon" style characteristic of nineteenth-century Russian music and attempted to reproduce faithfully the non-Western melodies, rhythms, and phrasings he heard. Many passages in the quartet imitate the sonorities of native Caucasian instruments. Insistently repeated rhythms, particularly in the opening movement, contribute to the work's primitive character.

The forceful principal theme of the opening movement is an actual Kabardian folk song, here scored to imitate the region's native plucked and percussive instruments. The Adagio (E minor) opens with an ardent cello statement based on a Kabardian love song. Tremulous accompaniment figures at its center imitate the kemange, a Caucasian stringed instrument. The wildly vigorous final Allegro is based on a Kabardian mountain dance.

*Sonata in D Major for Flute and Piano, Opus 94 (1944); arranged by Lera Auerbach for Violin, Cello, and Piano (2018)*

Moderato
Scherzo: Presto
Andante
Allegro con brio

Optimistic about victories at the Russian front, in the summer of 1943 Prokofiev left Moscow for an extended stay at a subsidized artists' quarters in the Ural Mountains. In this relaxing atmosphere he composed his charming Opus 94 flute sonata as a respite from work on three major scores that had occupied his attention the previous year (*Cinderella, War and Peace,* and the film score for *Ivan the Terrible*). He wrote of the sonata's composition: "Perhaps this was inappropriate at the moment, but pleasant. I had wanted to write a work for the neglected flute, and I wanted this sonata to have a delicate, fluid, classical style."

Opus 94 has had a history of successful transcriptions. After its premiere, violinist David Oistrakh requested that the work be arranged as a violin sonata. Auerbach's welcome 2018 transcription for piano trio creates additional performance opportunities.

The sonata form first movement develops two graceful, exuberant themes with pungent sonorities that suggest the influence of Mussorgsky. The delightful Scherzo, animated by exchanges of rhythmic patterns, is varied by a contemplative melody at its center. The brief Andante begins with a simple and serene melody. After an agitated section, the calm mood returns. The virtuoso rondo finale develops with wit and energy.

ALFRED SCHNITTKE
B. NOVEMBER 24, 1934 IN ENGELS, VOLGA-GERMAN REPUBLIC,
D. AUGUST 3, 1998 IN HAMBURG

Often considered the successor to Shostakovich, Alfred Schnittke is one of the most frequently performed twentieth-century Russian composers. Perhaps because of his German heritage, his dramatic, highly expressive compositions combine stylistic elements from both the Austro-German and Russian traditions. Schnittke created a significant body of chamber works, many of which explore procedures he continued to use on an expanded scale.

*Piano Quintet (1976)*

Moderato
In Tempo di Valse
Andante
Lento
Moderato pastorale

Schnittke began work on his Piano Quintet immediately after the death of his mother and completed it four years later. Commenting on the work's complex composing process, he states: "There were many variations and sketches. Eventually in early 1976 I found the second movement, the B-A-C-H waltz. Suddenly and astonishingly everything came together, and I was able to complete the work."

Schnittke continues: "The first and last movements frame an elaborate waltz inspired by Pushkin's *Eugene Onegin*. In the first movement, after a piano introduction, the string quartet develops in an expressive crescendo over the piano, increasing from a small cluster to a thumping organ point.

"The second movement develops in canonical, intertwining waltz motions and freezes into static trill passages. The third movement begins with fluid string sounds; an accelerando, emerging by repetition of quarter note motives, leads to a final ostinato in 5/4 time. The Lento goes from pianissimo to extreme fortissimo to create an eruption of despair. The finale, motivated by pain and nostalgia, is a *passacaglia* with fourteen repetitions of a soft horn motive, fading away in an almost tuneless continuation."

*String Trio (1985)*

Moderato
Adagio

Schnittke wrote his Trio for Violin, Viola, and Cello as a commission for the Alban Berg Foundation in honor of the Berg Centenary and recast the work for piano trio in 1992. The Trio suggests the influence of Berg both in its dense, virtuoso writing and in its structure, essentially a transformation of the opening material into a complex set of variations.

Schnittke's biographer Marija Bergamo describes the Trio: "Schnittke here exploits a thematic nucleus to create a clearly structured and homogeneous whole. With great virtuosity, he reformulates this nucleus in various ways, from atonal to tonal contexts. He incorporates features heard in Berg's music: the role of the fourth and seventh in melodic structure and harmonic tension; the variation principle; aphoristic brevity; and a strong polyphonic element in the part writing.

"This is a masterpiece of thematic metamorphosis in a lucid

periodic sequence and an aggressive synthesis of various styles. Schnittke has given us a work that exemplifies his conviction that composing is not merely a cerebral activity but also a moral endeavor. Here he shares deep roots with Alban Berg."

SOFIA GUBAIDULINA
B. OCTOBER 24, 1931 IN CHRISTOPOL,
TATAR AUTONOMOUS SOVIET SOCIALIST REPUBLIC

*String Quartet No. 3 (1987)*

Tatar-Russian composer Sofia Gubaidulina began studies at the Kazan Conservatory and completed them at the Moscow Conservatory, where she was awarded a Stalin Fellowship and praised by Shostakovich for her exceptional promise. An unapologetic avant-gardist, Gubaidulina was blacklisted in 1979 by the Union of Soviet Composers, but the following year she caught the attention of influential European composers and performers. Recognized with honorary degrees from Yale and the University of Chicago, Gubaidulina has resided since 1992 in Hamburg, where she is a member of its music academy.

Profoundly committed to her Russian Orthodox faith, Gubaidulina seeks to connect to higher powers through the artistic process, and she has devised a personal symbolism to achieve this synthesis. For her, the path toward the Divine is achieved through small increments; therefore her music is distinguished by narrow chromatic motives and glissandi rather than melodic phrases based on traditional intervals. She avoids tonal centers in favor of pitch clusters and the convergence of melodic voices. Many of her forms are based on the Fibonacci sequence, in which each succeeding time interval is equal to the sum of the two that preceded. Her varied influences include electronic music, world improvisation techniques, J.S. Bach, and Anton Webern. Gubaidulina has remarked, "I am the place where East meets West."

String Quartet No. 3 is constructed in two continuous sections. The first explores a range of plucked sounds: conventional pizzicato, glissando, trilled glissando, and the percussive "Bartók pizzicato" (the string is lifted and snapped against the fingerboard). In the latter section the players begin to use their bows with various colorful techniques: glissandi, playing with the wood of the bow, left hand pizzicato against continued bowing. The cello's return to pizzicato signals the coda, a closing sequence of nearly inaudible glissandi.

ANTANAS REKAŠIUS
B. JULY 24, 1928 IN PAVANDENĖ, LITHUANIA,
D. OCTOBER 4, 2003 IN VILNIUS, LITHUANIA

*String Quartet No. 3 (1976)*

Largo
Lento
Allegro

Declared a free nation in 1918, then subsequently reannexed by the Soviet Union but with self-rule restored in 2004, Lithuania has asserted its independence through its arts. Often called the "Mephisto of Modern Music," Rekašius created energetic works that brazenly disregard the conventions of Soviet musical life. His bitter irony and celebration of the random have turned many of his performances into subversive events. A champion of the aleatory school (from the root *alea*, Latin for "dice"), Rekašius composed much of his anti-rational "chance" music with the collaboration of his performers. Critical recognition occurred late in his career with the release of recordings in the United States.

The prolific Rekašius created a large body of compositions that includes six string quartets. His critically acclaimed String Quartet No. 3 (twelve minutes duration) reveals elements that recur in numerous Rekašius compositions: glissandi; slow, swelling pulsations; jazz and aleatory techniques; pounding percussive patterns; extremes of dynamics; intense rhythmic drive. *Fanfare* critic Benjamin Pernick observes: "It all works. Nothing is ever belabored, nothing ever goes on too long. Rekašius has the acute timing of a skilled photojournalist and a master wallpaper-hanger's ability to camouflage seams."

ARVO PÄRT
B. SEPTEMBER 11, 1935 IN PAIDE, ESTONIA

### *"Fratres" (1977), transcribed for String Quartet (1989)*

A rugged nation of numerous islands, rocky beaches, and old growth forests, Estonia won independence from Soviet Russia in 1918 but was reannexed; it regained self-rule in 1991 after the USSR's dissolution and joined the European Union and NATO in 2004. The country is well known for its encouragement of modernist arts.

Arvo Pärt began his career in the 1960s as a serialist influenced by avant-garde middle European trends. In the 1970s Pärt began to incorporate elements of Renaissance polyphony, medieval modes, and Gregorian chant into his works. Gradually he formulated a highly individual style that he called "empiric Sonorism," which is modernist without renouncing traditional harmony. A special stylistic element is "tintinnabula," rapid repetitions and overlaps of chord tones to create the illusion of glittering clusters. Pärt himself described his writing: "I build with the most primitive materials—with the triad, with one specific tonality. The three notes of the triad are like bells. And that is why I call them tintinnabulation."

Pärt initially wrote *Fratres* (Brothers) for violin and piano, but he soon rescored it for other instrumental combinations. The work revolves around three main voices—the high, middle, and low "brothers." Essentially a set of ornamented variations on a chorale theme initially heard in the lowest notes of the solo violin arpeggios, the shimmering *Fratres* creates an aura of mystical contemplation.

# NINE

# The Mediterranean

Named in the Middle Ages from the Latin words for "middle of the earth," the Mediterranean Sea is surrounded by nations that share common geology, climate, and access to trade routes. These ties have led to centuries of cultural exchange that impacted development of the Western arts. The music of Italy, Spain, and Turkey grew from Grecian roots that spread along the "superhighway" of the Mediterranean. Although mutual influences continued throughout the rise and fall of empires, the musical arts essentially evolved ethnically to create individual styles.

## ITALY

Long devoted to opera, Italian composers at the beginning of the twentieth century rebelled against the genre's perceived excesses and sought to restore the simpler grandeur of Italy's Renaissance/ early Baroque tradition up through Claudio Monteverdi (d. 1643). The reforming group included Gian Francesco Malipiero, Alfredo Casella, Ildebrando Pizzetti, and Ottorino Respighi—who alone gained a popular following for his brilliantly scored synthesis of elements ranging from Gregorian chant to Debussy's Impressionism (see below).

At mid-century a serialist group influenced by Germany's Darmstadt School and Karlheinz Stockhausen emerged that focused on electronic procedures and, ideally, the communication of social values. These composers—Luciano Berio (see below), Luigi Nono, and Bruno Maderna—eventually returned to traditional methods of sound production, often with a linguistic connection to their works. The serialism of the Viennese School influenced Luigi Dallapiccola, who wrote quietly intense chamber works such as *Divertimento in quattro esercizi* (Divertimento in Four Exercises) for soprano, flute, oboe, clarinet, viola, and cello (1934) that merged techniques of Anton Webern with contemporary Italian poetry to create clear and lyrical twelve-tone structures.

Italy's rapidly expanding postwar film industry, which required a steady output of quasi-operatic scores, offered opportunities for its neoromantic composers. Alessandro Cicognini, classically trained at the Milan Conservatory, produced film scores in collaboration with directors such as Vittorio De Sica; since much of his work is scored for small ensembles, it has the potential for chamber performance.

Notably, Italy has produced significant women composers, such as the neo-romantic Emilia Gubitosi, who pursued a successful career in Naples, and the postmodernist Sonia Bo (see below).

OTTORINO RESPIGHI
B. JULY 9, 1879 IN BOLOGNA,
D. APRIL 18, 1936 IN ROME

## *"Quartetto dorico"* (1923)

Since his works were championed by Toscanini, Ottorino Respighi became the most internationally successful Italian composer of his generation. Respighi is best known for his early symphonic poems *The Pines of Rome* and *The Fountains of Rome*, lavish programmatic works that display his brilliant sense of instrumental color. Because of his fluent and sensuous manner of expression, Respighi has often been compared to his literary contemporary, the extravagant Gabriele D'Annunzio. Yet Respighi sought more than grand effects. Rigorously trained in various European capitals, he admired the harmonic nuances of Debussy and Strauss. Devoted to early music, Respighi also intended to invigorate his works through musical gestures derived from ancient Italian roots.

Respighi's *Quartetto dorico* (Doric Quartet) derives both its name and its archaic quality from the pervasive use of the Dorian mode—a medieval church note pattern close to the D minor scale but with a flatted seventh. Perhaps inspired by the free tempo changes in the late Beethoven quartets which Respighi performed as a violinist, the Doric Quartet is structured as a continuous fantasia with adjustments of meter articulating the four classic divisions of the string quartet—allegro, scherzo, slow movement, finale. The first section, in sonata form, offers an exposition, development, and recapitulation of two contrasting themes. The two central sections are interludes, first energetic then lyrical. The conclusion resembles a baroque *passacaglia*, with the upper strings weaving figuration over a bass line pattern with alternating four- and three-pulse units.

MARIO CASTELNUOVO-TEDESCO
B. APRIL 3, 1895 IN FLORENCE,
D. MARCH 16, 1968 IN BEVERLY HILLS

*Quintet in F Major for Guitar and String Quartet,*
*Opus 143 (1950)*

Allegro, vivo e schietto
Andante mesto
Scherzo: Allegro con spirito, alla Marcia
Finale: Allegro con fuoco

Trained at the Cherubini Royal Conservatory in Florence, the neo-romantic Castelnuovo-Tedesco was acclaimed as one of Italy's most promising young composers during the 1920s. With the rise of Fascism, his music, much of it inspired by his Jewish heritage, was banned from performance. With the assistance of Arturo Toscanini and Jascha Heifetz, Castelnuovo-Tedesco emigrated to the United States, where he described his life as "suspended like a cloud between two continents." MGM Studios offered him a contract for movie scores, and he became a prolific composer of this "American genre," as he termed it, and mentor to a generation of film composers such as Henry Mancini and John Williams. Castelnuovo-Tedesco assumed United States citizenship in 1946, but remained a frequent visitor to Italy, which often presented his premieres of traditional concert works.

Recognized as one of the foremost classical guitar composers of the twentieth century, Castelnuovo-Tedesco was a pianist by training. He began his creation of over one hundred works for guitar after meeting virtuoso Andrés Segovia, with whom he maintained a lifelong friendship. The vibrant Guitar Quintet, suggestive of Latin fiestas, American jazz, and French impressionism, has been called a landmark composition that has led to the post-1950s proliferation of guitar chamber works.

The Quintet's opening movement, "lively and openhearted," fully integrates the string lines with the guitar, whose role smoothly alternates between accompanying voice and soloist. Andante mesto, "slow and mysterious," is a thoughtful lament that begins with a remarkable second violin soliloquy. Near its quiet conclusion, the atmosphere grows languid. The Scherzo, "fast and spirited; marchlike," begins with emphatic rhythms that conjure Latin festivity. The rhapsodic cello line creates a moment of poetic reflection, and the movement ends with piquant pizzicato chords. The Finale, "fast and with fire," develops two themes with inventive counterpoint, a favorite technique of its composer. Fervency builds toward the coda, and the movement ends with a high, rising scale.

LUCIANO BERIO
B. OCTOBER 24, 1925 IN ONEGLIA, ITALY,
D. MAY 27, 2003 IN ROME

*"Circles" for Soprano, Harp, and Two Percussionists with Drums, Gongs, Cymbals, Marimba, Chimes, and Vibraphone, based on three poems by E. E. Cummings (1960)*

Influenced by the modernist pioneers Karlheinz Stockhausen and Pierre Boulez, Berio stood at the cutting edge of Europe's post-war avant-garde scene. Berio crafted the work for the supple voice of his wife, mezzo-soprano Cathy Berberian, who also assisted as percussionist. Aaron Copland invited Berio to premiere *Circles* at the 1960 Tanglewood Festival, and Berberian made her American debut at the occasion.

Berio wrote: "I had no intention of writing a series of vocal pieces with harp and percussion accompaniment. Rather I was interested in elaborating the three poems in a circular way so that a unified form resulted, where the different levels of meaning, the vocal action, and the instrumental action would strictly condition each other, even on the plane of phonetic qualities. The theatrical aspects of the performance are inherent in the structure of the work itself, which is, above all, a structure of actions to be listened to as theatre and viewed as music."

Based on the 1920s work of the avant-gardist Edward Estlin Cummings (1894–1962), who signed his name as "e e cummings," *Circles* sets three of his surrealist poems, fragments of which are here quoted:

1. stinging / gold swarms / upon the spires / chants the litanies the / great bells are ringing with rose / the lewd fat bells / and a tall / wind / ...
2. riverly is a flower / gone softly by tomb / rosily gods whiten / befall saith rain / anguish / of

> dream-send is / hushed / in moan-toll where / night
> gathers / morte carved smiles / cloud-gloss is at
> moon-cease / soon / verbal must flowers close / ...

3. n(o)w / the / how / dis(appeared cleverly)world
   / iS Slapped:with;liGhtninG / ! / at / which(shall)
   pounceupcrackw(ill)jumps / of / THuNdeRB / loS-
   So!M iN / -visiblya mongban(gedfrag- / ment ...

Berio's music is a soundscape that pivots around the shapes of
the poetic lines. Since the work develops as a succession of syllables that are exploited as pure sound, individual phrases are
obscured. The singer must execute challenging leaps, upward
and downward glissandi, and distorted vowel sounds as she
declaims the text. The instrumentalists are positioned behind
the singer, who gradually moves backwards until she is partially encircled by them. Their virtuoso cadenzas articulate the
poetic structure.

## SONIA BO
### B. MARCH 27, 1960 IN LECCO, ITALY

Composer, pianist, and conductor Sonia Bo received her
degrees at the Santa Cecilia Academies in Milan and Rome. She
has taught composition at various Italian universities and the
Conservatorio di Milano, and she has won numerous first prizes
at international competitions for works in a variety of genres. She is
known for Spectralism (from the Latin root *spectrum*, plural *spectra*),
a luminous merging of tone colors drawn from a continuous range
of overtones that finds its counterpart in the optical phenomenon
of the rainbow. Bo has composed using electroacoustic procedures,
and her music reflects these characteristic sounds through traditional instruments.

## *"Frame Toccata" for Flute, Clarinet, Violin, Cello, and Piano (2009)*

A form popular during the Baroque era, the toccata is a "touch" piece (from the Italian *toccare*, to touch) composed to demonstrate the performer's skill. A structurally free form, the toccata typically offers virtuoso elements such as rapid figuration and an extended note range. Bo's *Frame Toccata* (freely translated from the Italian as "Toccata of Myself," six minutes duration) develops with ethereal sound effects grounded by a prepared piano, which alters sound quality by objects placed between the strings. Flute techniques include flutter-tonguing and high whistles; the strings frequently play *col legno* (with the wood of the bow). All instruments execute glissandi (continuous glides between notes) and elaborate flourishes of note clusters. The work fades to a gentle conclusion with a melodious statement in the strings.

## SPAIN

Early twentieth-century Spanish composers were closely influenced both by Romanticism and Impressionism, but they were also receptive to their own native traditions. A persistent advocate for folk nationalism was Felipe Pedrell, who taught that "Spanish art music must develop from the music of the people." He influenced a generation that included Enrique Granados and Manuel de Falla, who advised: "Folk music is most satisfactorily treated not by using authentic tunes but by 'feeling' them, by realizing the foundations on which they rest and conveying their essence in music of one's own."

In 1930, a group of eight Madrid-based composers and musicologists banded together to form *El Grupo de los Ocho* (The Group of Eight), modelled on the revolutionary *Les Six* in Paris. The Eight's New Objectivity movement aimed to free Spanish music from ethnic and literary associations and to bring Spain into the modernist European orbit through the neoclassical techniques of Hindemith and Stravinsky. Alternatively known as *El Grupo de Madrid*, it was expanded to nine members: Julián Bautista (1901–1961), Falla's student Ernesto Halffter (1905–1989), his brother Rodolfo Halffter (1900–1987), Salvador Bacarisse (1898–1963), the writer Juan José Mantecón (1895–1964), Fernando Remacha (1898–1984), Gustavo Pittaluga (1906–1975), Falla's student Rosa García Ascot (1902–2002), and her husband Jesús Bal y Gay (1905–1993). The group was forced to disband during the Spanish Civil War (1936–1939) and by the beginning of World War II, six had left Spain. Most continued to compose, but their contributions are little known; a thesis or article is needed to trace the history and scattered productions of these exiles. Rodolfo Halffter, who fled to Mexico and befriended composer Carlos Chávez, created the group's most significant known chamber music. His vibrant four-movement Opus 24 String Quartet (1958) develops with the Spanish Neoclassicism of Falla and the rhythmic verve of Chávez.

Spain's postwar composers returned to a style based on folk tradition as heard in Falla (then in exile in Argentina following Franco's victory in the Civil War). Works for Spain's beloved classical guitar continued to flourish, and contributions to its literature written by composers such as the Romero family of performing guitarists have been influential. Often these works are extended culturally through Latin American elements; for example, Pepe Romero's *De Cádiz a la Habana* (2013) for guitar quartet is based on the flamenco rhythm of *colombianas*—a mixture of Colombian folk melody with the rhythmic structure of the Cuban *guajiras* (originally a poetic genre from Andalusia)—and the Spanish *rumba gitana* (gypsy rumba).

Zarzuela, a seventeenth-century Spanish operatic form with spoken dialogue, has continued into the twentieth century with dramatic chamber arrangements by composers such as Federico Moreno Torroba (see below). In recent years postmodernist composers such as Gustavo Díaz-Jerez (see below) have explored new techniques such as Spectralism and tone colors influenced by electronics.

Revered as the founder of the modern Spanish school of composition, Enrique Granados began his career as a concert pianist following two years of study in Paris. After meetings with nationalist composer and folklorist Felipe Pedrell, Granados began to explore Spanish folk idioms. He then created a substantial body of work—seven operas, numerous piano and orchestral pieces—reflecting Spain's colorful native traditions. *Goyescas*, his final opera, was premiered in 1916 at the Metropolitan Opera, an honor that ironically ended his promising career. Although Granados disliked travel and rarely ventured far from Spain, he chose to attend the New York performance and then to perform a piano recital at the White House for President Woodrow Wilson. The extended voyage cost Granados his life, since on his return to Spain his ship was torpedoed by a German submarine in the English Channel. Although secure in a lifeboat, Granados dove into the waters to rescue his struggling wife. Neither of them survived.

*Piano Quintet in G Minor, Opus 49 (1895)*

Allegro
Allegretto quasi Andantino
Largo—Molto presto

Granados wrote his Opus 49 Piano Quintet and Opus 50 Piano Trio early in his career, a time when he was influenced by German romantic tradition. Both were premiered together in Madrid with resounding success. Granados wrote to his wife: "It was a night of true glory.... It was the first time a living Spanish composer's chamber work was performed in the Salon Romero." These melodious, well-crafted works have continued to maintain popularity.

Opus 49 has been described as "the happiest of all G minor chamber works." The ebullient Allegro, cast in sonata form, begins with a unison declamatory statement of the first theme; a tranquil second theme follows in the major mode. At the development, the first idea is expanded imitatively. It returns in original form, and the movement concludes with abrupt chords.

Muted throughout, the second movement achieves a haunting quality that evokes Moorish Spain. A central episode (A major) provides contrast before the return of the main themes.

After its brief and slow introduction, the virtuoso finale, driven by emphatic rhythms, hurtles forward with several interruptions by gypsy melodies. Themes from the opening movement return, and the movement concludes succinctly on two G minor chords.

MANUEL DE FALLA
B. NOVEMBER 23, 1876 IN CÁDIZ, SPAIN,
D. NOVEMBER 14, 1946 IN ALTA GRACIA, ARGENTINA

*Concerto for Harpsichord, with Flute, Oboe, Clarinet, Violin, and Cello (1926)*

Allegro
Lento (giubiloso ed energico)
Vivace (flessibile, scherzando)

Like his compatriot Granados, Manuel de Falla credited his teacher Felipe Pedrell for instilling the native Iberian spirit that infuses his compositions. Pedrell, also a composer, gave his students insights into the deepest roots of Spanish music, a venerable tradition that predates the gypsy elements often associated with it. Later, during his seven years in Paris Falla befriended Debussy and Ravel, and the three composers were mutually influential.

Attracted to the harpsichord because of its resemblance to the Spanish guitar, Falla wrote his chamber concerto (1923, completed in 1926) for Wanda Landowska, who had rescued that keyboard instrument from oblivion. A rugged and austere work, the concerto showcases the distinctive sonority of the harpsichord, which at moments evokes the sound of the guitar.

Although constructed according to classical principles, the concerto reflects the influence of Stravinsky, particularly in its polytonal (two keys heard simultaneously) outer movements. Of these, the opening Allegro develops a fifteenth-century Spanish song, "De los álamos vengo, Madre" ("I come from the poplar trees, Mother"), and the concluding Vivace moves with joyous dance rhythms. The emotional center of the work lies in the remarkable Lento, which bears Falla's inscription as an expression of faith: "In the year of the Lord 1926, on Corpus Christi Day." This deeply mystical and concentrated movement is intended to be heard and felt as a tonal prayer.

JOAQUÍN TURINA
B. DECEMBER 9, 1882 IN SEVILLE,
D. JANUARY 14, 1949 IN MADRID

The poetic son of an Italian genre painter, Joaquín Turina abandoned early studies of medicine and moved to Madrid, where he met Manuel de Falla and with him resolved to create musical reflections of Spanish life. In 1905 he relocated to Paris, where he enrolled at the Scola Cantorum and studied with the French Romanticist Vincent d'Indy, a follower of César Franck. After his return to Spain in 1914, Turina achieved popular success with works based on traditional Sevillian and Andalusian themes. Despite hardships during the Spanish Civil War, when he was persecuted by the Republicans, Turina survived to enjoy an honored career as composition professor at the Madrid Conservatory.

## *"Scène andalouse" (Escena andaluza) for Viola, Piano, and String Quartet, Opus 7 (1912)*

Crépuscule du soir: Allegretto mosso
A la fenêtre: Andantino mosso

Homesick for Seville and his girlfriend, grieving for both recently deceased parents, Turina began to write tone portraits of Spain soon after his arrival as a student in Paris. He sent the young woman a postcard: "How much I recall Andalucia! All my life and hopes are there." Begun in a moment of strong emotion but completed under the surveillance of his professors, *Scène andalouse* (Andalusian Scene) reveals the influence of Franck in its harmonic structures and d'Indy in its fine craftsmanship. A painterly work, its two movements portray a scene that begins at twilight ("Crépuscule du soir") and continues with a serenade at a lady's window ("A la fenêtre"). The solo violist assumes the role of the suitor; the strings and piano convey both atmosphere and the responses of the lady.

The work opens with a glittering piano solo evoking perfumed gardens and sparkling fountains. The viola enters with an ardent theme followed by a gracefully accompanied serenade to the lady, who responds through florid melodies in the strings supported by richly chromatic figuration in the piano. A suave and elegant *habanera* (a slow and sensuous Cuban dance) emerges. Numerous changes of tempo, texture, and dynamics create drama and atmosphere. The themes of the first movement are subtly echoed in the second movement, a continuation of the lovers' dialogue at the window. Propelled by quickly changing and asymmetrical rhythmic patterns, the movement's rapturous themes unfold with warm sonorities.

*Piano Trio No. 2 in B Minor, Opus 76 (1933)*

Lento—Allegro molto moderato—Allegretto
Molto vivace
Lento—Andante mosso—Allegretto

Turina's second piano trio, a work of gentle emotion and subtle elegance, belies the political and economic difficulties of the times. Before his return to Spain, Turina had constructed the framework of the trio at the Scola Cantorum of Paris, where he studied with the French romanticist Vincent d'Indy, a follower of César Franck. The influence of Franck is clearly heard in the trio's pervasive cyclic structure, a means of unifying the movements through a recall of themes.

A brief and hushed introduction leads into the first movement's main theme, a flowing melody that suggests Iberian influence. Florid melodies in the strings, marked "suave and expressive," overlay richly chromatic figuration in the piano, directed to be played "cantando." Numerous changes of tempo, texture, and dynamics lend drama to this atmospheric movement.

The second movement is written in a rapid quintuple meter, a favorite rhythm of Turina. The muted strings, articulating rapid repeated notes, contribute a breathless quality. A long-short rhythmic pattern underpins sections of melody that progress modally in parallel blocks. A fortissimo piano passage in octaves, followed by a dramatic pause, signals the slower contrasting middle section (triple time); the opening material returns.

As in the trio's opening movement, a short lento introduction prefaces the finale. The movement's expressive themes move through a variety of tempo changes. At its conclusion the main theme is transformed from a smoothly flowing melody to a rapid and emphatic statement.

FEDERICO MORENO TORROBA
B. MARCH 3, 1891 IN MADRID,
D. SEPTEMBER 12, 1982 IN MADRID

Composer and conductor Federico Moreno Torroba is best known for his stage works and his contributions to the Zarzuela, a light form of Spanish opera. His varied works for classical guitar have been performed by the Romero family, Andrés Segovia, and other notable artists. Romantic works deeply rooted in the Spanish folk tradition, his guitar compositions require virtuoso technique.

## *"Estampas" for Guitar Quartet (1979)*

Bailando un fandango charro
Remanso
La siega
Fiesta en el pueblo
Amanecer
La boda
Camino del Molino
Juegos infantiles

Moreno Torroba worked closely with the Romero Quartet as he composed his picturesque guitar works, including *Estampas* (Images). Written while Torroba was serving as Director for the Academia de Bellas Artes de San Fernando, *Estampas* was one of his later works. Its eight movements comprise an album of small portraits or scenes of Spanish life: "Bailando un fandango charro" (Dancing a Horseman's Fandango) refers to a festive country dance; "Remanso" (Backwater or Quiet Pond) illustrates a peaceful lakeside scene; "La siega" (The Harvest) quotes traditional folk melodies as does "Fiesta en el pueblo" (Festival in the Village); "Amanecer" (Dawn) is an evocative daybreak portrait; "La boda" (The Wedding) is a musical wedding celebration ending with a fascinating excursion through everyday Spanish life; "Camino del Molino" (Road of the Mill) conjures the steady turning of a mill through melodic repetitions and ostinato figuration in the accompaniment; "Juegos infantiles" (Children's Games) suggests gently playful games that progress, pause, and then resume.

### GUSTAVO DÍAZ-JEREZ
### B. FEBRUARY 1970 IN TENERIFE, CANARY ISLANDS

One of the foremost Spanish composers and pianists of his generation, Díaz-Jerez studied at the Conservatorio Superior of Santa Cruz de Tenerife and the Manhattan School of Music. His style is described as "algorithmic Spectralism," tonally luminous work achieved through a set of rules that define an operational sequence. A wide timbral range is an important goal of his method, which is derived from the mathematical disciplines of number theory and psychoacoustics. Díaz-Jerez quantifies the melodic, rhythmic, and timbral elements obtained through his processes and transcribes the results using traditional instruments. Despite its manipulations, the essence of his original concept remains intact, giving the listener a glimpse of a unique and affecting tonal world.

## "Tephra" for Violin, Viola, Cello, and Piano (2012)

Tephra, Greek for "ash," is a geological term for rock fragments and particles ejected during a volcanic eruption; tephra cones are a natural feature of Díaz-Jerez's once volcanically active environment. His composition Tephra is meticulously organized by its mathematical program, but it achieves significant emotional force as its momentum builds. The work begins descriptively as the piano line suggests minute falling particles through percussive, pointillistic note groups against sustained harmonies in the strings. The conjunction of string effects such as ponticello (playing at the bridge), *bariolage* (alternation of notes between adjacent strings), and harmonics creates an ineffable atmosphere. The intrusion of faster note values, rapid tremolando passages, and forte passages in the strings' upper registers varies the level of intensity as the work develops.

## TURKEY

Once the core of the Byzantine Empire and a significant portion of the Ottoman Empire, Turkey became an independent nation in 1923. Its diverse musical heritage reveals both the classical tradition of the Ottomans and a rich folk culture that reflects its position at the crossroads of Eastern Europe, Central Asia, and the Middle East. From the mid-twentieth century its music has been profoundly shaped by the late romanticist Ahmet Adnan Saygun (1907–1991) and musicologist Kemal İlerici (1910–1986), who developed a harmonization system based on intervals that reflect the Makam, Turkey's distinctive set of modes and scales (heard in İlhan Baran's *Dönüşümler*, see below). A student of both these pioneers, Baran during his thirty-five-year teaching career exerted strong influence on composers such as Kamran Ince (see below). With Baran's guidance many young composers have synthesized Western elements with Turkish culture.

İLHAN BARAN
B. JULY 10, 1934 IN ARTVIN, TURKEY,
D. NOVEMBER 27, 2016 IN ANKARA

One of Turkey's most significant modernist composers, Baran was born in a remote northeastern town near the Georgian border. Frequently moving with his military father to different regions of

Turkey, he gained exposure at an early age to its varied musical culture. At sixteen Baran entered the Ankara State Conservatory, where he studied composition with Ahmet Adnan Saygun and Turkish music harmony with Kemal İlerici. After graduation Baran continued composition studies with Henri Dutilleux in Paris, where he flourished in the experimental atmosphere of the 1960s. His works at this time included electronic compositions, several of which received encouraging Parisian premieres. After his return to Turkey he was appointed professor at his alma mater and subsequently at Bilkent University.

## "Dönüşümler" (Transformations) for Piano Trio

Fantasia: Poco rubato—dolcissimo—calmato—
    con passion—con elevazione
Dönüşümler I: Ben ritmo—pesante—con fuoco
Dönüşümler II: Grazioso—con amore
Dönüşümler III: Deciso—ben ritmo—con fuoco
Dönüşümler IV: Barbaro—sempre ffff e ben marcato—deciso
Dönüşümler V: Con grazia ma poco marcato—sempre ben ritmo
Dönüşümler VI: Con fuoco
Dönüşümler VII: Affetuoso— con delicatezza—
    poco misterioso—lontano
Dönüşümler VIII: Allegro tanto possibile—
    maestoso—perdendosi

Baran's contributions to the chamber repertoire are little known, but his rarely performed *Dönüşümler* is an important addition to the piano trio genre. *Dönüşümler* merges Turkish folk rhythms and modalities with Western minimalism to create a multi-faceted kaleidoscope of sound. The work unfolds freely, but it mimics a set of variations on a theme consisting of rhythmic and melodic patterns initially stated by the piano in the opening Fantasia. Although each Transformation is remotely related to the opening theme, the treatment of each becomes increasingly complex as different melodic and percussive elements are introduced. Ultimately the work's eight transformations go beyond Western variation form—the progressive "transformation" of gestures creates a continuously evolving work that conjures, in Baran's words, "a kind of atmospheric state of mind."

The designations of the various sections, many of which connect without pause, are translated as:

Fantasia: Very sweet—calm—with passion—uplifting
Transformation I: Very rhythmic—heavy—with fire
Transformation II: Graceful—with love
Transformation III: Decisive—very rhythmic—with fire
Transformation IV: Barbarous—always extremely loud and
    emphatic—decisive
Transformation V: With grace and not emphatic—
    always very rhythmic
Transformation VI: With fire
Transformation VII: With strong affect—delicate—a bit
    mysterious—heard from far away
Transformation VIII: As fast as possible—majestic—slowing
    gradually and dying away

KAMRAN INCE
B. MAY 6, 1960 IN GLENDIVE, MONTANA

Ince has been praised by the Los Angeles Times as "that rare composer able to sound connected with modern music and yet seem exotic." Raised in Turkey, where he studied with İlhan Baran, Ince continued his education in the United States at Oberlin and Eastman. He maintains connections in Turkey through his co-directorship of MIAM (Center for Advanced Research in Music) at the Istanbul Technical University.

Ince describes his style: "Although my music has become more developmental, that is not what I live for. Psychological effects, reactions, blocks, the use of time, different perceptions, and play with memory are what I am about." His music can be described as post-minimalist in that it utilizes essentially repetitive patterns and avoids traditional tonalities. Ethnic influences are particularly strong in his work, and he has on occasion combined Turkish and Western instruments in his ensembles.

### "Waves of Talya" for Flute, Clarinet, Violin, Cello, Piano, and Percussion (1988)

Commissioned by the Koussevitzky Foundation, *Waves of Talya* was named one of the best chamber music works by a living composer in *Chamber Music* magazine (June 2000). The composer writes: "Talya is the ancient name of Antalya, the Mediterranean coast city of Turkey, where majestic mountains meet the dazzling, warm coast. I visited there on many occasions as a child, and I was always in awe of the big waves that irresistibly crashed on the pebbly shores."

*Waves of Talya* is a dynamic tone poem that conjures strong images of churning waves through restless, *fortissimo* accented passages contrasting with briefly gentler passages that suggest water receding. Momentum quickly rebuilds with successions of accented chords and fervent passagework. Fast note repetitions in the upper registers of the winds suggest sparkles among the pebbles of the shore. Varied densities of scoring, rhythmic syncopation enhanced by metric shifts, rapid changes of dynamics from very, very soft (marked *niente*, or nothing) to very loud convey the grandeur and wildness of the coast.

FAZIL SAY
B. JANUARY 14, 1970 IN ANKARA

## Woodwind Quintet, "Alevi dedeler raki masasında," Opus 35 (2010)

Andantino tranquillo—Presto fantastico
Andantino tranquillo—Moderato
Andantino
Presto—Andantino

A virtuoso pianist, Fazıl Say balances his active performing career with composing in a variety of genres. His delightful and programmatic Quintet ("Alevi Fathers at the Raki Table"), commissioned by Konzerthaus Berlin, received its premiere in 2011. Say comments: "In four short movements following each other without pause, the Quintet humorously describes an everyday scene in an Anatolian village: Alevi fathers drinking raki at a well-laid table. An andantino ritornello in irregular meters returns in all movements to provide the thematic context for an eventful action."

Say's work conjures the atmosphere of Turkey's very male ritual of sharing drink and conversation at the local taverna. Octave doublings among the instruments, common in Turkey's ethnic music, create strong and heavy melodic weight that suggests the importance of the elders' meeting. The long legato lines that recur throughout the work in the *ritornello* passages suggest their familiar themes of discourse. The modal harmonic progressions could be heard in the regional tunes played on the traditional instruments of tavern bands. Repetitive figuration, varied by moments of piquant imitation, reflect the progressing rhythms of a pleasant evening with the *Alevis*, a significant Islamic sect.

# TEN

# British Soundscapes

England's tradition of outstanding literary arts influenced its musical composition in the early half of the twentieth century. Many composers embraced a written narrative, often one that reflected their worldviews, as both a starting point and a guiding force for their works. Ralph Vaughan Williams set six operas, fifty choral works, and over one hundred songs to texts that conveyed his liberal humanitarianism. A devotee of gothic tales, Edward Elgar drew inspiration from their sylvan "wood magic," which his wife sensed emanating from his studio as he composed his three significant chamber works in 1918. Arnold Bax, a poet and author as well as composer, loved Celtic literature and is said to write as if he were illustrating its legends. Benjamin Britten, as Arthur Hutchings states, "is at his best when a plot, text, or vocal line provides the thread that clarifies his texture and integrates his technique." All these composers most probably felt their purely instrumental works were enhanced by subliminal story.

After World War II the visual arts provided additional inspiration. From the middle of the twentieth century, British artists significantly impacted the art world; and Britain's composers were keenly aware of the cultural currents their works parallel. Figurative painters such as the darkly expressive Francis Bacon (1909–1992) and the bold portraitist Lucian Freud (1922–2011) achieved emotional effects that were emulated in the musical field, and, as the New Tate Gallery reveals, composers welcomed cooperation with compatible visual artists in multi-media projects.

Harrison Birtwistle, the father of two artists, composes work controlled by sound blocks that for many listeners evoke discernable imagery, most probably by intention; he states that his work has a "geographical" component that connects it to an imaginary scene. Thomas Adès writes much work that conjures known visual images, such as *Arcadiana*, and evokes picturesque events, such as *Catch* (see both below). The portrait of Adès by Phil Hale—who conceives visual art as "having breathing life akin to music"—was a seven-month-long project that now hangs in the National Portrait Gallery.

RALPH VAUGHAN WILLIAMS
B. OCTOBER 12, 1872 IN DOWN AMPNEY, GLOUCESTERSHIRE,
D. AUGUST 26, 1958 IN LONDON

*Quintet in C Minor for Piano, Violin, Viola, Cello, and Double Bass (1903)*

Allegro con fuoco
Andante
Fantasia (quasi variazioni)

Because of his deep assimilation of British Isles folk song and his appreciation for the modalities heard in ancient British music, Ralph Vaughan Williams wrote numerous works distinguished by their "Englishness." Acclaimed as the re-creator of his country's musical vernacular, Vaughan Williams achieved a reputation as one of Europe's most distinctive musical personalities by the beginning of World War I. He weathered a long and self-critical apprenticeship period. When Vaughan Williams wrote his early C minor Quintet, he already had composed four of his most famous songs and a cantata set to words by British poet Dante Gabriel Rosetti. But the quintet's heavily marked and erased score suggests that he did not feel control over the chamber medium. Revised over the course of two years, the quintet was finally premiered in December 1905 by some of the finest musicians in London. Although successful performances followed, Vaughan Williams withdrew the work in 1918. He did not altogether repudiate its material, since he quarried the Fantasia movement for themes to develop in his 1954 violin sonata.

Perhaps because of his perfectionism, Vaughan Williams's early unpublished works all carry an embargo against performance. However, because of intense interest in his music written before 1908, after a forty-year hiatus his widow Ursula agreed to the publication and performance of certain selected works, among which was the 1903 Quintet. Its first modern performance (1999) was held in London in association with the conference "Vaughan Williams in a New Century." In 2002 the quintet was published by the British firm Faber Music Ltd.

Created for the same combination of instruments as Schubert's "Trout" Quintet, the 1903 Quintet develops with the free Romanticism and the atmosphere of open-air freshness characteristic of Vaughan Williams throughout his career. The tempestuous first movement offers strong contrasts of mood and dynamics. After extensive exploration of the opening lyrical theme, first heard in Vaughan Williams's favorite viola voice, an emphatic idea is played in unison by all instruments. This motto recurs in the following movements as a unifying device.

The Andante, marked to be played "tenderly," offers expressive interludes for the piano. After a more agitated central section and interesting harmonic excursions, the movement closes quietly with a muted statement in the strings.

The Fantasia develops like the Elizabethan fantasy, a rhapsodic one-movement work that improvises on a principal motive. The movement opens with the theme (related to the strongly accented motto heard in the first movement) played in unison by all the strings. The piano offers a solo response. Designated "smooth and without expression," this soft beginning suggests an entrance from a remote point of time and distance. The ensuing sections, identified as "almost variations" by Vaughan Williams, unfold with sharp contrasts of tempo, expressive atmosphere, and tonality. The movement closes in the same quiet atmosphere as its beginning.

### String Quartet No. 2 in A Minor (1944)

Prelude: Allegro appassionato
Romance: Largo
Scherzo: Allegro
Epilogue: Andante sostenuto

Dedicated to violist Jean Stewart, Vaughan Williams's orchestral student at his annual Leith Hill Festivals, String Quartet No. 2 prominently features her instrument in all four movements. The viola begins each movement with the primary thematic statement and closes the first three movements with a motivic solo line. Composed between work on his major symphonies, the bold harmonic shifts of movements 1 and 3 anticipate those heard in Symphony No. 6.

The work begins with a sweeping statement for solo viola, soon followed by tremolo passages with quick harmonic shifts that underscore its tempestuous mood. A *tranquillo* passage leads to a solo viola statement of the opening theme. The songful Romance (G minor) again opens with a solo viola statement, here marked "without vibrato" to conjure the timbre of an ancient viol. Cast in three-part song form with a central section in D flat major, the movement ends with a calm viola statement.

The Scherzo (F minor) begins with a forceful viola statement from a theme used in *49th Parallel* (1941), a British war film for which Vaughan Williams wrote the music; the other instruments, muted, play softly *sul ponticello* (on the bridge) to create a subdued background. A viola solo in its upper register leads to a quiet conclusion. The concluding Epilogue (D minor to D major) is marked "Greetings from Joan to Jean," a reference to Vaughan Williams's incomplete film project on George Bernard Shaw's life of Joan of Arc. Slow and sustained, the movement concludes with an atmosphere of serenity.

GUSTAV HOLST

B. SEPTEMBER 21, 1874 IN CHELTENHAM, GLOUCESTERSHIRE,
D. MAY 25, 1934 IN LONDON

A shy musical rebel whose personal motto was "Always ask for advice but never take it," Gustav Holst composed in a variety of genres diversely influenced by the German romanticists Richard Wagner and Richard Strauss, the impressionists Claude Debussy and Maurice Ravel, and English madrigal. His lifelong friend Vaughan Williams also shaped Holst's individual style by sharing English folksongs that he had enthusiastically collected during his travels through the countryside; he asserted that Holst's directness of expression grew from his absorption of their natural simplicity. Holst also benefitted musically from his friendship with colleague and hiking partner Arnold Bax, who introduced him to astrology, the inspiration for his orchestral suite *The Planets*. A noted teacher at several institutions that included Morley College, Holst impacted the development of composers such as his daughter Imogen and, later, Benjamin Britten.

*Wind Quintet in A flat Major, Opus 14 (1903)*

Allegro moderato
Adagio
Minuet (and Canon)—Trio
Theme and Variations: Poco allegro e cantabile

The Allegro moderato develops two leisurely, songful themes with free imitation and lively counterpoint. The impressionist influence of Debussy is heard in its harmonies, often based on whole-tone scale patterns. Adagio, cast in three-part song form with a faster central section, develops a noble English folk-inspired melody with an impressionist touch; one detects harmonic echoes of Ravel's *Pavane pour une infante défunte* (1899). The energetic Minuet is varied by its flowing central Trio section and its contrasting major/minor modalities. The finale, Theme and Variations, offers full statements of its folklike theme, altered primarily through rhythmic shifts and piquant accompaniments.

## *Terzetto for Flute, Oboe, and Viola (1925)*

Allegretto; Andante
Un poco vivace

Holst's daughter Imogen, a modernist composer and Gustav's biographer, praised the Terzetto as his best work of chamber music because of its insouciant atmosphere and boldly experimental harmonies. The diaphanous Allegretto is a dreamlike movement that suggests the impressionist influence of Debussy's *Prélude à l'après-midi d'un faune* (1894). Its polytonal harmonic scheme requires the three individual lines to be played simultaneously in different keys (A major, flute; F minor, oboe; and C major, viola).

The second movement, Un poco vivace (a bit lively), continues the polytonal harmonic framework. A delightful evocation of English country dance, its playful main theme is developed imitatively and animated by piquant rhythmic treatment.

EDWARD ELGAR
B. JUNE 2, 1857 IN BROADHEATH,
D. FEBRUARY 23, 1934 IN WORCESTER

England's most significant composer of the late Romantic tradition, Elgar contributed three important works to the chamber repertoire—the Opus 82 Violin Sonata, the Opus 83 String Quartet, and the Opus 84 Piano Quintet. Elgar wrote all three works simultaneously beginning in 1918. His wife Alice had recently relocated the couple to a quiet cottage in Sussex, and Elgar, recovering from a throat operation, was delighted with its situation. Alice heard new sounds in the emerging works, the first chamber music that Elgar had written in thirty years—greater harmonic simplicity and an autumnal mood that she poetically described as "wood magic."

## String Quartet in E Minor, Opus 83 (1918)

Allegro moderato
Piacevole (poco andante)
Finale: Allegro molto

The E minor quartet unfolds with opulent lyricism. The opening movement, cast in sonata form, develops two serenely expressive themes with colorful shifts of register and harmony. Its long-breathed melodies unfold in spacious measures of 12/8 meter; its supple rhythms fluctuate with subtle variations of detail. The warmly lyrical second movement (C major, marked *dolce* or sweet) was said to be a favorite of Alice. Its dual themes suggest English folksong; near the conclusion the first theme returns with all instruments muted, and the tempo gently slows with the marking *morendo* (dying).

The vibrant finale (E minor) opens with the marking *risoluto* (resolute). Two themes, ornamented with passagework marked *brillante* (brilliant), are explored in sonata form. At its development

(A major) the melodic lines, now more chromatic, are made restless by continuously shifting tempos. The opening theme returns with vigorous passagework (*marcato*, each note emphasized) and expressive leaps. A soft *ponticello* passage (played at the bridge) creates a moment of calm before the recapitulation (marked *risoluto*). The *brillante* passagework returns together with new extensions marked *con passione* (with passion) and *con fuoco* (with fire). The movement concludes with a fortissimo coda designated "always increasing in tempo and dynamics."

## Piano Quintet in A Minor, Opus 84 (1918)

Moderato—Allegro
Adagio
Andante—Allegro

Elgar's home looked onto an eerily twisted group of white trees, a continual source of fascination for him. Local legend held that the trees were the ghosts of Spanish monks who had practiced black magic in the area. His literary interests at this time, encouraged by a visit from Algernon Blackwood, the noted author of horror tales (whose frightening story "The Willows" involved trees) fueled his imagination. Elgar then requested that several novels of Edward Bulwer-Lytton (notorious for his opener "It was a dark and stormy night...") be sent to his remote cottage. Both he and Alice were enchanted by Bulwer-Lytton's *A Strange Story*, in which true love and witchcraft collide in an English village. Alice suggested the source of the quintet's brooding atmosphere in a diary entry: "E. wrote more of the wonderful Quintet. Sad disposed trees and their dance and unstilled regret for their evil fate.... Lytton's *Strange Story* seems to sound through it too."

Although the local gothic legend influenced the atmosphere of Opus 84, the anxieties of war doubtless contributed to the work's dark undercurrents. World War I had entered its closing phase as composition began, and Elgar doubted that England's familiar way of life could continue. Throughout the entire work two themes continuously interweave—an ominous plainchant motif suggesting the beginning of a Requiem Mass; and a lilting, nostalgic theme conjuring the elegance and vivacity of the Old Europe.

The Quintet opens with an aura of mystery as the piano quietly intones the stark main theme in octaves (*serioso*) and the strings utter a subdued accompaniment. The graceful second idea, which the violins play in thirds, resembles a Spanish dance theme. In the Allegro section, the two themes are recast and developed with harmonic richness. At the atmospheric conclusion, the strings and piano, now in its lowest register, engage in dramatic dialogue to create a sense of awe.

The three-part Adagio (E major) begins with a viola solo of poised elegance. The other strings join and interweave to create textural richness. Echoes of the opening movement themes return with variations; an elegiac motif is introduced by the first violin and answered by the cello. A calmly contrasting section (F major) features the viola, soon joined by the other strings. The original harmonies (C sharp minor/E major) return and the movement grows in fervency and sweep. After a statement of the plainchant motif, the movement closes in a hushed atmosphere.

The Finale's introduction reprises motifs from the opening movement. The ensuing Allegro develops two passionate themes in sonata form. Echoes of the first movement themes reappear and intertwine with these new ideas. A muted recapitulation of the nostalgic "Spanish" theme leads to the extended coda, which continuously accelerates until its "grandioso" conclusion.

ARNOLD BAX
B. NOVEMBER 8, 1883 IN STREATHAM, LONDON,
D. OCTOBER 3, 1953 IN CORK, IRELAND

Although his life experience was deeply English because of his London upbringing, training at the Royal Academy of Music, and knighthood from King George VI in 1937, the late romanticist Arnold Bax drew his inspiration from Ireland's literature and seascapes. A staunch supporter of Irish independence, Bax wrote both political tracts and fiction under the pseudonym "Dermot O'Byrne." He became a significant figure in Dublin's literary circles even as he continued to compose. In his 1943 memoirs Bax wrote: "I worked very hard at the Irish language and steeped myself in its history and saga, folk-tale, and fairy-lore. Under this domination my musical style became strengthened. I began to write 'Irishly,' using figures and melodies of a definitely Celtic curve."

Exempt from military service during World War I because of a heart condition, Bax produced a large body of instrumental works during his early career; he was considered England's pre-eminent symphonist until his reputation was overtaken by Ralph Vaughan Williams and William Walton in the 1940s. Bax's romantic sensibilities did not resonate with post-war modernists, and his music gradually fell into nearly complete neglect. His compositions, recently rediscovered, are now actively promoted and recorded by the Sir Arnold Bax Trust, founded in 1985.

Bax wrote that in his early years he "wallowed" in Wagner, but he also studied closely the works of Richard Strauss; the expressive chromatic harmonies heard throughout his quartets reveal similar late romantic tendencies. His penchant for florid passagework suggests the picturesque influence of Franz Liszt's tone poems.

## String Quartet No. 1 in G Major (1918)

Allegro semplice
Lento e molto espressivo
Rondo

Bax dedicated his G major quartet to Edward Elgar, whom he had visited at his home. The chromatically enriched harmonies and vigorous rhythmic drive heard throughout this first quartet suggest that Bax, a violist and chamber musician, was acquainted with Richard Strauss's youthful String Quartet in A Major, Opus 2 (1880). Occasional pentatonic gestures suggest the haunting themes of Dvořák's late quartets. Double stops contribute a full, orchestral quality.

The joyous opening movement develops two graceful ideas in sonata form. In the development the mode changes to G minor in a forceful passage marked "very rhythmical"; the opening ideas are then varied in passages designated "very neat and precise." At the coda the tempo accelerates to create a dynamic conclusion.

The songful Lento (D major) unfolds with luxuriant harmonies and dynamic nuance. Its center section is muted and played *sur la touche* (on the fingerboard) to impart a thin, transparent color. The rondo finale conjures a vigorous Irish jig. A modal change to G minor, an extensive *ponticello* passage (played at the bridge), and myriad adjustments of tempo animate this colorful movement. At the coda the tempo accelerates to create a vivacious conclusion.

## String Quartet No. 2 in E Minor (1925)

Allegro—Tempo vivace
Lento, molto espressivo—Poco allegro
Allegro vivace—Lento

Bax wrote his second quartet simultaneously with his somber Second Symphony; a sober mood continues into his second quartet, which has never achieved the popularity of the first. Like his first quartet, the second is structured with three balanced movements, the outer ones framing a contrasting inner movement.

The remarkable solo cello introduction presents four ideas that are developed over the course of the opening Allegro; the viola then joins, and after an interval the violins enter. The various themes are explored in sonata form. Syncopated figures energize the long cantabile (singing) lines heard throughout.

Perhaps because of Bax's personal difficulties, unease prevails in the Lento. The main theme, intoned in the viola's darkly low register, suggests pensive Irish song. The theme is spun out and continuously varied by metric shifts and brooding changes of modality. At its center Bax quotes a fragment from *A Romance,* his 1918 piano work written for Harriet Cohen, who had induced him to leave his wife and children.

The primary theme of the cello recitative heard at the work's beginning is now transformed into the rapid dance theme of the expansive finale. The sonorous chords of the muted middle section provide contrast. Fast and harmonically unsettled, the wild Irish dance continues with two vigorous fugato passages. Earlier ideas are combined at the animated concluding coda to unify this varied and intense composition.

BENJAMIN BRITTEN
B. NOVEMBER 22, 1913 IN LOWESTOFT, SUFFOLK,
D. DECEMBER 4, 1976 IN ALDEBURGH, SUFFOLK

The leading British composer of the mid-twentieth century, Benjamin Britten is widely famed for his operas and song settings—but he also wrote string quartets, three of them numbered, that deserve more attention. Each develops with modernist techniques realized with rigorous logic and clarity. All exude a particular Englishness because of his deep absorption of Elizabethan heritage and the Anglican tradition. While permeated with dissonance, these compositions are grounded by extensive areas of tonality. Always seeking his own voice, Britten has created luminous works with an undercurrent of narrative.

## *String Quartet No. 1 in D Major, Opus 25 (1941)*

Andante sostenuto—Allegro vivo
Allegretto con slancio
Andante calmo
Molto vivace

A pacifist, Britten spent much of World War II in the United States as Artistic Ambassador. He and his companion, the great tenor Peter Pears, were hosted by the English duo pianists Ethel Bartlett and Rae Robertson at their San Diego area home. Britten set up a studio in the tool shed to escape their robust piano practice; there he wrote his first numbered string quartet within three months as a commission for Elizabeth Sprague Coolidge. "It was short notice and a bit of a sweat, but I'll do it as the cash will be useful," he wrote. After its successful premiere, Britten received the Library of Congress Medal for this quartet, which was hailed as a milestone in his composing career.

Coolidge had commissioned Bartók's String Quartet No. 5 seven years earlier, and certain of its gestures are heard in Britten's Quartet No. 1. Allusions to Beethoven's late quartets appear in both compositions—the chorale theme of Bartók's slow movement references Beethoven's Opus 132; Britten's quick alternations of slow and fast passages in his first movement mirror the opening of Beethoven's Opus 130. Britten's quartet opens with an ethereal area that resembles Bartók's "night music," soft, dissonant passages intended to evoke the murmur of a mysterious forest. In Britten's slow Andante sostenuto, the high, close pianissimo intervals of the upper strings (simultaneously F sharp-G sharp-A) against the D major cello pizzicato creates the ineffable, somewhat sinister, atmosphere of night. The following Allegro vivo, in a loud dynamic, introduces propulsive, syncopated rhythms. The two sections alternate with variations throughout the movement.

In the brief scherzo, "lively with momentum," a rhythmic pattern is established in a soft dynamic; the viola interrupts the momentum with brusque interjections. The following Andante calmo (B flat major), cast in an asymmetrical 5/4 meter, conjures the swell of the sea for some listeners. The movement develops with pungent dissonances that are mitigated by the strong tonality of the cello line. At its center an animated cello passage (*declamato*, declaiming) is joined by the viola to create a dual duet with the two violins. The movement concludes *dolce* (sweet) in a triple piano dynamic.

The hammered bow strokes of the rapid finale create Bartókian energy. Unexpected pauses recall similar surprises in the quartets of Haydn. Near the conclusion, rising scale passages in the violins accentuate the forceful thematic statements, and the work ends with an exhilarating coda.

### *String Quartet No. 2 in C Major, Opus 36 (1945)*

Allegro calmo senza rigore
Vivace
Chacony: Sostenuto

In July 1945 Britten and Yehudi Menuhin toured Germany as a piano and violin duo to play for concentration camp survivors. Soon after his return, Britten wrote his String Quartet No. 2, a work ostensibly composed to commemorate the 250th anniversary of Henry Purcell's death but also one that testifies to the intensity of his recent experience. The quartet, perhaps his most popular chamber work, was completed in October 1945 and premiered that November in London.

Classically structured in sonata form, the quartet opens with calm statements of three melodious themes, each beginning with the wide interval of the tenth and accompanied by a sustained chord forming the interval of a tenth. An *animato* section is followed by a quiet statement with ghostly atmospheric effects created by glissandi and harmonics over sustained notes. An *energico* passage leads into an episodic development section, in which tranquil and agitated passages alternate. After a brief restatement of ideas and a coda, the movement ends quietly with cello pizzicati "like a harp" punctuating the softly sustained lines of the other instruments.

The Vivace (C minor) is a demonic scherzo that is no less ferocious because it is played with mutes throughout. Its aggressive theme, introduced fortissimo by the first violin, is consistently accompanied by pianissimo arpeggiated figures. Emphatic chords punctuate this opening section. In the contrasting trio section (F major) the first violin introduces a theme in long note values, an augmentation of the movement's primary theme. The scherzo returns in the same F major key, but the theme is now a pianissisimo murmur in the upper registers of the violins and viola; arpeggiated figures in the cello accompany. Strongly accented chords in the transition passage signal the opening theme's return to its original key.

The Chacony, a Tudor English respelling of the baroque *chaconne,* pays homage to Purcell. The form consists of variations on a slow, triple-time ground, which here is a nine-measure melody initially played by the unison strings. The twenty-one variations that follow are separated into four groups by cadenzas for the cello, viola, and first violin. Britten writes: "The sections may be said to review the theme from (a) harmonic, (b) rhythmic, (c) melodic, and (d) formal aspects. The first group presents six variations based on a developing harmonic scheme. The second group of six, introduced by a cello cadenza, varies the rhythmic patterns.

A viola cadenza leads to the third group, six variations based on a countermelody heard in the second violin. The first violin plays the final cadenza, which introduces the final three variations, which together form a coda to the movement."

## String Quartet No. 3 in G Major, Opus 94 (1975)

Duets: With moderate movement
Ostinato: Very fast
Solo: Very calm
Burlesque: Fast—con fuoco
Recitative and Passacaglia (La Serenissima)

In October 1975 Britten began work on his third and final string quartet, a medium he had ignored for thirty years. Britten had recently suffered a small stroke during heart surgery, and his right hand had become slightly impaired. His musicologist friend Hans Keller, who had long hoped to hear another Britten quartet, suggested that "now is the time for four staves." Britten wrote this Opus 94 quartet for his longtime friends in the Amadeus Quartet and completed it during his November visit to Venice—the location perhaps inspiring incorporation of material from his 1973 opera *Death in Venice* into the last movement. Although Britten had the satisfaction of hearing the work in rehearsal, the Amadeus Quartet premiered the quartet a few days after his death in 1976.

Keller, the work's dedicatee, states that in Quartet No. 3 "Britten ventures into the Mozartean realm of the instrumental purification of opera." Throughout his long career, Britten had placed the highest value on the human voice, and portions of his final quartet develop with the direct simplicity of song. However, the quartet's first four movements also suggest the abstract modernist influence of Bartók and Shostakovich.

The opening movement, "Duets," develops six duo pairings centered on the interval of the second. "Ostinato," a scherzo movement, is based on a series of energetically syncopated intervals of the seventh. "Solo," the slow central movement, pays tribute to the virtuosity of Amadeus Quartet violinist Norbert Brainin. Its calm and ethereal violin line is supported by triadic arpeggio figures for the other players. "Burlesque" conveys sardonic humor through dissonant melodies underpinned by brusque rhythms.

"La Serenissima" offers themes from Britten's final opera, *Death in Venice*. The opening cello recitative recalls the *barcarolle* accompanying Aschenbach's gondola rides. In the *passacaglia* section, important opera motifs are heard over the persistent ground bass. The work concludes, as Britten said, "with a question"—an ambiguous chord that denies full harmonic closure and instead casts doubt on the protagonist's future. Despite its uncertainty, the ending conjures a still and serene atmosphere.

IMOGEN HOLST
B. APRIL 12, 1907 IN RICHMOND,
D. MARCH 9, 1984 IN ALDEBURGH, SUFFOLK

*String Quintet for Two Violins, Viola, and Two Cellos (1982)*

Prelude
Scherzo
Theme and Variations

The daughter of Gustav Holst, Imogen Holst was taught and encouraged by her father, whose reputation was later enhanced by her several books on his life and music. Studies with Vaughan Williams at the Royal College of Music also influenced her style, which reveals a similar love of folksong, strong interest in English music of the sixteenth and seventeenth centuries, and flair for innovation. Early in her career Holst's works were broadcast and performed together with works by other young British women composers such as Elisabeth Lutyens. In the 1940s Holst joined the Dartington Hall faculty and established it as a major center of music education. In 1956 Benjamin Britten appointed her as his co-director for the Aldeburgh Festival, and inevitably Holst became a part-time composer. After her retirement, she resumed composition and at age 74 created her acknowledged masterpiece, the String Quintet—a work she thought "made her a real composer."

Holst's quintet was warmly praised by *The Guardian* (2009): "Early Michael Tippett and Gerald Finzi are perhaps Holst's closest matches stylistically, but it's the String Quintet that really shows off her independence, with its rustic depictions in its first two movements, and a complete change of mood in the finale, which is a set of variations on the last theme written in her father's notebook."

The Prelude opens with a sustained C in the full ensemble, a suggestion that the group is tuning in preparation. This warmly lyrical movement develops with hints of Impressionism in its harmonies, occasionally built on the whole tone scale (six tones rather than the traditional seven of common practice) heard in Debussy. The players offer a succession of exquisite solo moments characterized by expressive leaps and gentle resolutions. The Scherzo (F major) is a light and playful movement animated by rapid bow repetitions, piquant pizzicato interjections, ornamental trills, and passages of lively imitation.

The Theme and Variations, a tribute to her adored father, is a statement of subtly nuanced beauty. The solo viola intones the searching and elegiac theme, heard initially in B minor. Separated by brief pauses, its variations develop Gustav's motif through rhythms suggestive of folk dance and rhapsodic soliloquys, often accompanied by a single sustained note. At the final variation the harmony changes to C major, an upward shift that conveys luminous ascendancy.

GERARD SCHURMANN
B. JANUARY 19, 1924 IN JAVA, DUTCH EAST INDIES,
D. MARCH 24, 2020 IN HOLLYWOOD HILLS, CALIFORNIA

## Piano Quartet No. 1 (1986)

Ricercare: Andante con affetto
Capriccio: Allegro molto
Corale: Largo

A British descendant of the prolific seventeenth-century composer Georg Caspar Schürmann, Gerard Schurmann (anglicized name form) largely taught himself the craft of composition. He gained fluency, as well as the ability to conjure a specific emotional atmosphere, during his early employment by the British film industry, for which he composed thirty-two scores. After devoting himself solely to his own compositions, Schurmann produced intensely expressive works through lyrical, harmonically colorful language. Once the neighbor of painter Francis Bacon, Schurmann was inspired by him to write his descriptive 1968 orchestral work *Six Studies of Francis Bacon*. He has written numerous chamber works that have received their premieres in the United States, where he relocated in 1981.

Schurmann discusses his quartet: "The Ricercare, named for a popular early music form, is characterized by intermittent canonic devices, giving the music a searching quality (ricercar= "to search out"). It opens quietly with one of the principal subjects, a short melodic phrase, played in canon by the strings. The piano joins after one bar with a broader version of the same materials in octaves. A brief antiphonal idea quickly builds to a second, more assertive melodic idea announced fortissimo by the strings, after which a series of integrated sections develops and restates the material in various juxtapositions. The movement comes to rest in a slow, more extended canon.

"The Capriccio (a free and lively form) keeps relentlessly to a basic fast tempo throughout. Most of the music stems from a simple but intense little theme that first appears almost immediately in the violin. It consists of two symmetrical phrases of four bars each, connected and followed by three bars of ascending runs for the piano. The transformation of this material proceeds along essentially dramatic lines, contrasting strong declamatory episodes with some quieter, less vehement passages. A forceful coda ends the movement angrily.

"Corale (choral) indicates a more unified expression in the music, which is predominantly of a lyrical nature. It returns to the material of the opening Ricercare, but although the work ends in the way that it began, the final feeling is one of quiet resignation and peace."

## HARRISON BIRTWISTLE
### B. JULY 15, 1934 IN ACCRINGTON, LANCASHIRE

Awarded a British knighthood in 1988, Sir Harrison Birtwistle is one of Britain's most acclaimed contemporary composers. After studies at both the Royal Manchester College of Music and Princeton University, Birtwistle established his reputation with two works, the opera *Punch and Judy* and *Verses for Ensembles*. A form of expanded chamber music, *Verses for Ensembles* (woodwind quintet, brass quintet, and percussion, 1969) develops partially as chance music that for some listeners suggests the practices of Charles Ives. After composing the work's largest section, Birtwistle cut it arbitrarily into smaller pieces, which he then arranged randomly. Connecting links of introductions, epilogues, and internal material were inserted to give unity and coherence to the work. He achieved an overall structure of "verse and refrain," a popular song form in which a soloist offers a theme and the larger group responds as a unit. In performance the work exhibits an intriguing visual element; the instrument groups are set in symmetrical ranks and the soloists are arrayed around them. The players migrate between positions to suggest arcane ritual.

*An Imaginary Landscape* (1971), a powerful work for brass, percussion, and double basses, evokes brilliant, often otherworldly images; conceived for symphonic forces, it belongs to the chamber world as an outlier because of its narrow range of instrumental families. Its construction in blocks of sound suggests the influence of Edgard Varèse (1883–1965), known as the first composer to conceive sound groups as objects independent from the traditional possibilities of development and variation. The name alludes to John Cage's set of 1950s electronic works with the same title but signals Birtwistle's penchant for geographically orienting his listener in space. He terms the work a "processional," and the music unfolds similarly as horizontal scenes in a frieze. The instruments are grouped so that they can clearly respond to one another as units. At the final section they merge to intone a quiet chorale, an elegiac tribute to his departed mother.

Birtwistle describes his strongly pictorial style: "One starts, stops, moves around, looks at the overall view, fixes one's attention on a particular feature or on a detail of that feature or on a fragment of that detail or on the texture of that fragment." He often compares a work's abstract structural scheme to a scenic walk in which a central reference point is glimpsed from different angles. Like an exploratory excursion, Birtwistle's core musical idea is altered, varied, and distorted as the work progresses; one does not necessarily return to its starting point. Throughout his work one hears assemblages of instrumental sonorities and densities that accumulate to define an imagined musical space.

## Clarinet Quintet (1980)

An accomplished clarinetist, Birtwistle frequently writes works showcasing his instrument's three distinctive registers—the mysterious low chalumeau, the trumpet-like clarion, and the high altissimo. His choice of the clarinet in A rather than the more brilliant woodwind in B flat allows the player to execute a darker, more veiled tone quality that blends effectively with its string quartet partners. Written in one continuous movement, the quintet is cast in very free sonata form; motivic ideas at the beginning expand to create an exposition, and the strings as a group begin a section of development. There is a recapitulation of ideas and a quiet concluding coda. A theatrical exploration of a diverse tonal landscape, colorful effects are heard throughout the quintet—rapid dynamic and timbral changes, abrupt pointillistic interjections that suggest the influence of Anton Webern, buzzing effects that conjure an insect horde from Bartók's "night music." Since the work suggests a strong visual component, an effective performance might be paired with screenings of contemporary art.

## "Five Distances for Five Instruments," for Flute, Oboe, Clarinet, Bassoon, and Horn (1992)

Birtwistle's jubilant and fast-paced wind quintet (13 ½ minutes) suggests animated conversation that overcomes the barrier of distance. Written for the Ensemble Intercontemporain, the score asks its players "to sit as far apart as is practically possible." Challenging for musicians accustomed to close interaction so that individual auditory cues can be easily discerned, as well as spectators forced to consider the music with altered visual perspective, the work has been described as "a scriptless musical theater, teeming with individual sonic characters."

The distanced players begin to play independently of one

another but gradually their monologues come together as a full discussion. At the rhythmically intricate concluding section their unique lines contract and expand in turn, each instrument waiting for its opportunity to speak until the quiet closing.

## "Hoquetus Irvineus" for String Quartet (2014)

Hoquetus, or hocket, is Latin for "hiccup." An important means for enlivening works of the French Ars Nova era (fourteenth century), hocket is an interrupted effect achieved by splitting a single melody into fragments so that notes and rests alternate among voices. Influenced by the great master Guillaume de Machaut (1300–1377) and his *Hoquetus David*, Birtwistle has created a playful homage of four minutes duration. Syncopated note groups, separated by dramatic pauses, cascade then wind down and come together with chords, animated motion that perhaps reflects their dedicatees—"Irvine and his lovely boys."

THOMAS ADÈS
B. MARCH 1, 1971 IN LONDON

Heralded as one of the twenty-first century's brightest talents, British composer, conductor, and pianist Thomas Adès was appointed the Benjamin Britten Professor of Composition at the Royal Academy of Music shortly after his graduation from King's College, Cambridge. In 2000 he became the youngest person to win the Grawemeyer Award for Composition, and in 2017 five of his compositions received accolades as the greatest works of the past two decades by the Italian magazine *Classic Voice*. His compositions have been the focus of contemporary music festivals in France, Finland, and Sweden.

## *"Catch" for Clarinet, Violin, Cello, and Piano, Opus 4 (1991)*

*Catch* encompasses both brilliantly playful music and inventive theater in a brief, single movement. It has been compared to Stravinsky's *L'Histoire du soldat* (Soldier's Tale, 1918), also a musical narrative. Adès offers a description: "*Catch* structures itself around various combinations of the four instruments. There are several games going on: at the start, the clarinet is the outsider, the other three are the unit, then, after a decoy entry, the clarinet takes the initiative. All four then play jovial 'pig-in-the-middle' with each other. The clarinet is then phased out leaving a sullen piano and cello, with interjections based on the clarinet's original tune. This slower passage gradually mutates back into fast music, and this time the game is in earnest: the piano is squeezed out, only to lure the clarinet finally into the snare of its own music."

## *"Arcadiana" for String Quartet, Opus 12 (1994)*

Venezia notturna
Das klinget so herrlich, das klinget so schön
Auf dem Wasser zu singen
Et ... (tango mortale)
L'Embarquement
O Albion
Lethe

Adès conceived the seven movements of *Arcadiana* (freely translated as "idyllic pastorale") as a series of short evocations to be played without pause. He states that each of the movements is intended to conjure "an image associated with ideas of the idyll, vanishing, vanished, or imaginary." Throughout the work Adès alludes to works of earlier composers but does not directly quote them. The opening movement, "Venice at night," suggests its mysteriously shimmering water reflections. The title of Movement 2,

"That sounds so pretty, so lovely" references the aria from Mozart's *Die Zauberflöte* (The Magic Flute, 1791); there is a suggestion of Papageno's bells and the presence of the Queen of the Night. Movement 3, "To sing on the water," alludes to Franz Schubert's D. 774 *Lied* (1823), which describes a water scene and then reflects on the passage of time. Adès states that Movement 4, "Deadly tango," was inspired by Nicolas Poussin's baroque 1638 painting *Et in Arcadia ego*, in which idealized shepherds are gathered around a tomb. The movement begins with a grotesque parody of the classic tango but becomes a funeral march. Movement 5, "The Embarkation," inspired by Jean-Antoine Watteau's large rococo painting *The Embarkation for Cythera* (1717), hints impressionistically at Debussy's *L'Isle Joyeuse* (1904). Movement 6, "O Albion," refers to the poetic and archaic alternate name for Britain; marked to be played *devotissimo* (with much devotion), it offers homage to Elgar's "Nimrod" movement from his *Enigma Variations*. The final movement, "Lethe," refers to the classical river of Hades whose waters granted oblivion to all who drank from it.

## Piano Quintet, Opus 20 (2000)

Historical forms appeal to Adès, a composer with a lively interest in early music, and his remarkable quintet is largely informed by classical tradition. Although cast as a single movement, it falls into sections that echo traditional sonata form—an opening allegro section, which is repeated; a slower section that is often lushly romantic; and a faster, agitated section that accelerates dramatically into the concluding coda. Although complex, its harmonies are recognizably tonal. But the quintet's true originality is heard in its rhythmic transformations of the thematic material. This is often achieved through nonstandard time signatures—such as 1/5 or 4/7. Consistent metrical juxtapositions in the strings and the piano lines, with each group articulating vastly different rhythms, create a shimmering texture. The quintet's widely nuanced range of dynamics and tempos reinforces its profoundly individual vision.

The quintet earned highest critical praise from *The Guardian* (2003): "It is a piece that seems simultaneously familiar and strange: its large-scale architecture and many of its melodies seem to allude to classical and romantic repertoire, but every element is transfigured by the processes Adès visits on his material.... The piece sounded especially clear, concise and powerful. And the final climax was a shattering moment, as the music hurtled towards its emphatic final bars."

# ELEVEN

# Cultural Fusion in Latin America

In his lecture "A Latin American Composer" at Harvard's 1958 Charles Eliot Norton speaker series, the eminent Mexican composer Carlos Chávez asserted: "For us in Latin America, who have lived the life of our countries, a study of the past is not necessary. The past is present. We knew of abstractionism and so-called 'primitivism' long before such trends were the fashion in Europe. They are in our eyes and ears, and the legacy came directly to our hearts. Indeed, a country like Mexico creates in one the feeling of man's association with the earth for thousands of years. This link with the remote past is deep and subconscious."

Perhaps because of strong connections to the land and its traditions, nationalism prevailed in Latin America following the countries' new independence in the nineteenth and early twentieth centuries. Composers often relied on specific native folkloric elements for the substance of their works, either through direct quotations of material or assimilation of its structure. These heartfelt compositions earned substantial international recognition. However, the major twentieth-century composers—the Mexican Chávez, the Brazilian Villa-Lobos, and the Argentinian Ginastera—were not exclusively nationalistic but rather sought to fuse their native traditions with European techniques. Although generally standing within tonal tradition, these composers followed current trends of Impressionism, Neoclassicism, and serial techniques, effectively combining them with native Indian/ Mestizo tradition.

During the 1960s, a decisive break with nationalism occurred as Latin composers began to explore electronic resources and avant-garde techniques. In the early twenty-first century, composers such as Guastavino and Golijov substantially returned to tonally oriented, melodic work that fuses Latin America's folk traditions with elements of romanticism.

## MEXICO

After the burst of patriotism following the Revolution of 1910, an emerging "Aztec Renaissance" drew from both Spanish and traditional Mexican cultures to create the style of "Mestizo Realism." The new government gave muralists such as Diego Rivera massive walls for public art, and they chose to paint revolutionary scenes in this nationalist style. Composers understood the impulse generating Mexico's significant pictorial arts scene, but the path toward a similar national music was elusive. Chávez writes that a central idea was "to write simple, melodic music with a peculiar Mexican flavor that would have a certain dignity and nobility of style." Eventually Mexico's music, once dominated by derivatives of Italian opera, was liberated by new techniques that began in Europe but were realized with its own distinctive energy. The geographical distance from Europe's traditions offered an advantage for developing an individual style.

CARLOS CHÁVEZ
B. JUNE 13, 1899 IN MEXICO CITY,
D. AUGUST 2, 1978 IN MEXICO CITY

A leading exponent of Mexican nationalist music, Carlos
Chávez (whose full name was Carlos Antonio de Padua Chávez
y Ramirez) was widely regarded as Mexico's foremost twentieth-
century composer and conductor. As Director of the National
Conservatory and National Institute of Fine Arts, founder of the
National Symphony Orchestra, and longtime journalist for the
leading Mexico City newspaper *El Universal,* Chávez exerted
strong influence on Mexico's musical development. His early
work was described as "profoundly non-European" because of its
evocations of pre-conquest Indian culture. Later, Chávez experimented with Neoclassicism in works such as the percussive ballet
*H.P.* (Horsepower, 1932). However, like his painter contemporary
Diego Rivera, Chávez's social conscience motivated him to connect
to his compatriots through Mexican elements. It has been observed
that his chamber works reflect his environment—the harsh and
craggy landscapes of the forbidding Mexican plateau.

*Sextet for Two Violins, Viola, Two Cellos, and Piano (1919)*

Lento
Allegro con brio
Andante
Presto scherzando
Allegretto

Chávez's youthful sextet, written before his influential travels
to major European arts centers, is characteristic of his earliest phase,
a time when he sought to emulate Robert Schumann. A piano
prodigy, Chávez wrote the work for his own performances; the
string scoring, while competent, is not always idiomatic for the
instruments. Although essentially connected to nineteenth-century

Romantic tradition, the sextet reveals a festive folk spirit that foreshadows Chávez's mature work. Vigorous rhythms with flexible tempos, colorful harmonic shifts, and playful pizzicati animate this vivacious sextet. The themes often develop through imitation or direct repetition rather than inventive reworking, a suggestion that Chávez was still mastering his craft.

## String Quartet No. 1 (1921)

Allegro
Adagio
Vivo
Sostenuto

This compact work (fourteen minutes) shows the influence of Debussy and Stravinsky but indicates Chávez's emerging individual voice. As Chávez composed the quartet, he was becoming aware of the Mexican Renaissance, an efflorescence of mural painting that celebrated native themes. His recent friendship with José Vasconcelos, the charismatic politician/philosopher who crafted widely influential essays on the nature of modern Mexican identity, forged his solidarity with the movement.

The opening Allegro creates a sound world that is tonal yet modern. It develops two themes with a full and animated texture that hints of Debussy's Impressionism. The Adagio opens with an elegiac cello soliloquy; its central theme is developed imitatively and combined with other motifs. After a forceful passage, the dynamic level fades to pianissimo and the movement closes with a chord of piquant dissonance.

Vivo (lively) is a festive and playful movement that evokes Mexico's popular music. The cello introduces a pastoral idea that is treated imitatively by the other instruments. The final Sostenuto (sustained) is a slow and meditative lament that concludes with pungent dissonance.

## String Quartet No. 2 for Violin, Viola, Cello, and Double Bass (1932)

Allegro moderato
Scherzo
Largo, liberamente
Moderato

The use of the double bass grounds Quartet No. 2 with a deep foundation. The opening movement develops a lively staccato theme with imitation and repetitions to reinforce the line. A capricious movement that suggests the impressionist influence of Debussy, the Scherzo features a vivacious interplay of pizzicati. The contrasting Largo (marked "freely") is a reflective movement that develops with contrapuntal lines.

The whimsical finale opens with a series of short notes that appears to be a quest for the theme, which, once achieved, develops through imitation and direct restatement of ideas. Its dissonant melodic intervals and rapidly scurrying imitative phrases echo Bartók's "night music." Syncopated rhythms near the end animate this C major work.

## String Quartet No. 3 (1943–4)

Allegro
Lento
Allegro

The opening Allegro's vigorous rhythms and supple folklike melodies suggest the influence of Bartók. The pervasive joyous melodies conjure a festive atmosphere. A reflective movement, the Lento develops a serene theme, first heard in the violin, that is supported by sustained harmonies and dovetailed accompanying lines in the other strings. The final Allegro begins and concludes with a festive fanfare. Rhythmic syncopation energizes the flow, and emphatic unison passages reinforce the theme at the work's conclusion.

## SILVESTRE REVUELTAS
### B. DECEMBER 31, 1899 IN SANTIAGO PAPASQUIARO, D. OCTOBER 5, 1940 IN MEXICO CITY

Established as a violinist and conductor, Revueltas began to compose during the last decade of his life after encouragement from his friend and mentor Carlos Chávez. Revueltas's early death from pneumonia (complicated by alcoholism) before the full realization of his talent was a profound loss for Mexico's arts community. An obsessive experimenter, Revueltas aspired to a synthesis of imagined Mayan Indian music with modernist rhythmic and harmonic techniques heard in Bartók's string quartets and Stravinsky's *Rite of Spring*. He eventually achieved his own dynamic primitivism that drives the compositions toward his trademark "fireworks" conclusion, a pyrotechnical succession of runs and flourishes. Revueltas's style is widely perceived to reflect the temperament of contemporary Mexico. Although his music does not directly quote Mexican folksong, Revueltas achieves convincing local color through tuneful, occasionally shrill melodies that might be heard at village festivities. Dissonant harmonies suggest the raw vitality of popular street music.

Revueltas's four string quartets were written within a short time frame at the beginning of his compositional career. Brief works of nine to thirteen minutes duration, the quartets develop with intensely energetic passages varied by moments of broad lyricism.

## *String Quartet No. 1 (1930)*

Allegro energico
Vivo

Revueltas's first string quartet reveals the picturesque influence of his mentor Carlos Chávez, to whom it is dedicated. The opening movement is structured in three sections that resemble classical "song form" (ABA). The two outer sections are forceful and rhythmically aggressive; the central section, which suggests the chromatic practices of Alban Berg, offers a lyrical contrast. The rapid concluding Vivo, also structured in three fast-slow-fast sections, is a virtuoso tour de force for its players.

## *String Quartet No. 2, "Magueyes" (1931)*

Allegro giocoso
Molto vivace
Allegro molto sostenuto

Revueltas dedicated his brief second quartet (ca. ten minutes duration) to his close friend Aurora Murguía. The score was eventually published with substantial changes of uncertain origin twenty years after its composition. Its subtitle "Agave Plants," the cactus base for tequila, is possibly a nationalist gesture; but Revueltas was attracted to strong drink, which unfortunately shortened his life. At the beginning of the quartet, Revueltas quotes a motif from a popular song of the same name: "I pray to heaven to dry up the *magueyes*, because these agaves are the source of my misfortune. I am very drunk and nothing makes me happy, because the woman I love does not love me."

Revueltas's second string quartet unfolds with a variety of propulsive rhythms, colorful tonal effects, and edgy dynamic shifts. The opening movement is constructed in simple two-part form with minimal thematic development. The second is cast in three sections (fast-slow-fast); its main theme is foreshadowed in the first movement. The compact finale (37 measures long) concludes with Revueltas's typically vibrant "fireworks" coda.

## String Quartet No. 3 (1931)

Allegro con brio
Lento, misterioso y fantastico
Lento—Allegro

Revueltas's forcefully colorful third string quartet was not published until 1995, fifty-five years after his death. A fervent work that suggests the influence of Bartók, the quartet opens with strident passagework. A solo cello recitative slows the momentum; its ensuing lyrical motif is extended by the violin and returned to the cello. The pace accelerates, and percussive chords lead to full-textured, energetic passagework.

The solo cello introduces the Lento, a "mysterious and fantastic" movement that conjures an eerie atmosphere. Pizzicati spontaneously punctuate the suspended melodic lines, supported by ethereal impressionist harmonies that echo Debussy. The finale begins with a reflective passage for cello that leads steadily to emphatic declamatory dialogues among all instruments.

## String Quartet No. 4, "Música de feria" (1932)

Allegro—Lento—Allegro giocoso—Allegro

"Música de feria" (Music of the Fair), Revueltas's final quartet, is often regarded as one of his most significant works. Cast in one continuous flow with a duration of nine minutes, the quartet falls into four sections that correspond to the traditional movement sequence of fast-slow-scherzo-fast. The quartet's motifs are developed with dense textures made colorful through pizzicati and harmonics. The concluding coda (Presto y frenético) builds to a "fireworks" conclusion that is an emblem of Revueltas's style.

JAVIER ÁLVAREZ
B. MAY 8, 1956 IN MEXICO CITY

## *"Metro Chabacano" for String Quartet (1991)*

Known for his striking combinations of international styles and his bold instrumental colors, the prolific Álvarez has been praised by fellow composer John Adams: "Álvarez's music reveals influences of popular culture that go beyond the borders of our own time and space." The inspiration for *Metro Chabacano* came from an earlier work that Álvarez had written for his parents as a Christmas present in 1986. Álvarez revised this work five years later and dedicated it to the Cuarteto Latinoamericano, a leading proponent of Latin American chamber works. Its premiere occurred at a Mexico City subway station—the Metro Chabacano—during the grand opening of an enormous kinetic art installation by Marcos Límenes, one of Mexico's most recognized artists. The composition, played live for the ceremonies, aired continuously on Mexican radio for the following three months.

A brief, single movement work, *Metro Chabacano* develops fragmentary melodic ideas against a driving background of continuous eighth notes. Although the perpetual motion backdrop gives the illusion of simplicity, the solo passages played by each instrument in turn are intricate and complex.

ARTURO MÁRQUEZ
B. DECEMBER 20, 1950 IN ÁLAMOS, SONORA

## *"Homenaje a Gismonti" for String Quartet (1993)*

Born in the state of Sonora, Mexico, Arturo Márquez began his piano and music theory courses in California. He continued studies at the National Conservatory in Mexico City and the Instituto Nacional de Bellas Artes in the composition workshop. He developed a passion for chamber music during his two years of advanced study in Paris. A 1988 Fulbright Grant enabled him to explore electroacoustic music at the California Institute of the Arts.

An eclectic, Márquez draws from a wide variety of Latin American musical traditions. In an interview Márquez stated his main concerns: "the constant search for special sonorities and colors, as well as the exploration of traditional instruments through new forms of execution."

*Homenaje a Gismonti* is a tribute to Brazilian painter Egberto Gismonti, who is known for his exuberant depictions of tropical scenes. Márquez writes: "In this work I follow a spontaneous and natural manner of composition to reflect Latin musical elements. *Homenaje* has decidedly been influenced by the music of Rubén Blades, Oscar D'León, the fiddlers of the Huasteca region in Mexico, as well as the Veracruz and Venezuelan harpists."

## BRAZIL

Brazilian culture was controlled by the Portuguese royal court for three hundred years. Shortly before Brazil won independence in 1822, Emperor Don João VI furthered Europe's arts influence with the "French Artistic Mission," a retinue of Parisian artists and musicians who established an Academy in Rio de Janeiro to imbue the local court with French culture. The Mission's influence waned after Brazil achieved independence, but an affinity for French styles lingered. At the end of the nineteenth century a new cultural identity began to emerge through the fusion of French Neoclassicism with Brazilian folk and Indian elements, set against the backdrop of the country's magnificent and varied natural environment.

Brazil's modernist movement was launched in 1922 by the first "Week of Modern Art Festival," which encompassed all arts. The leading nationalist composer Villa-Lobos and his colleagues held premieres introducing a fusion of European harmonic practice with folklore to create "genuine Brazilian" expression. These efforts generally met hostility from their traditionalist audiences; composers then returned to more conventional techniques until the late 1930s, when they adopted the twelve-tone approach of Arnold Schoenberg. During the 1960s the *Música Nova* (New Music) wave focused on serialism and electronic music. In the post-millennium era, trends encompass both experimental and traditional methods, often energized by rhythmic elements from Africa and the Far East.

HEITOR VILLA-LOBOS
B. MARCH 5, 1887 IN RIO DE JANEIRO,
D. NOVEMBER 17, 1959 IN RIO DE JANEIRO

The imaginative and prolific Villa-Lobos dominated Brazilian music for half a century. He created nearly one thousand works in all genres, often accompanied by extravagant stories to explain their origin. Essentially self-taught, he remained a lifelong eclectic receptive to all influences. His early friend Darius Milhaud, a French cultural attaché in Brazil before he became a member of *Les Six*, introduced Villa-Lobos to the works of Debussy and the French modernists. Villa-Lobos explored the colorful materials of both his native folk tradition and Brazilian popular music to create the basis for his unique national style—a beguiling mix of Brazil-ian-African-Portuguese folk and popular music, Impressionism, and jazz.

Awarded a Brazilian government grant for study in Paris in the 1920s, Villa-Lobos established himself as a conductor. He quickly became the darling of French avant-garde circles, who admired the exotic modernism of his harmonically pungent and rhythmically propulsive works. The approach of war motivated his return to Brazil, where he wrote the majority of his seventeen string quartets—still largely unknown in both Europe and the United States—and his nine acclaimed *Bachianas Brasileiras*.

### String Quartet No. 3, "Quarteto de pipocas" (1916)

Allegro non troppo
Molto vivo
Molto adagio
Allegro con fuoco

Written when Villa-Lobos was in Rio de Janeiro, Quartet No. 3 brought the emerging composer to the attention of the public and the critics. The quartet is remarkable for its air of spontaneity, its rhythmic energy, and the simple beauty of its melodies. Because of an insistent left hand pizzicato figure in the second movement, which creates a sound that suggests corn popping in a closed pot, the work is often referred to as the "Popcorn Quartet."

### String Quartet No. 5, "Quarteto popular No. 1" (1931)

Poco andantino
Vivo e energico
Andantino—Tempo giusto e ben ritmato
Allegro

Villa-Lobos wrote his Quartet No. 5 shortly after he had compiled a large collection of Brazilian children's melodies. He states that the work, subtitled "Quarteto popular," "makes joyful use of children's themes, which, when transformed, find freedom within the traditional quartet format." The various tunes, among which are "What beautiful eyes" and "Let's go behind the mountain, little doll," are generally light and uncomplicated; harmonics convey cheerful whistling. A somber mood is conjured in the slower passages. The final movement reiterates the theme "The miaowing cat" to suggest a music box.

### "Quinteto em forma de chôros" for Flute, Oboe, Clarinet, Bassoon, and Horn (1928)

Villa-Lobos's *Quinteto* suggests the improvisatory freedom of an actual Brazilian *chôros*, a band of street musicians who perform dance music at carnival celebrations and other festive occasions. One of his most popular works, the *Quinteto* achieves a striking effect through its strong instrumental color and rhythmic energy.

The work was premiered in 1930 at Paris's Salle Chopin. Villa-Lobos subsequently altered its scoring to replace the original English horn with the more usual French horn in the wind ensemble. The work combines the neoclassical ideas that Villa-Lobos absorbed during the Parisian phase of his career with the spontaneous spirit of Brazilian native music.

### "Bachianas Brasileiras"

Villa-Lobos revered J.S. Bach as "the universal source of music." As homage he wrote nine *Bachianas Brasileiras* (Brazilian suites in the style of Bach) between 1930 and 1945, all inspired by the atmosphere of the Baroque master's work. A virtuoso cellist who understood his instrument's deeply expressive qualities,

Villa-Lobos scored the first and fifth works of the set for eight cellos with the addition of a soprano for number five. Although both are true chamber works, the remaining *Bachianas Brasileiras* are classified as duos or orchestral compositions. Like Bach's suites and partitas, the essence of each is a dance suite preceded by a prelude and concluded with a fugue. Each movement is given two titles in Portuguese, the first Bachian and the second Brazilian, to reflect their dual origins—free adaptations of baroque devices now fused with national folk music.

## *"Bachianas Brasileiras" No. 1 for Eight Cellos (1930)*

Introdução (Embolada)
Prelúdio (Modinha)
Fuga (Conversa)

"Embolada" (lit. "embolden") is a popular art form of Northeast Brazil; it consists of two participants who improvise fast metrical verses of speech/song with tambourine accompaniment and vie for the winner's "crown." This introductory movement (C minor) unfolds as a series of energetic dialogues among the cellos, paired two to a stand. The discourse is delineated by measures of *rallentando* (slowing) and changes of tempo. A slower central section (F major) creates a three-part structure.

"Modinha," a traditional Brazilian nostalgic song, functions as a second prelude to the work. A leisurely three-part song form movement in D minor, Modinha features a sublime cello solo in its central section.

"Conversa" (conversation) is a vigorous fugue (B flat major) that creates an ongoing dialogue among the paired cellos. As in the first movement, the discourse is varied by slower, contemplative sections.

## "Bachianas Brasileiras" No. 5 for Soprano and Eight Cellos (1938/1945)

Ária (Cantilena)
Dança (Martelo)

"Ária," the initial section, is perhaps Villa-Lobos's most renowned composition. Rescored for guitar and solo voice by the composer and popularized by folksinger Joan Baez, it secured the composer's fame in the 1970s. Villa-Lobos dedicated the work to Arminda Neves D'Almeida ("Mindinha"), whom he would marry in 1948; the text was written by Ruth Valladares Corrêa, the soprano/poet who premiered the work in Rio de Janeiro. Harvey Officer here translates from the Portuguese:

> Lo, at midnight clouds are slowly passing, rosy and lustrous,
> O'er the spacious heavens with loveliness laden.
> From the boundless deep the moon arises, wondrous,
> Glorifying the evening like a beauteous maiden.
> Now she adorns herself in half unconscious duty,
> Eager, anxious that we recognize her beauty,
> While sky and earth, yea, all nature with applause salute her.
> All the birds have ceased their sad and mournful complaining;
> Now appears on the sea in a silver reflection
> Moonlight softly wakening the soul and constraining hearts
> To cruel tears and bitter dejection.

The eight cellos, paired two to a stand, briefly introduce the Cantilena (A minor), an ethereal duet between the solo cello and the soprano's vocalise. The singer declaims the poem's words in the animated central section; after they conclude, she continues the theme with soft humming to create a quasi-instrumental duet with the solo cello.

After an eight-year hiatus, Villa-Lobos composed "Dança" (C major), the work's contrasting second section. Structured as an *embolada*, a rapid patter song of Brazil's Northeast, the movement is subtitled "Martelo" (Hammer). Steadily underpinned by short, repeated notes, the percussive flow is interrupted by brief slower sections. Manuel Bandeira wrote the lyrics, a sentimental tribute to the beauties of the Cariri Mountains, a Brazilian preserve with numerous bird species. The text includes a list of their species and suggests their birdsong: "La! Lia! Lia! Lia! Sing more to remember Cariri!"

RAIMUNDO PENAFORTE
B. JULY 20, 1961 IN RECIFE

*Piano Trio, "An Eroica Trio" (1998)*

Astor
Maurice
Capiba

The prolific composer and multi-instrumentalist Raimundo Penaforte has written for and collaborated with notable performers in a variety of genres. Penaforte has toured Colombia with the Afro-Cuban band La Tipica Nova. Popular in the United States, he was both Artistic Director and keyboardist for the first Brazil-New York Jazz Festival at Town Hall.

Penaforte describes his piano trio: " 'Astor' is a movement that combines the rhythmical aspects of tango music. Despite its connection with Piazzolla, the title has no hidden intentions to turn this movement into a traditional tango.

" 'Maurice' was inspired by the slow (*passacaglia*) movement in Ravel's Piano Trio. Again, there are no planned similarities to Ravel's music. The name here functions as a title only.

" 'Capiba' is the only movement that bears a resemblance to the composer's music whose name is given in the title. On a beautiful Sunday morning I found myself seated in front of the computer, with a cup of coffee in my hands and my uninvited gray and white cat on my lap. As the computer downloaded the art section of my hometown newspaper, I could not believe what my eyes were seeing on the screen. There was a picture of the Northeast Brazilian composer Capiba, seated on a chair with a cup of coffee and a gray and white cat on his lap."

## VENEZUELA

### INOCENTE CARREÑO
B. DECEMBER 28, 1919 IN PORLAMAR, VENEZUELA,
D. JUNE 29, 2016 IN CARACAS

*String Quartet No. 1 (1974)*

Introducción: Andante con moto
Scherzo: Quasi presto
Finale: Allegro maestoso

One of Venezuela's most significant musical personalities, Carreño has pursued a multifaceted career. He has been a French hornist and conductor of the Venezuela Symphony Orchestra, Director of the José Ángel Lamas Music School in Caracas, and a composer of numerous prizewinning works.

Carreño's various chamber works all combine dissonance and rhythmic ostinato with his characteristic folk-based lyricism. He describes his String Quartet No. 1: "This is a simple work that develops an atmosphere of diaphanous sonorities and lyricism. The Quartet consists of three continuous movements. The

Introduction begins with a slow three-measure theme, presented in the first violin, that employs all pitches of the chromatic scale arranged to form a tone row. During the course of the movement, the tone row is presented in a series of transformations (retrograde and inversion) and appears as vertical harmonies and horizontal melodies. Most of the time the row appears in its original form.

"A three-note motif appears later in the movement and leads directly to the Scherzo. The motive alternates with the opening theme and undergoes transformations of diminution and augmentation. The Finale, which opens solemnly, presents elements of the initial twelve-note row."

## ARGENTINA

After Argentina won its independence from Spain in the early nineteenth century, it essentially continued European artistic traditions. A national style began to emerge in the 1920s with an efflorescence of modernist visual painting and the support of numerous forward-thinking journals. A specifically Argentinian music closely followed with a merging of pre-Hispanic Indian traditions, Mestizo influences, and developments such as the tango—creating works that imaginatively evoke the land and people of Argentina.

ALBERTO GINASTERA
B. APRIL 11, 1916 IN BUENOS AIRES,
D. JUNE 25, 1983 IN GENEVA

Alberto Ginastera is internationally recognized as one of the most significant creative artists in twentieth-century Latin American music. Aaron Copland, his mentor in the United States, encouraged him to forge his own nationalistic style by fusing new European techniques with Argentinian native elements. Throughout his career, Ginastera steadily evolved from a folklorist to a sophisticated modernist who infused his freely tonal structures with bold timbres and dissonances that heightened their implicit psychological states.

During his youth in Buenos Aires, Ginastera absorbed Argentina's vibrant *gauchesco* folk culture—lore that eulogized the *pampas* (the land) and its nomadic *gauchos*, cowboys who stubbornly resisted civilization and progress. Inspired by their nineteenth-century narratives, Ginastera based much of his early works on native Argentinian themes and rhythms. As he evolved stylistically toward his own Neo-expressionism, Ginastera continued to color his compositions with atmospheric evocations of the Argentinian countryside.

## *String Quartet No. 1, Opus 20 (1948)*

Allegro violento ed agitato
Vivacissimo
Calmo e poetico
Allegramente rustico

Throughout String Quartet No. 1 Ginastera exploits characteristic Argentinian dance rhythms, especially the *malambo*, the rapid, foot-stamping dance of the *gauchos*. Elements of local *criollo* (Spanish-American) tradition are heard in the second and fourth movements, in which the melodic units conform to the *copla*, the eight-syllable quatrain of popular folklore.

The first movement ("violently fast and agitated") is a tour de force of nervously energetic thematic lines underpinned by rapid note repetitions. The fleet scherzo achieves moments of piquant delicacy through harmonics and bowing effects such as *col legno* (playing with the wood of the bow). In the third movement, "calm

and poetic," Ginastera creates a tone poem for his beloved countryside, the *pampas*. The rondo finale ("cheerfully rustic") evokes
popular Argentinian dance.

## *String Quartet No. 2, Opus 26 (1958)*

Allegro rustico
Adagio angoscioso
Presto magico
Libero e rapsodico
Furioso

Ginastera comments that Quartet No. 2 marks the beginning
of his "New Expressionism," an homage to earlier expressionists
such as Alban Berg, who sought to convey a wide range of psychological experience through intensely wrought melodic lines and
dramatic harmonic color. Described by Argentinian music critics
as "a parade of writing types," the work develops with a rich and
expressive harmonic vocabulary: polytonal procedures with two
key centers heard simultaneously, serialism, and quarter tones.
The quartet achieved both critical and popular success following
its premiere at the First Inter-American Music Festival, held in
Washington, D.C., in 1958.

Structural symmetry is heard in the quartet's five-movement
organization. The two outer movements, identical in tempo and
meter, reflect the dynamism of the *malambo*, the *gaucho*'s rapid and
energetic dance. The first slow movement, an "anguished adagio," is
a five-part song that expresses profound sadness. The central movement, Presto magico, conveys a fantastic, surreal mood through
bold and varied instrumental sonorities. The fourth movement,
"free and rhapsodic," consists of a theme with three variations
crafted as cadenzas for the individual instruments. The dazzling
virtuosity and percussive rhythms of the Furioso finale bring the
work to an exciting conclusion.

## String Quartet No. 3, Opus 40 (1973)

Contemplativo
Fantastico
Amoroso
Drammatico
Di nuovo contemplativo

Ginastera wrote his final string quartet shortly after his marriage to cellist Aurora Nátola and their move to Geneva. The work was inspired by Arnold Schoenberg's Opus 10 String Quartet (1908), which also features the soprano voice. Praised by *The Strad* as "a reflective and mysterious melodic invention," the work emerged as Ginastera composed within the constraints of serial composition but, like its prototype, develops with romantic warmth. The four poems flexibly alternate between song and speech to emphasize their meaning and create a magical atmosphere. The second movement is scored for instruments alone.

> *La Música* (movement I), Juan Ramón Jiménez (1881–1958)
> In the tranquil night,
> You are the rain, pure melody,
> Keeping the stars alive—
> Like lilies in a fathomless vase.
> Suddenly, like the flowing
> From a heart that breaks
> The passionate outburst
> Shatters the darkness—
> Like a woman who might sobbingly
> Open the balcony wide to the stars
> In her nakedness, with eagerness to
> Die without a reason,
> Which might be but a mad abundant life.
> The strength of music!
> How it vanquishes the monstrous darkness!
> The strength of music!
> Vial of magic purity; sonorous, grateful

Weeping; lovely black moon—
All, like rain eternal within human darkness;
Secret light along margins of mourning—;
With mystery
Which seems, Oh, to be love!
Music;
—woman unclad,
Crazily running through the spotless night!

*Canción de Belisa* (movement III), Federico Garcia Lorca (1898–1936)
Love, love.
Between my secret thighs,
The sun swims like a fish.
Calid water through the rushes,
Love.
Cock crow and the night is fleeing!
Do not let it go, Oh no!

*Morir al sol* (movement IV), Rafael Alberti (1902–1999)
The soldier lies supine. The woods
Come down to weep for him each morning's dawn.
The soldier lies supine. A little brook
Came down to ask for him.
To die under the sun, to die
Seeing it above,
Its splendor broken
Through the shattered panes
Of a single window
Whose sill is fearful
Of framing a sorrow-stricken
Brow, eyes full of
Dread, a cry ...
To die, to die, to die,
Beautiful dying, the body
Falling to earth, like
A fully ripe peach,
Sweet, needed ...
The soldier lies supine. Only a dog
Barks furiously at him.

*Ocaso* (movement V), Juan Ramón Jiménez
Oh, what a sound of gold will now remain,
Of gold that's going to eternity;
How sad is our listening as we strain
To hear the gold that goes to eternity
This silence that is going to remain
Without its gold that goes to eternity!

*Translations by Eloise Roach*

## Piano Quintet, Opus 29 (1963)

Introduzione
Cadenza I per viola e violoncello
Scherzo fantastico
Cadenza II per due violini
Piccola musica notturna
Cadenza III per pianoforte
Finale

At the time Ginastera wrote his Opus 29 Quintet, his ideal was to convey the maximum expressive effect within a strictly constructed framework. Obsessed by problems of form ("a work without form is a work deformed," he stated) in Opus 29 he intersperses cadenzas between movements to achieve balance and unity. Like Bartók, Ginastera explores each instrument's potential for creating startlingly colorful effects. He strives to suggest the supernatural and the surreal, particularly in the ethereal Scherzo fantastico movement. The finale, "A little night music," is a direct reference to Bartók's ineffable "night music" passages, evocations of a mysterious woods.

ASTOR PIAZZOLLA
B. MARCH 11, 1921 IN MAR DEL PLATA, ARGENTINA,
D. JULY 5, 1992 IN BUENOS AIRES

The son of Italian émigrés to Argentina, Astor Piazzolla spent most of his childhood in New York City, where he was diversely exposed to jazz, works of J.S. Bach, and the tango music which his father listened to every night after work. After his father bought an accordion-like bandoneon from a pawn shop, Piazzolla writes: "I became a child prodigy on this tango instrument. I even played Bach on it by adapting the music written for piano." After returning to Argentina at age sixteen, he performed in tango clubs and began classical composition studies with Alberto Ginastera. Piazzolla soon won a scholarship to study in Paris with Nadia Boulanger, a teacher known to shape careers according to the student's natural voice. Although Piazzolla had hoped to become a "mainstream" composer in the European tradition, Boulanger encouraged him to write tangos rather than to compose in a more academic style. He ultimately produced 750 works of astounding variety, all based on the tango.

Piazzolla's tangos, far more rhythmically and harmonically adventurous than traditional tangos, initially caused an uproar among his countrymen, who considered the form to be sacrosanct. Yet his beguiling and sonorous tangos ultimately earned him the name "El Gran Astor" in Argentina.

*"Tango Ballet" for String Quartet (1956)*

Titulos
La calle
Encuentro-Olvido
Cabaret
Soledad
La calle

Piazzolla composed his *Tango Ballet* for his revolutionary group Octeto Buenos Aires, which expanded the traditional tango sextet (two bandoneons, two violins, bass, and piano) by including cello and electric guitar. The group became notorious for its aggressive sound effects and savage rhythms, often achieved by using the string instruments as percussion. The virtuoso and highly nuanced *Tango Ballet* is a programmatic suite that evokes a nighttime encounter in six movements: "Titulos" (Title), an introduction; "La calle" (The Street), which conjures the energetic atmosphere of Buenos Aires; the mysterious "Encuentro" (Meeting); "Cabaret," where tango appears in its purest form; the melancholy "Soledad" (Solitude); a varied reprise of "La calle." Piazzolla subsequently transcribed the work for both orchestra and string quartet.

## *"Histoire du Tango" for String Quartet (1986)*

Bordel 1900
Continental Café 1930
Night Club 1960
Concert d'aujourd'hui

Perhaps in response to the hostile reception for his revolutionary *Tango Nuevo*—which incorporated jazz elements, an expanded harmonic palette, and non-traditional instruments into the traditional form—Piazzolla wrote *Histoire du Tango* (History of the Tango), which traces the evolution of Argentinian tango in four sections. Piazzolla provides commentary:

" 'Bordel 1900.' The tango originated in Buenos Aires in 1882 and first was played on the guitar and flute. Arrangements then included the piano and later the bandoneon. This music was full of grace and liveliness. It depicts the good-natured chatter of the French, Italian, and Spanish women who peopled these bordellos as they teased the policemen, sailors, thieves, and riffraff who came to see them. This is a playful tango.

" 'Continental Café 1930.' This is another age of tango. People stopped dancing it as they did in 1900 and preferred simply to listen. Tango became more musical and romantic. This tango has undergone total transformation: the movements are slower, harmonies are new and often melancholy. Tango orchestras now consist of two violins, two bandoneons, a piano, and a bass. The tango is sometimes sung as well.

" 'Night Club 1960.' This is a time of rapidly expanding international exchange, and the tango evolves again as Brazil and Argentina come together in Buenos Aires. The bossa nova and the new tango are moving to the same beat. Audiences rush to night clubs to listen earnestly to the new tango. This marks a revolution and profound alteration in some of the original tango forms.

" 'Modern Day Concert.' Certain concepts in tango music became intertwined with modern music. Bartók, Stravinsky, and other composers reminisce to the tune of tango music. This is today's tango and the tango of the future as well."

## *"Four for Tango" for String Quartet (1988)*

By the time Piazzolla wrote his *Four for Tango* for the legendary Kronos Quartet, he was absorbed with creation of *Tango Nuevo*—a New Tango that developed with extreme dissonance, complex chord structures, free treatment of the basic tango rhythm, and non-standard instrumental scoring. This departure from classical dance roots profoundly disturbed aficionados of the traditional tango form, long embedded in the Argentinian soul. Nevertheless, he persevered with his vision. As Argentinian cellist Antonio Lysy writes: "Piazzolla was a probing and thoughtful musician who had high ambitions. In his youth he often struggled to find his compositional identity. Yet he would eventually, through his performances, virtuosity, and creativity, become the man to redefine 'tango' as we know it today."

The work opens with brash harmonies and unusual sound effects such as rapid, high glissandi and forceful bow hammerings. At its center a beguiling tango melody emerges and is sustained against its vociferous accompaniment. At the brief coda the work returns to the hammered bow strokes and high violin glissandi heard at the beginning.

OSVALDO GOLIJOV
B. DECEMBER 5, 1960 IN LA PLATA, ARGENTINA

## "Last Round" for String Nonet (1996)

Movido, urgente
Lentissimo: Muertes del Angel

Osvaldo Golijov spent his early youth in Argentina, where he was surrounded by classical chamber music and the new tango style of Astor Piazzolla. After several years in Israel, he moved permanently to the United States in 1986. Golijov is the winner of two Grammy Awards, a MacArthur Fellowship, and has received numerous commissions from major ensembles and institutions.

Golijov writes about his Nonet: "Astor Piazzolla, the last great tango composer, was at the peak of his creativity when a stroke killed him in 1992. He left us, in the words of the old tango, 'without saying goodbye,' and that was the day the musical face of Buenos Aires was abruptly frozen. Piazzolla condensed all the symbols of tango in his accordionlike bandoneon, which was by turns raised, battered, and caressed during the dance.

"I composed *Last Round* in 1996. Friends heard a sketch of the second movement, which I had written in 1991 after hearing the news of Piazzolla's stroke, and they encouraged me to write more. The title is borrowed from Julio Cortázar's short story on boxing.

My work imagines that Piazzolla's spirit has the chance to fight one more time (he used to get into fistfights throughout his life). The piece is conceived as an idealized bandoneon. The first movement represents the act of a violent compression of the instrument and the second ["Deaths of an Angel"] a final, seemingly endless sigh. But *Last Round* is also a sublimated tango dance. Two quartets confront each other, separated by the focal bass, with violins and violas standing up as in the traditional tango orchestras. The bows fly in the air to suggest inverted legs in crisscrossed choreography, always attracting and repelling each other, always in danger of clashing, always avoiding this with the immutability that can only be acquired by transforming hot passion into pure pattern."

CARLOS GUSTAVINO
B. APRIL 5, 1912 IN SANTA FE, ARGENTINA,
D. OCTOBER 29, 2000 IN SANTA FE, ARGENTINA

*"Las Presencias No. 6: Jeromita Linares," for Guitar and String Quartet (1980)*

Argentinian cellist Antonio Lysy writes: "The voice of Carlos Guastavino was perhaps the most quietly distinctive in 20th-century Argentinean music. Vigorously rejecting the stylistic radicalism of Alberto Ginastera and his younger compatriot Mauricio Kagel, he followed in the footsteps of nineteenth-century nationalists such as Julian Aguirre and Alberto Williams. Yet Guastavino was a no less influential figure for the younger generation of composers— particularly in popular music—growing up in Argentina in the 1960s and 1970s. He dismissed atonality and musique concrète, believing that music should be based on melody and harmony. 'I love melody,' he once said. 'I love to sing. I refuse to compose music only intended to be discovered and understood by future generations.' "

Guastavino established his reputation as a vocal writer; over half of his 300 works are delightful songs, some winsome or tinged with sadness. In the 1980s he wrote a series of instrumental *Presencias* (Characters), picturesque studies of persons and places meaningful to him. One of his few works scored to include string quartet, *Jeromita Linares* is named for the elderly Spanish lady who was Guastavino's neighbor during his youth in Santa Fe. He remembers her home as a simple *rancho* with many flowers, which she grew in oil cans, and chickens; the young Carlos used to visit her to buy eggs. Cast in one continuous movement, the work is varied by a slow central section. Although the work does not quote folk themes, it develops with the engaging Argentinian character heard in his art songs.

TWELVE

# China: Tradition Unbound

For thousands of years China's legends and their interpretation through music conveyed the high ideals that were accepted as the bedrock of its civilization. Traditional Chinese culture encompassed a world in which philosophers and poets engaged in a quest for harmony with the *Tao*, or the "Way" of the universe. Tales of valor and virtue conjured the deep spirituality that connected heaven and earth. During the Cultural Revolution (1966–1976), that exalted worldview was rejected by the Communist regime, which focused on massive industrial, agricultural, and labor growth. In recent years China's unique musical heritage has been successfully revived—but Western elements are increasingly insinuated into its performances. In numerous contemporary works China's ancient instruments—the plucked pipa and qin and the reed instruments suona and sheng—are scored together with Western strings and winds. This expanded tonal palette enables profound reinterpretations of traditional themes as well as original compositions with a wide emotional range. One senses in China's new music the soul of an ancient civilization interpreted with sensitivity to current trends.

Significant programs have introduced China's contemporary chamber music to a receptive audience. The biannual Ding Yi Chinese Chamber Music Festival, inaugurated in 2013 in Singapore, offers a series of master classes, workshops, and concerts showcasing the wide range of chamber arts created throughout China. Important premieres by composers such as Chen Yi are heard during the Festival. Since 2012 Ding Yi has also sponsored the triennial Composium, an international composition competition and symposium festival for the encouragement of new Chinese chamber music. Composers Chen Yi and Zhou Long advise the New York-based Music in China program, winner of the Adventurous Programming commendation from Chamber Music America and ASCAP. Since 1984, Music in China has promoted Chinese music both traditional and cross cultural through far-reaching educational programs and prestigious competitions.

## CHEN YI
### B. APRIL 4, 1953 IN GUANGZHOU, CHINA

Barely a teenager when the Cultural Revolution overtook China, Chen Yi (family name Chen) secretly continued her music studies with her piano dampened by a blanket and a mute on her violin. Assigned to years of hard labor in remote rice fields, she continued to play her violin; without regret she insists that the experience gave her a broad awareness of her motherland, its people, and its music. When the school system was restored in 1977, she enrolled in Beijing Central Conservatory and became the first Chinese woman to receive a Master of Arts degree in composition. While in residence, she learned to sing hundreds of Chinese folk songs collected from more than fifty provinces and twenty ethnic groups. She states that these songs are a mirror of daily life, "reflecting the people's thoughts, sentiments, local customs, and manners.... Sung in regional dialects, they use the idioms of everyday speech with their particular intonations, accents, and cadences." This vast trove of songs has provided a continuing source of material for her evolving body of work.

Brought to the United States by Chou Wen-Chung (see below), she earned a Doctor of Musical Arts degree with distinction from Columbia University and soon was awarded a Guggenheim Fellowship for Creative Arts. She is now recognized as one of the most important composers of her generation. Chen Yi writes: "I express my feelings through my music, which combines Chinese and Eastern musical materials and media. The inspirations and ideas behind the pieces are mostly Chinese. But the instrumentations of the pieces usually come from the musicians in America who commission them."

## "Shuo" for String Quartet (1994)

From the composer: "*Shuo* is written for string quartet or string orchestra, and it is approximately twelve minutes in duration. The word 'shuo' in Chinese means 'initiate.' It represents the first day of every month in the lunar calendar. In my piece *Shuo* I applied initial materials taken from Chinese folk music, in terms of tunes and mountain sing-song gestures, and I developed them for string instruments. The pentatonic lines (based on the five-note scale, a variable reduction of the seven-note Western scale and the framework most often heard in folk-based music) are woven vividly in different layers to paint a delicate Oriental landscape. Based on the first movement of my 1982 string quartet, the work is dedicated to Professor Wu Zu-Quiang, my composition teacher at the Central Conservatory of Music in Beijing, who guided me to find my own voice in new music creation."

A varied musical portrait, *Shuo* alternates ethereal passages that evoke the interior serenity of Chinese scroll paintings with extroverted areas that conjure animated scenes. The work begins with a low groundwork of sustained chords and tremolos, from which a high, melismatic violin cadenza gradually emerges. The vigorous section following suggests the American influence of Aaron Copland, also a tonal painter of broad landscapes. An accelerated tempo leads to a recapitulation of the violin cadenza, then the faster ensemble passagework. *Shuo* concludes with the flourish of an emphatic chord.

## *"Ning" for Pipa, Violin, and Cello (2001)*

Often called the Chinese lute because of its similar structure and plucked performance, the pipa has remained a popular instrument for the two thousand years of its existence. Legend tells of its invention for a homesick Han Dynasty princess who required a soothing instrument to play on horseback. Its versatility allows it to conjure a variety of narratives. A variety of pipa techniques—known as "flipping, sweeping, circular fingering, wringing, rolling, and halting"—can both create percussive sounds imitative of horns and drums and also conjure numerous shades of emotion implicit in the story.

*Ning* (Peaceful) integrates the Chinese pipa into a western trio anchored by the violin and cello. Described after its premiere as "melancholy and terribly visceral," *Ning* evokes China after World War ll. A traditional song, "Jasmine Flowers," is buried within the work's texture. Long tunes on the violin and cello join the restless, high-pitched melody of the pipa. A sorrowful yet hopeful mood pervades this lament for a homeland ravaged by war.

## *"From the Path of Beauty" for String Quartet (2009)*

The Bronze Taotie
The Rhymed Poems
The Secluded Melody
The Dancing Ink

Originally a seven-part cycle for chorus and string quartet, Chen Yi rescored *From the Path of Beauty* as a four-movement work for string quartet alone. Adept at using Western instruments to evoke the sounds of Chinese vocal music, Chen Yi supports the string quartet voices with traditional Chinese scales and ornaments. Each movement depicts an aspect of one of China's great dynasties. Strongly atmospheric, *From the Path of Beauty* has been described as "a miniature universe with a seemingly endless variety of sonorities, textures, and moods."

The quartet version is based on movements I, IV, VI, and II of the 2008 seven movement song cycle. From Chen Yi: "The music conveys the history of beauty in Chinese arts, from the ancient totems to the figurines, from poetry to calligraphy, from dance to music—from the thoughts to the spirit. It's expressively deep and colorfully rich, lyrical yet dramatic."

"The Bronze Taotie," inspired by the bronze taotie from the Shang dynasty, ca. 1600–1046 BCE, is also the first movement of *The Ancient Beauty*, an orchestral work combining Chinese and Western instruments. Chen Yi writes: "Taotie are the fierce animal-like patterns on bronze wine vessels used in primitive sacrificial ceremonies during the Shang dynasty. The ferocious beauty of the bronze art represents the irresistible force of historic inevitability." Beginning with a single note that grows to a tone cluster, the movement evokes ancient ritual.

"The Rhymed Poems" is an instrumental realization of two Mandarin poems by Li Qingzhao from the Song dynasty, 960–1279 CE. The movement conveys the contrasting atmospheres of two verses that conjure love, rain, wine, and regret through intricate dovetailing of voices and spectral effects such as finger tapping.

"The Secluded Melody," originally scored for qin (ancient seven-string Chinese zither), explores a slow melody over pentatonic harmonies. Pitch material drawn from the qin work "Secluded Orchid in the Mode of Jie Shi" (Six Dynasties period, 222–590 CE) is developed polyphonically.

"The Dancing Ink" depicts swirls of calligraphy through fleet imitative passages. Chen Yi writes: "The strings have woodwind-like running passages representing the exaggerated shapes and gestures in Chinese cursive from the Tang dynasty (618–907 CE)."

## "Sound of the Five" for Solo Cello and String Quartet (1998)

Lusheng Ensemble
Echoes of the Set Bells
Romance of Hsiao and Ch'in
Flower Drums in Dance

Chen Yi writes: "The work is written for Western instruments that will reproduce the sound and style of the Chinese traditional instruments. Lusheng is an ancient mouth organ with bamboo pipes. Villagers of various minorities in Southwestern China often play together while dancing in lusheng ensembles to celebrate spring holidays. The lusheng instruments range from bass (twenty-three feet long) to soprano (about twelve inches long). The lead player performs with the smallest lusheng and dances in complicated movements around the ensemble, which responds with colorful pentatonic harmonies in the background.

"The history of set bells can be traced back to the pre-Qin period (Shang dynasty, ca. 1600–1046 BCE). Made from bronze, every bell produces two tones (played in different positions), which can form different intervals. Grouped from three to sixty-four bells as a set, it is a melodic instrument played in court orchestras. Hsiao is a vertical bamboo flute which carries lyrical melodies through delicate lines. Ch'in is a two-thousand-year old Chinese seven-string zither, which has a rich repertoire in the history of Chinese music and literature. Flower drum has membranes on both ends, and it is also the name of a popular folk dance. Groups of people play the flower drums hung on their waists while dancing; the sound is strong and passionate.

"In the first movement, the solo cello plays the lead role and the quartet represents the ensemble. Imagining the bell sound from a distance, the five strings merge with mysterious harmonies in the second movement. In the third movement the cello transmits a lyrical sense to express the composer's love for humanity. The string quartet, sounding like an energized ch'in, symbolizes Nature. The finale returns to an energetic scene. The rhythmic design is inspired by traditional Chinese percussion ensemble music. Making the drum sound, the string quartet accompanies the singing cello, building up momentum and leading the music to a lively ending."

CHOU WEN-CHUNG
B. JULY 28, 1923 IN YANTAI, SHANDONG, CHINA,
D. OCTOBER 25, 2019 IN NEW YORK CITY

*String Quartet No. 1, "Clouds" (1996)*

Andante con moto
Leggierezza
Largo nostalgico
Presto con fuoco
Andante con moto

Honored as a "true twenty-first century global musician," composer, teacher, and cultural ambassador Chou Wen-chung (family name Chou) emigrated to the United States in 1946 and received his musical education at the New England Conservatory and Columbia University. During the seven active decades of his career, he achieved a synthesis of progressive Western idioms with his Asian heritage. An intellectual force in the Chinese-American community, he explored the theories of Yin-yang, the *I Ching*, and Daoism, as well as the practice of brush calligraphy, and qin (Chinese zither music), pivoting their relationship to both early and modern European music theories. His unique body of work, an expression of traditional Chinese aesthetic in contemporary language, has had a huge impact on the development of modern Asian music. He encouraged his many acclaimed students to study their own cultures closely. His ultimate goal was to achieve a confluence of many cultures firmly grounded in the traditional understanding of each.

Chou Wen-chung writes: "For decades I have explored ways to synthesize the concepts and practices of Eastern and Western music. Because of its exceptional homogeneity, the flow of the sound of a string quartet—like that of the music for the qin (zither)—is a close aural equivalent to the flow of ink in brush calligraphy. I believe calligraphy is the foundation of all artistic expression in China and that qin music is the essence of Chinese musical expression. In my quartet I attempt to fuse my musical thoughts with the legacy of the string quartet.

"The title 'Clouds' refers to the quality shared by cloud formations and calligraphy: the continual process of change. The phenomenon of mingling and melting clouds—in transformation, aggregation, and dispersion—is the aesthetic impetus for the musical events and progressions in the quartet.

"This ephemeral phenomenon is expressed through variable modes based on the permutations in the *I Ching* (*Yi jing*, or *Book of Changes*), the concepts of yin-yang duality, and various modal theories of the East and West. The quartet's overall structure, as well as its inner sections, is also related to the transformation and interaction of the changing modes in motion. Each of the movements progresses through its own modal succession and tonal continuity.

"The Asian flavor of the second movement results from the various pizzicato and *saltando* (jumping) sounds that recall Asian string instruments. These timbres result from the close juxtaposition of ascending and descending orders of each modal segment.

"The third movement is reminiscent of the poems of Li Qingzhao (1084–ca. 1155 CE). One of China's great musical poets, she was a master of alliteration and other auditory effects. The frequent reiteration of pitches in this movement is the result of shared common tones between the ascending and descending orders. Expressive slides, mutes, and different types of vibrato contribute to the mood that echoes Li's poetry. (Li is known by her pen name, Yi'an, which coincidentally is the name of my wife, to whom this quartet is dedicated.)"

ZHOU LONG
B. JULY 8, 1953 IN BEIJING

Winner of the 2011 Pulitzer Prize for his opera *Madame White Snake*, Zhou Long (family name Zhou) began his musical career as composer-in-residence for the National Broadcasting Orchestra of China. Brought to the United States to continue composition studies with Chou Wen-chung, Zhou Long soon became Director of the group Music in China, expanding its goals to encompass contemporary Chinese works that reflect contemporary Eastern and Western practice. A composer of numerous chamber works, many inspired by Chinese literature, Zhou Long writes: "Verses of poetry might give you the frame; movements of calligraphy may give you the rhythm; an ancient dark ink painting may give you space, distance, and layers; a variety of sound sources may give you color. Finally, craft ensures your own full expression."

*"Poems from Tang" for String Quartet (1995)*

Hut Among the Bamboo
Old Fisherman
Hearing the Monk Xun Play the Qin
Song of Eight Unruly Tipsy Poets

Zhou Long describes his *Poems from Tang*, a merging of Eastern and Western musical traditions: "The four movements are inspired by the works of four poets from China's Tang dynasty (618–907 CE). Tang dynasty arts were cultivated and intellectual, and its poets created distinguished new literary forms within an ancient civilization.

"In *Poems from Tang*, I have conceived the string quartet as an expanded ch'in, a traditional Chinese seven-stringed plucked zither long associated with sages and scholars. The sophisticated technique of ch'in playing, exemplified in the earliest ch'in manuscript from the Tang dynasty, involves various ways of plucking the strings and the use of ornaments to produce changes in sonority, intensity, dynamics, range, and timbre. My composition for string quartet intends to capture these special gestures and to reflect the undercurrent of tranquility and meditation heard in ancient Chinese melodies.

"The first movement is based on the poem 'Hut among the Bamboo' by Wang Wei (701–761): Sitting among bamboos alone / I play my lute and croon carefree. / In the deep woods where I am unknown, / Only the bright moon peeps at me.

"The poet plays with abandon on his ch'in but feels dissatisfied, sensing that his music is somehow incomplete. Looking toward the sky, he is inspired to howl, and this spontaneous expression delights him. Against patterns of silence punctuated by quiet harmonic clusters we hear his improvisatory music-making. The movement begins quietly, with muted instruments. The low, sustained tones of the cello and high harmonics of the other strings create an eerie feeling of space and emptiness, suggesting the depths and isolation of the secluded woods. The harmonic motive, accompanied by high-pitched tremolo or pizzicato passages and sharply accented pinging sounds, depicts the quavering leaves of the bamboo and other forest sounds. The opening tempo is slow, but as the poet begins his lusty howling, represented by descending glissando clusters, the tempo accelerates.

"The second movement is based on the poem 'Old Fishermen' by Liu Zongyuan (773–819), a government official and outstanding thinker and writer during the middle of the Tang dynasty. He was removed from his post for advocating reform, but he never became despondent. He traveled the mountains and valleys of Southwestern China, creating many excellent works. In 'Old

Fishermen' he wrote: The old fisherman moors at night by western cliffs / At dawn draws water from the clear Xiang / Lights fire with southern bamboo. / Mists melt in the morning sun / And the moon is gone. / Only the song reverberates in the green of the hills and waters. / Look back, the horizon seems to fall into the stream / And the clouds float aimlessly over the cliffs.

"I wrote the third movement as I began a residency at the Rockefeller Foundation's Bellagio Center on Lake Como, where I heard bells of villages and churches echoing off the mountains and water from morning until evening. These haunting sounds reminded me of a verse by Li Bai (701–762): I seem to hear the moaning of pine trees / as if from a thousand valleys. / My wayfaring heart is cleansed by the flowing stream; / its soft cadence, lingering still, / Fuses into distant chiming of a frost-cold bell.

"The movement opens with harmonics that simulate the sound of bells. Pizzicati create the effect of echoes off the mountains and lake. Tremolos suggest the moaning of the wind in the pines, and varying pitches and dynamics conjure oscillating sound waves coming close then receding. Rondo in form, the movement ends with sounds that resolve in the distance.

"The fourth poem is based on a verse by Du Fu (712–770) that affectionately describes the drunken behavior of eight fellow poets: Unrestrained, undisciplined, humorous, and eloquent; / Riding on the horse, faltering steps in enjoyment; / Drawing on the paper, spattering ink as dancing dragon; / Howling toward the sky, citing poems, feeling indignant.

"The movement is scherzo in form (ABA). The movement begins ad libitum, but with drink the tempo gradually increases to a fast and wild climax, at which point the poets are completely uninhibited and unruly. The movement ends with eight identical fortissimo chords, one for each poet, separated by eight measures of rest. We hear the faltering sounds of the drunken poets, who try ever harder to recite until eventually, despite themselves, they collapse into silence."

## *"Spirit of Chimes" for Piano Trio (1999)*

From the composer: "Written for the Peabody Trio's participation in A Musical Celebration of the Millennium, sponsored by Chamber Music America, this piano trio was inspired by the sounds of the earliest surviving instruments from ancient China— bells, chime stones, and Jiahu bone flutes (ca. 7000 BCE)—which are also the world's oldest extant playing instruments. Although no examples of early Chinese music before the Tang dynasty have survived to modern times, my fascination with the acoustic characteristics of these ancient instruments fired my imagination. In this work, I have translated the real sounds of these instruments and combined them with my own inspiration with the hope that my music can give them new life."

BRIGHT SHENG
B. DECEMBER 6, 1955 IN SHANGHAI

During the Cultural Revolution, Bright Sheng (family name Sheng) spent seven years in Qinghai Province, once part of Tibet. He closely observed its folk traditions, and he preserved its themes by scoring them for the available piano and percussion. His trove of Qinghai folk music has remained a steady inspiration for his compositions. After graduating from the Shanghai Conservatory with training in Chinese classical music, Bright Sheng continued his education at Queens College and Columbia University, where he studied with Chou Wen-chung as well as Leonard Bernstein. He has participated in the Silk Road Project, which encompasses music of different cultures, and has made research trips along the route to collect historical material and themes.

Bright Sheng is a sensitive melodist, and this gift can be well appreciated in *Seven Tunes Heard in China* (1995), scored for solo cello, and his acclaimed opera, *Dream of the Red Chamber* (2016), based on a popular eighteenth-century Chinese novel. Bright Sheng admires Bartók, and in his four string quartets that influence is apparent. Like Bartók, he creates a fusion of folk and art music through subtle interweaving of their diverse elements. Inspired by his country's characteristically vibrant folk tunes and rhythms, their essences and energies pervade his work.

### String Quartet No. 4, "Silent Temple" (2000)

I.

II.

III.

IV.

From the composer: "In the early 1970s I visited an abandoned Buddhist temple in northwest China. As all religious activities were completely forbidden at the time of the Cultural Revolution, the temple, renowned among the international Buddhist community, was unattended and on the brink of ruin. The most striking and powerful memory I had from this visit was that, despite the temple's appalling condition, it remained a grand and magnificent structure. The fact that it was located in snowy mountain ranges added to its dignity and glory. Standing in the middle of the courtyard, I could almost hear the praying and chanting of the monks, as well as the violence committed against the temple and the monks by the Red Guards.

"To this day the memories of this visit remain vivid. And I use them almost randomly as the basic images of the composition. As a result, the quartet develops through four short and seemingly unrelated movements, which should be performed without pause."

ZHAO LIN
B. 1973 IN XI'AN, CHINA

## *"Red Lantern" for Pipa and String Quartet (2015)*

Prelude: Moonlight
Wandering
Love
Death
Epilogue

Zhao Lin (family name Zhao) was born in the northwest prov-ince of Shaanxi, recognized as one of China's cradles of civilization. Xi'an, its capital of thirteen feudal dynasties for over 1000 years, holds the archeological site of the first Qin Emperor's Mausoleum, which houses the thousands of clay soldiers known as the Terra-cotta Army. In the first century BCE Xi'an became the starting point for the Northern Silk Road, an essential trade route from China to Europe. Zhao Lin's association with the contemporary Silkroad Ensemble, the world music group begun by Yo-Yo Ma, is especially appropriate.

After composition studies at the Central Conservatory in Beijing, Zhao Lin composed for the National Traditional Orchestra of China, which deploys ancient Chinese instruments in Western settings. In 2004 he began to collaborate with Yo-Yo Ma on the Silk Road project. His duo concerto, written for cellist Yo-Yo Ma and sheng virtuoso Wu Tong, was premiered in Shanghai in 2013. Influenced by his composer father Zhao Jiping, Zhao Lin has also written numerous award-winning film scores for Chinese cinema. In 2001 father and son established the studio ZHAOs, where they collaborate on Chinese film projects. Zhao Lin currently resides in Beijing.

Zhao Lin writes: "This piece is a tribute to my father, the com-poser Zhao Jiping, and to the great tradition of music from China.

*Red Lantern* is derived from my father's original music, scored for the great Zhang Yimou film *Raise the Red Lantern* (1991). Inspired by Chinese traditional Beijing Opera, this work explores its unique musical style and language with the many colors of our traditional music. The quintet is a suite of stories that take place in a traditional Chinese courtyard through the centuries. It tells an emotional story of Chinese family relationships in older times and the impact of the family's isolation from society."

TAN DUN
B. AUGUST 18, 1957 IN CHANGSHA, HUNAN PROVINCE

*Concerto for String Quartet and Pipa (1999)*

Andante molto
Allegro
Adagio
Allegro vivace

Tan Dun (family name Tan) has made an indelible mark on the world's music scene with a creative repertoire that spans the boundaries of classical music, multimedia performance, and Eastern and Western traditions. He has won numerous honors, including the Grammy Award, the Academy Award for Best Original Score (*Crouching Tiger, Hidden Dragon*), and Italy's Golden Lion for Lifetime Achievement. Also a visual artist, Tan Dun uses his creativity to raise awareness of environmental issues and to protect diversity; his string quartet *Water Heavens*, performed biannually in Shanghai, promotes water conservation. *Prayer and Blessing*, his response to COVID, was the featured premiere on UNESCO World Environment Day, and was broadcast to twenty-nine countries on June 5, 2020.

Tan Dun's vibrant Concerto for String Quartet and Pipa is a reduction of his 1994 Concerto for String Orchestra and Pipa, which originated with his theater piece *Ghost Opera*—a poetic five movement "music ritual" for string quartet and pipa, with water, metal, stone, and paper placed to reflect different time frames and spiritual realms. He describes this work as a "reflection on human spirituality, too often buried in the bombardment of urban culture and the rapid advances of technology." In composing *Ghost Opera*, Tan was inspired by childhood memories of the shamanistic "ghost operas" of Chinese peasant culture. In this ancient tradition, humans and spirits of the future, the past, and nature communicate with each other. Tan's *Ghost Opera* embraces this tradition, calling on the spirits of Bach (in the form of a quotation from the C sharp minor Prelude from Book II of the Well-Tempered Clavier); Shakespeare (a brief excerpt from *The Tempest*); ancient folk traditions; and nature (represented by the Chinese folk song "Little Cabbage"). Tan states that the Bach excerpt acts "like a seed from which grows a different counterpoint of different ages, different sound worlds, and different cultures." In the final movement the gradual transformation of the counterpoint brings the spirits of Bach and Shakespeare, the civilized world, and the rational mind, "this insubstantial pageant," into the eternal earth. The movements are played without pause.

## LEI LIANG
### B. NOVEMBER 28, 1972 IN TIANJIN, CHINA

Born into a musical family, Lei Liang (family name Liang) grew up in Beijing and began composing at age six. Also a pianist, his early works are among the required repertoire for national piano competitions in China and are widely used for piano pedagogy. Lei Liang came to the U.S. in 1990 for composition studies at the New England Conservatory and Harvard; his professors included

Harrison Birtwistle, Robert Cogan, Chaya Czernowin, and Mario Davidovsky. The recipient of many awards, Lei Liang has been heralded as "one of the most exciting voices in New Music" (*The Wire*). His large number of compositions has been described as "hauntingly beautiful and sonically colorful" (*The New York Times*). Lei Liang serves as Artistic Director of the Chou Wen-chung Music Research Center at the Xinghai Conservatory of Music in Guangzhou, China.

## *Trio for Piano, Cello, and Percussion (2002)*

Lei Liang writes: "The idea of this piece came to me while taking a walk around Fresh Pond in Cambridge, MA, during a snowstorm. I can never forget the scintillating sound of thousands of snowflakes quietly and violently hitting the dry leaves and pine needles. This moment inspired me to write the opening of the work.

"I was interested in discovering how an abstract idea can manifest itself in different musical appearances, be they rhythmical, harmonic, melodic, or textual. I wished to treat the idea (in this case, a numerical permutation using six numbers) as a living organism and see how far it could 'travel' during the course of the composition."

## *"Gobi Gloria" for String Quartet (2006)*

The composer comments: "*Gobi Gloria* belongs to series of compositions that grew out of my admiration for Mongolian music. A principal melody is played against its own inversion, retrograde, and retrograde-inversion in an otherwise mostly heterophonic texture. The piece alludes to various genres of Mongolian music that include the long-chant, as well as the music and dance and shaman rituals. It concludes with a rendering of a folk song that I heard during my visit to Nei Monggol region in 1996."

## *"Five Seasons" for Pipa and String Quartet (2010)*

Dew-Drop
Water-Play
Cicada Chorus
Leaves-Fall
Drumming

The composer comments: "The ancient Chinese devised a system of five phases (*wuxing*, also known as five elements) to describe generative and destructive interactions in nature. Each element is correlated to a season: the element wood is correlated to spring, fire to summer, metal to autumn, water to winter. In addition, the fifth element, earth, is correlated to *chanxia*, or long summer, which is the transitional phase between the summer and autumn.

"In this composition five chords are chosen from the ancient sheng (mouth organ) repertoire, now preserved in the *gagaku* music of Japan. These harmonies are foreshadowed in the second section, then appear in continuous succession—from extremely slow to extremely fast—serving as the harmonic basis of the last three sections.

"The piece starts with 'dew-drop,' the image of ice melting in early spring, evoked by pizzicati. The water-drops converge into streams and rivers, symbolized by rapid pulsations in the 'water-play' section. The middle section of the piece recalls the 'cicada chorus' that I heard in the long and hot summer days in Beijing where I grew up. This section is followed by the fall season, where downward bending notes of the strings capture the image of 'leaves falling' in slow motion. The Chinese pronunciation of winter, *dong*, is homonymous to a drumming sound, therefore the piece concludes with the quintet imitating percussions. The end of the piece may link back to the beginning of the piece, reflecting the cyclical nature of seasons.

"*Five Seasons* was completed during the rainy season in Osaka, Japan."

## "Listening for Blossoms" for Flute, Harp, Violin, Viola, Double Bass, and Piano (2011)

From the composer: "The sound of blossoms is a theme in both Chinese and Japanese traditional poetry, and it arose as part of the Taoist and Buddhist practice of meditation. If one contemplates in complete stillness, one can hear the blossoms. This piece was also inspired by the idea of layering of surfaces as well as an ambiguous and subtle world of time found in these poetic texts.

"*Listening for Blossoms* was begun while I was in residence in New York as a recipient of the Aaron Copland Award and completed at the American Academy in Rome. It was premiered in Los Angeles by the Southwest Chamber Music Ensemble in January, 2013."

## "Verge Quartet" for String Quartet (2013)

Lei Liang writes: "Originally scored for eighteen solo strings, *Verge* was composed on the verge of an exciting moment in my life: the birth of our son Albert Shin Liang. Albert's musical name—A, B (B flat), E, D (re)—asserts itself in different figurations and disguises as basic harmonic and melodic material. His heartbeat also makes an appearance in the form of changing tempi and pulsations. In a sense, I composed the piece to make a musical amulet for Albert.

"On a technical level, I was fascinated by the dialectical relationship between the convergence and divergence of musical voices found in the traditional heterophonic music of Mongolia. There, the functionality of a principal line and its accompaniment can interchange, and often not synchronously."

# THIRTEEN

# Australia:
# Insights From the Natural World

Once a British colony, Australia began to form an artistic identity after its six self-governing states formed a Federation in 1901. Yet an attachment to the traditions of Britain and the Empire persisted for several decades; folk and popular music continued to be influenced by Anglo-Celtic traditions, and its classical music echoed British taste. After World War II Australia became a more open society owing to its determined immigration policy of "populate or perish"—perceiving the security and developmental advantages of a larger population, the country welcomed several hundred thousand persons from all over war-ravaged Europe. Enhanced diversity ultimately sparked creativity in Australia's arts, and a new spirit of experimentation emerged. Composers drew inspiration from their incomparable natural landscape and their multi-cultural environment. Both Peter Sculthorpe, versed in ancient traditions that communicate the Australian Aboriginal Peoples' beliefs of Dream Time, and Ross Edwards, who derived scale patterns from Australia's bird calls, brought ritual elements into their works (see below). Other sonorities were explored beginning in the 1970s as Australia's art music evolved toward fusions of Southeast Asian elements, American jazz and blues, and the European avant-garde. These contemporary mergings constitute a unique world contribution.

Chamber music enjoys lively support in Australia. Musica Viva Australia, the country's leading chamber music organization and the largest entrepreneur of its kind in the world, has premiered numerous new works at its annual festival in Sydney. This national touring and presenting group, founded in 1945, sponsors a network of local branches throughout Australia and has steadily promoted awareness of its resources. Chamber Music Australia, founded in 1991, promotes new chamber works through its annual competitions. Other groups such as the Australian String Quartet and Synergy Percussion (see below) draw large and enthusiastic audiences. The Australian Music Centre, whose motto is "Breaking Sound Barriers," provides in-depth coverage of Australian art music through its accessible recordings, scores, interviews, and articles.

PETER SCULTHORPE
B. APRIL 29, 1929 IN LAUNCESTON, TASMANIA,
D. AUGUST 8, 2014 IN SYDNEY

## "Djilile" for Percussion Quartet (1986)

In the late 1950s anthropologists A.P. Elkin and Trevor Jones collected Aboriginal melodies from northern Australia. Sculthorpe subsequently adapted the ethnic song "Djilile," translated as "whistling duck on a billabong," for modern performance; he has made transcriptions for several instrument combinations as well as duo piano and cello. Sculthorpe writes: "*Djilile* illustrates the principle of dualism, present in almost all my music since the mid-fifties. Many of my works are also concerned with the environment and social issues. In *Djilile* my intention is to suggest that it is possible for the white Australian and the Aborigine to live together in a harmonious manner." The opening melody is a transcription of the original chant.

*String Quartet No. 11, "Jabiru Dreaming,"*
*with optional Didgeridoo (1990)*

Deciso
Liberamente—Estatico

Sculthorpe began to write string quartets during his early student days in Melbourne. His eighteen quartets combine Australian, European, and Asian influences to create images described by critics as "at once familiar yet exotic." A profound spiritual element pervades his work, which is largely structured through mythic pattern.

Quartet No. 11, *Jabiru Dreaming* has been critically recognized as "the first flowering of Sculthorpe's mature style." Influenced by the landscapes and peoples of far northern Australia, including the Torres Strait islanders, the quartet is part of a series that continued with its companions, *Island Dreaming* and *Quamby* (Quartets Nos. 13 and 14). For Sculthorpe, the word "dreaming" refers to the creation myths of the Aboriginal people, who believe that the world emerged over longs arcs of dreamtime. *Jabiru Dreaming* abounds with pentatonic dance tunes and the sounds of birds and insects.

Sculthorpe describes his quartet: "*Jabiru Dreaming* was written as a gift to France upon its bicentenary. In one movement, it takes its point of departure from three Aboriginal melodies collected by members of a French exploratory expedition in 1802. These melodies are the first examples of indigenous Australian music known to have appeared in Western notation.

"Jabiru Dreaming is a rock formation near the East Alligator River in Kakadu National Park. While the rock is regarded as sacred, there is nothing forbidding about it: on the contrary, in some way it seems to beckon and welcome.

"The living, indigenous music of the north of Australia has been part of my language since the late 1980s, and its incorporation is particularly evident in this quartet. The first movement contains rhythmic patterns found in the indigenous music of the Kakadu area. Some of these patterns also suggest the gait of the jabiru, a species of stork. The second movement is dominated by a chant, first stated by the cello in its original form. This movement is also a joyful one; it stems from my belief that Australia is one of the few places on earth where one might write straightforward, happy music."

*String Quartet No. 12, "From Ubirr,"*
*with optional Didgeridoo (1994)*

Sculthorpe's music reflects his Australian identity: "It is a natural choice to write music about the country and our history. It is who I am, what I am about." Many of his works suggest the vastness and the loneliness of the Australian landscape, as well as the sounds of its wildlife. Strongly attracted to the heritage of the indigenous Australians and their experience of the land, Sculthorpe also draws inspiration from Aboriginal peoples' history, language, and melody. He notes: "It's always seemed foolish not to take heed of a music that has been shaped by this land over many thousands of years."

Sculthorpe comments about his String Quartet No. 12: "Ubirr is a large rocky outcrop in Kakadu National Park, in northern Australia. It houses some of the best and most varied Aboriginal rock painting in the country. Many of the paintings have been proven to be the earliest known graphic expressions of the human race. They clearly demonstrate a caring relationship with the environment, and the Aboriginal belief that the land owns the people, not the people the land.

"The music of *From Ubirr* is derived from the orchestral work *Earth Cry* (1986). Like its progenitor, it asks us to attune ourselves to the planet, to listen to the cry of the earth as the Aborigines have done for many thousands of years.

"The work is a straightforward and melodious one with a total duration of ten minutes. Its four parts are made up of quick, ritualistic music framed by slower music of a supplicatory nature, and an extended coda. The slow music is accompanied by a didgeridoo pitched to E and the quick music by a second didgeridoo pitched to C. The instrument represents the sound of nature, of the earth itself."

ROSS EDWARDS
B. DECEMBER 23, 1943 IN SYDNEY

One of Australia's best known and most performed composers in all genres, Ross Edwards creates a unique sound world that, in his words, "seeks to reconnect music with elemental forces and to restore such qualities as ritual, spontaneity, and the impulse to dance." Profoundly connected to his ecological environment, Edwards has followed his own path as a composer by drawing musical shapes and patterns from Australia's natural world, including birdsong and the mysterious humming of summer insects. Aware of music's ability to promote enhanced perception, he states that "it is his responsibility as a composer to make full use of the planet's potent forces to communicate vividly and widely at the highest artistic level." He maintains a strong belief in the healing power of music, and to this end he has created a body of contemplative works inspired by the Australian landscape. Although his music is thematically universal in its preoccupations with humanity's elemental forces, it connects to his roots in Australia and celebrates its cultural diversity. As a composer living and working on the Pacific Rim, he is conscious of the exciting potential of this vast region and Australia's important position in it.

## "Tyalgum Mantras" for String Quartet, Percussion, and Didgeridoo (1999)

Written for the Australian ensemble Con Spirit Oz, *Tyalgum Mantras* belongs to the series of meditative pieces Ross Edwards began to compose in the 1970s. Works in this series—other examples of which are *Pond Light Mantras* (1991) for two pianos and *Yarrageh* (1989) for percussion and orchestra—have been described as "contemplations in sound." Each is designed as a mantra to focus the listener's attention inwards and to create a trance-like stillness.

*Tyalgum Mantras* was originally commissioned for the 1999 Tyalgum Festival in New South Wales. Edwards has scored the work for several combinations: shakuhachi (an end-blown Japanese flute), didgeridoo (a droning Aboriginal wind instrument), and percussion; for recorder, string orchestra, and percussion; and for string quartet, didgeridoo, and percussion. Edwards writes: "I think one of music's great blessings to humanity is its capacity to still the unquiet mind, to suspend the linear passage of time, and to promote the intuitive 'night' mode of consciousness which invites present-centered contemplation. When I was commissioned by the Tyalgum Festival in Eastern Australia to create a work for shakuhachi, didgeridoo, and percussion, I took the opportunity to explore the contemplative mode through techniques involving the repetition of sounds and shapes that might induce a sense of timelessness. At that time, I had no inkling that this would become one of my most widely performed works and would initiate a series of mantra pieces. The flexible scoring of *Tyalgum Mantras* has allowed many performance possibilities. It is often performed in the open air, in the desert; once, memorably, outside a Welsh castle by the sea at dawn; and in semi-darkened concert halls and candle-lit churches. Other possibilities await exploration."

## *"Tucson Mantras" for String Quartet, Percussion, and Didgeridoo (2008)*

Edwards writes: "In 2006, Peter Rejto took part in a large-scale performance of *Tyalgum Mantras* at the Four Winds Festival on the east coast of Australia, which also involved William Barton and Synergy Percussion. In inviting me to compose another mantra piece to close the 2008 Tucson (Arizona) Winter Chamber Music Festival, Peter specified the need for a celebratory conclusion. Accordingly, the long, ruminative, often intense string passages that follow the opening mantras have the effect of accumulating energy which joyfully explodes in the work's expansive conclusion.

"*Tucson Mantras* abounds with nature symbolism—shapes and patterns abstracted from birdsong and the mysterious sound world of insects and frogs. Drones remember the earth and there is music reference, by way of personal symbols, to an Earth Mother archetype that pervades all my work."

## *"Bright Birds and Sorrows" for Soprano Saxophone and String Quartet (2015, revised 2019)*

Songbird I
Chorale
Lullaby
Lament for the Sacred Earth
Sanctus
Laughing Dance (Songbird II)

*Bright Birds and Sorrows*, commissioned for and premiered at the 2017 Musica Viva Australia Festival, is a collection of short pieces that provides insight into the composer's personal vision as well as his outlook on the external world. Edwards's musical language has steadily evolved since his early decision to reject European modernism. Following his own intuition, Edwards has explored and given instrumental voice to sounds of the natural world. To convey both his personal mythology and his strong ecological focus, Edwards overlays his works with cross-cultural references to various chants and deities with environmental associations.

From the composer's notes:

Songbird I. "I've always been captivated by birdsong. Rather than try to replicate it in music, I usually allow my subconscious to work on it until it emerges as a sort of mythical transformation of what I've heard. Sometimes vestiges of the original remain, and when I'm working in the mountains I occasionally hear a fragment of my own music echoed from a tree! We have some expert mimics among Australian birds. There are two bird pieces in this suite. I composed the first as a ritualized response to a striking melodic outpouring of unidentified birdsong which happened to conform to the blues scale."

Chorale. "Over the sound of a distant chorale, filaments of melody begin to take shape, intertwine, and slowly spiral upwards, as if seeking an answer to some profound question that can't quite be defined."

Lullaby. "One of the most ancient forms of music is the lullaby, whose essential purpose is to bring sleep upon a child. Throughout all ages mothers have soothed and coaxed with gently rocking melodies and appropriate words. The melodies are usually simple, although in some cultures, especially some Asian ones, they can be elaborate and quite difficult to sing. A lullaby can also act as a vehicle for the mother to voice her concerns, so that a simple sentiment can be overlaid with strong emotion. My lullaby, while not without moments of intricacy and angst, always returns the mother's undivided attention to her child."

Lament for the Sacred Earth. "This somber piece is an expression of grief over the tragic descent of humanity's relationship with the earth from veneration to exploitation, placing the planet in grave danger."

Sanctus. "The mysterious, sacred earth is adored in this hymn to harmoniousness, wholeness, and the interrelationship of all things. The Sanctus of the Catholic Mass, alluded to in various ways, is interpreted here in an environmental context. The Latin word Sanctus, which translates as 'holy,' has an alternate meaning traced by 19th-century Jewish and English scholars as 'whole'—particularly relevant as we witness the disintegration of the environment. The Sanctus bell, traditionally used to underline the solemnity of the text, has been retained."

Laughing Dance (Songbird II). "There's a natural connection between laughter and spontaneous musical impulses, more so in the participatory ceremonies of indigenous peoples than in western art music. Like music, laughter is a universal language, and today there's even a movement called Laughing Yoga, emanating from India and fast spreading around the world. I originally conceived this exuberant miniature for bass clarinet and percussion. It caught on rather well, and I made this alternate version in the hope of widening the audience."

*"Four Inscapes": Quintet for Flute, Pipa, Percussion, Violin, and Cello (2018)*

Inscape with Frog and Bird
Dance of the Merciful Mothers
Floating Moon
Ritual Earth Dance

*Four Inscapes* was commissioned for the Tucson Winter Chamber Music Festival, where it was premiered in 2020. Edwards writes: "*Four Inscapes* is a poeticized fusion of my imaginings and observations of events and characteristic patterns ('inscapes') of human nature.

I. "Inscape with Frog and Bird is a personalized response to the natural world, in which healing sounds of flowing water are punctuated by imagined birdsong and the lone voice of a frog. Into this idyllic scene drifts a cello melody tinged with sadness, later to be joined by violin and flute.

II. "Dance of the Merciful Mothers. My music, essentially drawn from the ecological sound world of Australia's coastal regions, is overlaid with far-reaching cultural associations. This lively movement brings together universal symbols of nurturing and healing in the form of chant fragments relating to the European concept of Mother Mary and her East Asian counterparts.

III. "Floating Moon, for solo pipa, is a nocturne that pays homage to Guan-Yin, the graceful Chinese Goddess of Compassion, symbolized by the Tang Dynasty poet Po Chü-I as the moon's reflection floating in pure, clear water. Composed in simple three-part song form, it is based on a scale associated with the Japanese koto, a stringed instrument with similarities to the pipa as well as the European lute, Arabic oud, and many others from a diversity of cultures. The human family is well connected through music!

IV. "Ritual Earth Dance. The work concludes with an exuberant, celebratory *maninya*—a form of Australian dance-chant of my own invention—with spirited dialogue between pipa and darbuka, an Arabic goblet drum."

MICHAEL ASKILL
B. 1952 IN DURBAN, SOUTH AFRICA

Considered to be Australia's finest percussionist, Michael Askill is also a composer whose large body of music draws equally from both ethnic traditions and Western jazz, rock, and classical idioms. Askill is a founding member of Synergy Percussion, acclaimed as Australia's most vibrant and energetic contemporary group. Flexibly configured to allow expansion for specific projects, Synergy has a long history of commissioning works from Australian composers and performing them in worldwide venues.

## *"Lemurian Dances" for Percussion Quartet (1990)*

Askill writes: "The work was composed following a trip to the Philippines and is dedicated to my former teacher, Richard Smith. The legend of Lemuria proposes the idea of an Atlantis-like sunken continent in the Pacific that was the motherland of all mankind. The wide and unexplained distribution of lemurs (a small primate) in the region gave further fuel to the idea of a land mass that existed in the Indian Ocean between Madagascar and India millions of years ago."

Hypnotically steady rhythmic patterns underpin the syncopated melodic lines of the first three dances, all connected with subtle transition passages. The final two dances unfold with emphatic statements on the marimba and vibraphone with strong punctuations from the other members. The dazzling variety of instrumental colors creates a kaleidoscopic effect.

## *"No Rest From the Dance" from "Salome," for Percussion Sextet (2001)*

A strong narrative line is evident in Askill's ballet score *Salome* (1997), a rich fusion of motifs and rhythms inspired by the Middle East, Africa, and Asia. Askill describes the percussion ensemble piece he created from *Salome*: "*No Rest from the Dance* is based on rhythmic material from my score for Graeme Murphy's ballet. The rhythms in the opening sections are derived from the scenes of Salome being pursued relentlessly by the lustful King Herod while the chorus of dancers (representing King Herod's court) chant: 'Salome! Salome! Dance! Dance!' The steadier 'groove' section of the piece is based on an earlier part of the ballet featuring the young women of Herod's court."

CARL VINE
B. OCTOBER 8, 1954 IN PERTH, AUSTRALIA

*Fantasia for Piano Quintet (2013)*

Carl Vine first earned recognition as a dance composer with twenty-five scores to his credit. His vast catalogue now includes numerous symphonies, concertos, music for various media, and many chamber works. The longtime Artistic Director of Musica Viva Australia, Vine was appointed as Officer of the Order of Australia (AO) in 2014 "for distinguished service to the performing arts as a composer, academic, and artistic director, and to the support and mentoring of emerging performers."

The fantasia has been an important form since the late sixteenth century, at which time it was essentially a rhapsodic one-movement work exploring a single subject. Throughout the several hundred years of its existence, the fantasia has continued to suggest quasi-improvisational thematic development with spontaneous flights of imagination and abrupt changes of mood within a flexible structure.

Vine writes about his quintet, which was premiered at the 2013 Tucson Winter Chamber Music Festival: "I call this single-movement piano quintet Fantasia because it doesn't follow a strict formal structure and contains little structural repetition or recapitulation. The central section is generally slower than the rest and is followed by a presto finale, but otherwise related motifs tend to flow one from the other organically through the course of the work. It is 'pure' music that uses no external imagery, allusion, narrative, or poetry."

BRETT DEAN
B. OCTOBER 23, 1961 IN BRISBANE, AUSTRALIA

After graduating with highest honors from the Queensland Conservatorium, Brett Dean spent fourteen years as violist with the Berlin Philharmonic. He returned to Australia in 1999 to devote himself to composition. During his years in Germany, he absorbed the modernist techniques of significant central European composers, especially the Hungarians Béla Bartók, a pioneer of evocative instrumental effects, and György Ligeti, who constructed musical material from shifting densities and colors. Dean creates uniquely atmospheric works that develop with ethereal sonorities: rustling sounds achieved by playing on the instrument's wood with the bow; high harmonics combined with glissandi and forceful pizzicati; hints of the haunting didgeridoo in low cello lines. His poetic body of work draws much inspiration from literature and his natural environment. Dean's multi-textured compositions are frequently motivated by social issues.

## *"Epitaphs" for String Quintet (2010)*

Only I will know (... in memory of Dorothy Porter):
Gently flowing, with intimate intensity

Walk a little way with me (... in memory of Lyndal Holt):
Moderato scorrevole

Der Philosoph (... in memory of Jan Diesselhorst):
Slow and spacious, misterioso

György meets the "Girl Photographer"
(... in memory of Betty Freeman, homage à György Ligeti):
Fresh, energetic

Between the spaces in the sky (... in memory of Richard Hickox):
Hushed and fragile

Dean comments on *Epitaphs*, a set of musical obituaries for friends and colleagues who died in 2008–2009: "*Epitaphs* is a celebration of personal qualities, characteristics, and achievements ... also an expression of loss and contemplations of energetic lives fulfilled as well as lives cut short."

Each movement signals the lively characteristics of these departed friends. The first, for Dorothy Porter (Australian poet, 1954–2008), creates a magical, poetic atmosphere through glissandi and gently rustling repetitive figures. The second ("moderate and fluent"), for the freely verbal Lyndal Holt (Australian solicitor, academic, and author, 1962–2008), is punctuated by bold pizzicati to emphasize lines of discourse. The third movement, a tribute to his cellist colleague in the Berlin Philharmonic, Jan Diesselhorst (1954–2009), centers on a passionate cello soliloquy. The "fresh" fourth epitaph, for the spirited Betty Freeman (American arts patron, philanthropist, and photographer, 1921–2009), is also a homage to Hungarian composer György Ligeti (1923–2006). It features both a winsome violin melody and suggestions of Ligeti's darker modernism, as influenced by Bartók. The fifth epitaph quotes themes from the opera that Dean had hoped to produce with his friend Richard Hickox (British conductor and music director, former Artistic Director of Opera Australia, 1948–2008); it closes with a wistful passage that suggests calm acceptance.

DONALD HOLLIER
B. MAY 7, 1934 IN SYDNEY

Hollier studied composition at the New South Wales Conservatorium of Music and the Royal Academy of Music in London. After returning to Australia, he was appointed Music Director at Newington College and subsequently Head of Academic Studies at the Canberra School of Music. Devoted to full time composition since 1987, he has written prolifically in numerous genres, especially opera and oratorio.

## *Piano Trio No. 2, "Five Sea Songs" (2021)*

Song 1: Aubade
Song 2: Break, Break, Break, On Thy Cold Grey Stones, O Sea
Song 3: Dead Seamen
Song 4: Many Waters Cannot Quench Love
Song 5: Sea Fever

*Five Sea Songs* was commissioned by Musica Viva Australia. Before writing, Hollier consulted with Bernadette Harvey, the trio's pianist, who "wished for some water music." Initially planning a set of variations on Benjamin Britten's serene opening theme for *Peter Grimes*, Hollier decided instead "to use the theme to bounce onto other poems about the sea. The words of these poems were the impetus for each song."

Bernadette Harvey comments: "The theme for 'Aubade' (a welcome to dawn) is taken from Act I, scene I of Britten's opera *Peter Grimes*. Marked Lento, tranquillo, the movement shivers to life in the same manner as Britten's first sea interlude, with the theme in high pianissimo violin notes and colorful oceanic effects in the piano. Taken up by the cello, the theme arches gradually to forte and closes softly, conjuring the effect of the sea yawning and stretching into life at daybreak. The movement connects seamlessly into Song 2, a depiction of Nature's damaging violence and the cold indifference of the sea. Tennyson's poem 'Break, Break, Break, On Thy Cold Grey Stones,' an elegy to the loss of a close friend, inspired its turbulent mood. Cast in ternary form (ABA), the movement begins with a quiet arpeggiated piano figure that ascends in pitch and accelerates to the main Allegro tempo, propelled by loud and furiously undulating intervals. The contrasting middle section is a free but ferocious recitative.

"Songs 3 and 4 are seamed together. 'Dead Seamen' begins with the players speaking the words 'Dead seamen' from the poem 'Beach Burial' by Kenneth Slessor (1944), an Australian war correspondent. Dramatic and rhythmically incisive piano chords accompany these words to create a terrifying refrain. Between its four statements we hear the rocking of a boat in the strings' 6/8 rhythmic patterns and a wailing melodic line that dips and soars. The sea in this song takes the role of a vessel delivering the anonymous dead to the sandy shores of an Arab coastline during World War II.

"Song 4 is based on chapter 8, verse 7 of 'Song of Songs': 'Many waters cannot quench love. Neither can floods drown it.' It begins abruptly and brutally with an ascending and accelerating piano cadenza that conveys Water's attempt to drown or quench Love. The strings meet this powerful display with stoic melodic figures that hint of a popular melody, perhaps Jacob Gade's 'Jalousie.' The humorous closing G major pizzicato suggests that Love triumphs in the end.

"Song 5 is based on the poem 'Sea Fever' by John Masefield. Hollier sets the line 'I must go down to the seas again, to the vagrant gypsy life' with a rollicking, folklike melody (marked Rumbustious and Boisterous) and tavern-style rhythms. In this song the Sea represents a life lived fully and joyfully. Light-hearted and jocular, with drunken glissandi in the piano, hornpipe figures in the strings, rowdy dancing with audible foot stamping in the piano, the Song concludes with a wild fortississimo Presto."

# FOURTEEN

# American Pathfinders

---

**NORTH AMERICA BEFORE WORLD WAR II**

---

During the late nineteenth century, American composers steadily produced competent if not highly original chamber works, most reflecting German influence following the midcentury emigration wave. Since the United States lacked opportunities for systematic musical education, most aspiring composers travelled to the continent for training, ostensibly developing into minor European composers. A national voice began to emerge after philanthropist Jeannette Thurber established the nation's first music conservatory in New York City in 1892. Thurber had the good fortune to recruit Czech nationalist composer Antonín Dvořák as its director for three formative years. Believing that each country offered a uniquely valuable contribution, Dvořák urged American composers-in-training to find their individual voices. He beseeched his students to quarry the nation's rich trove of folk song and indigenous music. He stressed the value of environmental sounds, whether bird calls heard in nature or casual tunes and harmonies of the urban street.

During his time in the United States, Dvořák absorbed the rich diversity of Plains Indian and African-American culture. "American music should draw from these wellsprings," he insisted.

The "Americanisms" heard at the resoundingly successful New York premiere of his Symphony No. 9, "From the New World" (1893), gave composers the inspiration to forge similar paths. Its closing measures of nascent jazz rhythms on the proto-boogie chord E-G sharp-B-C sharp-E are arguably as influential for music's future as Wagner's enigmatic Tristan chord fifty years earlier.

Dvořák's students decisively impacted the development of American music. Arthur Farwell (1872–1952) is particularly significant both for his ethnographic studies of Native American music and his establishment of the first publication forum for American composers. He stated that his Wa-Wan Press (1902) offered opportunities for "new and daring expressions.... It includes a definite acceptance of Dvořák's challenge to go after our folk music." Composers sponsored by this imaginative press incorporated a wide range of folk, ragtime, and Latin American music into their works.

New Englanders Edward MacDowell, John Knowles Paine, and Horatio Parker impacted America's music by promoting composition teaching at its major universities. Training abroad now happened with altered focus. Paris offered the skillful guidance of Nadia Boulanger (1887–1979), the insightful composer, conductor, and teacher who urged her students to express their original ideas, ideally reflections of visions and concepts shaped in their home regions. One of her successes was Aaron Copland, who based works on specific American themes and rhythms derived from jazz—America's essential contribution to world music—but developed them with Europe's modernist techniques.

The Great War of 1914–18 became the cultural turning point for the United States. Affirmation as a major world power created a heightened national consciousness and the inevitable need for a vigorous and individual artistic expression. German or English preferences no longer dominated in a country that welcomed a diverse array of immigrants. The early arrivals of Ernest Bloch from Switzerland, Edgard Varèse and Charles Martin Loeffler from France, as well as the many esteemed composers fleeing conditions before World War II alerted Americans to continental trends and, most importantly, signaled a new internationalism. It is notable that several outstanding women composers finally achieved recognition.

CHARLES IVES
B. OCTOBER 20, 1874 IN DANBURY, CONNECTICUT,
D. MAY 19, 1954 IN NEW YORK CITY

## String Quartet No. 1, "A Revival Service" (1896)

Chorale: Andante con moto
Prelude: Allegro
Offertory: Adagio cantabile
Postlude: Allegro marziale

One of the great originals of music history, Charles Ives created a unique style that grew from deep roots in his New England past. His boldly imaginative works, all composed between 1891 and 1921, were an amalgam of classical ideas and spontaneous country tunes set to harmonies and rhythms of extreme complexity. Although he had studied composition at Yale with Horatio Parker, Ives became an insurance executive and composed only during weekends. None of his pioneering work was heard or even known before the 1920s; important public performances were held after 1939. His String Quartet No. 1, written in 1896, received its premiere as a complete work in 1957.

During his years at Yale, Ives supported himself as organist for New Haven's Centre Church. Three movements of his String Quartet No. 1, his first major work, were composed for church performances, but its first movement developed from a fugue he had written for Parker's composition class. Since he wrote the second and fourth movements for a revival, Ives titled his quartet

"A Revival Meeting." Because of its popular hymn quotations, it is also subtitled "From the Salvation Army."

The opening movement is based on two hymn tunes, "All Hail the Power of Jesus' Name" and "From Greenland's Icy Mountains." The cello announces the first theme, which is treated fugally by all instruments. The writing is simple and academically correct, as Parker would expect from his students.

Ives's originality emerges in the following three movements. Tired of standard hymns, Ives began to embellish them with the blessing of the Centre Church minister, who said "God will understand." Although the second movement retains its hymnlike character, the writing includes free paraphrases of early American favorites "Beulah Land" and "Shining Shore." The third movement grows even more daring. Based on the hymn "Come, Thou Fount of Every Blessing," Ives incorporates strong dissonances and abrupt jagged rhythms. The fourth movement, Postlude, begins with a quotation from the marchlike "Stand Up, Stand Up for Jesus," but a theme fragment from the Prelude interrupts. The movement soars to a climax (resolute and strongly marked) as the triple rhythm of "Come, Thou Fount of Every Blessing" clashes with the four-beat meter of a harmonically altered "Stand Up, Stand Up for Jesus."

AMY BEACH
B. SEPTEMBER 5, 1867 IN HENNIKER, NEW HAMPSHIRE,
D. DECEMBER 27, 1944 IN NEW YORK CITY

Amy Beach, the sheltered child of a mathematician father and pianist mother, showed early musical ability that was nurtured within the confines of her New England home. Although her parents were advised to send Amy abroad for study, she was trained in piano by her mother and later by Carl Baermann, a student of Franz Liszt. Beach took only one composition class during her life, a locally taught theory and harmony course. Her marriage at age eighteen to Dr. Henry Beach, twenty-four years her senior, brought further constraints. Dr. Beach objected to private composition tutoring, as well as her public piano performances, but he did encourage Amy to compose as an avocation using the models of classical scores from their own library.

As a self-taught composer Beach achieved astounding success. Her 1896 *Gaelic Symphony* was the first large-scale work written by an American woman and performed by American orchestras. Premiered by the Boston Symphony, it was acclaimed throughout the United States—but with her name listed on programs as "Mrs. H. H. A. Beach." Despite her gender, Amy was welcomed into the group of New England composers known as the Boston Six (see below), one of whom was Edward MacDowell. After her husband's death, Beach spent her summers composing at the MacDowell Colony in New Hampshire; her works of this time were most often premiered in New York at St. Bartholomew's Episcopal Church, where she was unofficially composer-in-residence. Beach composed with a free flow of ideas, creating over 300 mostly published works. Near the end of her life she generously stated that "being a woman presented no hindrance to her musical creativity."

*Piano Quintet in F sharp Minor, Opus 67 (1907)*

Adagio—Allegro moderato
Adagio espressivo
Allegro agitato—Adagio come prima—Presto

Since a grand piano was the favored centerpiece for spacious American halls (as well as homes), composers of the early century often scored chamber works to include it. Beach herself performed as pianist for the quintet's 1908 premiere, at which the work was critically praised as "truly modern" and "rhapsodic in the fashion of our time." Beach had performed the Brahms and Franck piano quintets, both endowed with prominent piano scores, and most probably these provided the models for her late romantic composition.

The opening movement, in sonata form, begins with a mysterious introduction remarkable for its range of dynamics and subtle changes of tempo. After a full pause, the Allegro presents two lyrical themes developed with flexible tempos and animated figuration throughout. After a fervent section marked *con fuoco* (with fire), the atmosphere changes to *dolce* (sweet) and the movement ends quietly.

The Adagio espressivo (D flat major) opens in a quiet dynamic with muted strings (*con sordino*) but gradually grows more intense. The cello offers significant solo moments throughout. After a solo piano statement marked *appassionato* (impassioned), the movement fades to a soft conclusion.

The forceful finale recalls themes from the first movement, now developed with richer harmonies. After a brief fugal area the final Presto, marked *furioso* (furious), hurtles toward a dramatic conclusion.

*Piano Trio in A Minor, Opus 150 (1938)*

Allegro
Lento espressivo—Presto—Tempo I
Allegro con brio

Strongly romantic in spirit, Beach's Piano Trio reveals the influence of Franck and especially Dvořák. The opening Allegro's somber primary theme, introduced by the cello and developed as a duet with the violin, suggests a Dvořák *dumka*, a flexible lament heard throughout his 1891 *Dumky Trio*, Op. 90. Over rippling piano figures the violin and cello develop two themes as an ardent duet in their upper registers. The mode changes to A major at the calm conclusion.

The second movement, Lento espressivo (slow and expressive) is constructed in ABA song form with serenely reflective sections framing a rapid and playful inner section. Intoned by the cello, the opening theme recalls the *dumka* effect of the first movement; the violin joins to create a rhapsodic duet. The finale, Allegro con brio, explores two contrasting ideas—a syncopated theme and a more lyrical idea that is extended into a songful aria for the strings. Momentum slows at a central interlude, but the spirited pace resumes and the movement concludes with a brisk flourish.

ARTHUR FOOTE
B. MARCH 5, 1853 IN SALEM, MASSACHUSETTS,
D. APRIL 8, 1937 IN BOSTON

*Piano Trio No. 2 in B flat Major, Opus 65 (1908)*

Allegro giocoso
Tranquillo
Allegro molto

Arthur Foote was an esteemed member of the Boston Six, an early twentieth-century group that also included Amy Beach, Edward MacDowell, John Knowles Paine, George Whitefield Chadwick, and Horatio Parker. Centered in New England, the group is considered pivotal for the establishment of a distinctively American idiom. The first American classical composer to be trained entirely in the United States, Foote is best known for his distinguished body of chamber music. Although grounded in late romantic tradition, his well-crafted works reveal elements of twentieth-century Impressionism.

Douglas Moore, the editor of Foote's cello compositions, writes: "The second trio was one of Foote's latest works, and it contains many harmonic twists and turns reminiscent of Wagner.

Its opening movement is a compact sonata form. The final seven measures of the movement are marked Tranquillo; this serves to set up the same mood and tempo marking for the next movement. The key of the second movement is D major, a third relation away from the original B flat major, and a demonstration of one of the Brahmsian influences on Foote. A middle section is hauntingly beautiful, with the piano doubling the violin melody two octaves higher. The last movement, marked Allegro molto, begins in a turbulent B flat minor and does not reach the original major key until a triumphant coda which briefly restates the theme of the first movement just before the end."

HENRY HADLEY
B. DECEMBER 20, 1871 IN SOMMERVILLE, MASSACHUSETTS,
D. SEPTEMBER 6, 1937 IN NEW YORK CITY

*Piano Quintet in A Minor, Opus 50 (1918)*

Allegro energico
Andante tranquillo
Scherzo: Allegro giocoso
Finale: Allegro con brio

Americanist and cellist Theodore Buchholz writes: "When asked to identify a great American composer, Richard Strauss replied, 'There is only one, Henry Kimball Hadley.' Hadley studied in Vienna before returning to the United States, where he achieved fame as both conductor and composer. Although Hadley's music is rarely played today, during his lifetime virtually every American orchestra performed his works. His piano quintet is perhaps his finest and most daring chamber composition, a bold entry into a relatively sparse genre.

"The first movement opens with a stentorian rising figure; this motive is a distant cousin to Dohnányi's Quintet though more anxious in its taut chromaticism. Strauss's influence can be felt in Hadley's dovetailed instrumental layering, each voice weaving in and out of the energetically rising texture. Just at the crescendo's breaking point, Hadley pulls out the proverbial rug of expected harmony, shifting the sands to a new tonal landscape.

"Gently rippling, lulling, and subliminal, the second movement is an impressionistic dreamscape. Hadley achieved this vivid effect with muted instruments and saturated harmonies that run from the page like watercolors. The middle section stirs with expressive solo melodies, then descends to the tender material from the movement's hypnagogic opening.

"Rhythmically askew, the third movement has just enough offbeat humor to be a scherzo in the tradition of Haydn and Mendelssohn. By leaning into the 'right' wrong notes—producing the bray of an instrumental heehaw—the joke is the difficulty of pinning the pulse on this donkey. The broadly sweeping middle section almost soars in grandeur, but it then bumbles back to the jauntiness of the movement's opening—a pretty good joke.

"The finale begins with a recall of the first movement, although its once angsty motive is now transformed into a joyful exclamation. Hadley's ability to modulate on a dime, from the sparkly A major to the purest C major, sets the stage for one of the loveliest cello solos in the piano quintet literature. The quintet ends triumphantly in A major but is tinged with subtle harmonic shadows from its original minor key—a reminder of how far the work has travelled in half an hour.

"Hadley's quintet is a rich and powerful work, full of tonal and dynamic quantum leaps, triumphant returns, and unexpected harmonic vistas. The scoring offers shining moments for each performer."

REBECCA CLARKE
B. AUGUST 27, 1886 IN LONDON,
D. OCTOBER 13, 1979 IN NEW YORK CITY

## Piano Trio in A Minor (1921)

Moderato ma appassionato
Andante molto semplice
Allegro vigoroso

Born in England to German-American parents, Rebecca Clarke claimed U.S. citizenship after establishing permanent residence in the United States on the eve of World War II. Clarke was trained at the Royal College of Music, where she became the first woman composition student of Charles Stanford, a difficult taskmaster notorious for discouraging all but the most committed candidates. Banished at a young age from her family home and cut off from funds, a cruelty detailed in her memoirs, Clarke left the College and embarked on a successful career as a professional violist. She found an encouraging friend and lively colleague in cellist May Mukle, an avid chamber musician known for her support of contemporary composers. To augment their paid engagements they frequently "barnstormed," finding their own venues, providing their own programs, and putting a collection plate at the back of the hall for contributions.

Clarke's compositional breakthrough came with her 1918 viola work *Morpheus*, premiered in Carnegie Hall and published under the male pseudonym "Anthony Trent" for marketability. Continuing to compose with this camouflage, she used the name "Trent" to enter her piano trio in the 1921 Berkshire Music Festival Competition. In a large field Clarke was the runner-up. Discovering the subterfuge, patroness Elizabeth Sprague Coolidge commissioned Clarke to write a work for the next Berkshire Festival. However, publishers gave her little support, and her output steadily declined.

During her last thirty-five years, she composed only one song. Recently there has been keen interest in the revival of Clarke's compositions. Patrons issued her unpublished manuscripts to celebrate her 90th birthday, and in 2000 the Rebecca Clarke Society was formed in Massachusetts to support the publication, performance, and recording of her music.

Although Clarke's harmonic language is conservative for its time, her development of motifs and textures is strikingly original. In the 1921 piano trio her themes are continuously recast both to unify the work and to achieve maximum variety and drama. The trio's three movements are linked by a recurring motto initially heard fortissimo in the piano and insinuated throughout the work. After the succinct motto (six 16th notes) has been developed through ardent passagework in the cello and violin, a calmer second theme marked *misterioso* enters. Both the motto and the second idea are interwoven and developed, and the movement concludes with a coda based on canonic treatment of the motto theme in the piano and cello.

The second movement ("slow and very simple") is muted throughout. It opens with a calm statement in the violin accompanied by the single reiterated note C in the piano. A second folklike theme is introduced by the piano with gentle string accompaniment that references the motto. The movement concludes with a tranquil violin restatement of its opening idea.

Enlivened by pizzicati, glissandi, and harmonics, the virtuoso finale moves with restless agitation through dramatic changes of register and metric pulse. Piquant interludes relieve the tumultuous passagework. Following a development based on the opening movement's primary theme, a spirited coda concludes the work.

ERNEST BLOCH
B. JULY 24, 1880 IN GENEVA,
D. JULY 15, 1959 IN PORTLAND, OREGON

## Piano Quintet No. 1 (1923)

Agitato
Andante mistico
Allegro energico

Ernest Bloch emigrated to the United States in 1916 and eight years later became an American citizen. Although known as a Hebrew nationalist because of his introspective *Jewish Cycle*, a set of epic compositions based on biblical subjects, Bloch remained an eclectic. He continuously explored facets of his musical personality while maintaining roots in the Central European late romantic tradition. In the 1920s, a period when he wrote much chamber music, he adopted a neoclassical aesthetic.

Suzanne Bloch, the composer's daughter, describes the genesis of the piano quintet: "The work started as sketches for a cello sonata, but these were put aside. A year later, Bloch found them and decided that the material he had jotted down, using quarter tones, needed heavier instrumentation—so transformed this into the quintet. He abandoned this project for a year, and then took it up again. He completed it by going in every Sunday to the empty Cleveland Institute of Music (he was then the director), where in solitude he could work undisturbed. He wrote: 'An Institute of Music without music is an ideal place!' "

Bloch himself said little about his quintet: "The music speaks for itself. The first movement is more objective than the second. The third is a kind of exotic dream." Strongly colored by rich timbres, the quintet abounds with string effects such as harmonics, glissandi, and passages played on the bridge or fingerboard. Quarter tones are transformed into piquant grace notes. The first two movements, played without pause, develop similar thematic material but create contrasting atmospheres, one strident and primitive, the second a languorous interweaving of three ideas that create an aura of mystical contemplation. The propulsive Allegro energico develops its two themes in sonata form. This barbaric, percussive finale ends with a note of serenity on a conventional C major cadence. Although critics have objected that this wild and free movement requires a similar conclusion, Bloch insisted that the ending must be calm. Over time, listeners have agreed.

ARTHUR SHEPHERD
B. FEBRUARY 19, 1880 IN PARIS, IDAHO,
D. JANUARY 12, 1958 IN CLEVELAND, OHIO

*"Triptych" for Soprano and String Quartet (1926)*

He it is
The day is no more
Light, my dear

Composer, conductor, and educator Arthur Shepherd was born in a small Mormon community near the Utah border. A piano prodigy, at the age of twelve he was sent to the New England Conservatory to begin advanced studies. After graduating with honors Shepherd spent eleven years in Salt Lake City, where he taught private piano lessons and conducted the Salt Lake Symphony. Having absorbed the advice of Dvořák, who urged American composers "to create a great and noble school based on native material," Shepherd vowed "to go after our folk music" to cultivate a specific American voice. While retaining an essentially European framework, Shepherd published American tune-based works such as *Horizons*, which includes the famous dying cowboy tune, "Bury Me Not on the Lone Prairie." His mature works reflect admiration for the romantic modalities of Vaughan Williams and the fine craftsmanship of Fauré. Shepherd stated that he remained a traditionalist because "he was unable to renounce the necessary inevitable beauty of the simpler euphonies."

Shepherd's most frequently performed work is his *Triptych*. Pervaded by a subtle chromaticism that suggests French influence, the work is a luminous set of songs supported by countermelodies in the string quartet. The songs are arranged to form a three-movement work with contrasting tempos (moderate-slow-fast).

Shepherd set the *Triptych* to poems of Rabindranath Tagore (1861–1941), a Bengali poet, painter, and composer who blended folk song with classical Indian music in his own works. Shepherd's *Triptych* is a setting of poems 72, 74, and 57 from Tagore's *Gitanjali* (Song Offerings), which was published in England (1913) with an introduction by William Butler Yeats. Tagore made his own English translation from the Bengali original.

"He it is, the innermost one, who awakens my being with his deep hidden touches. He it is who puts his enchantment upon these eyes and joyfully plays on the chords of my heart in varied cadence of pleasure and pain. He it is who weaves the web of this maya in evanescent hues of gold and silver, blue and green; and lets peep out through the folds his feet, at whose touch I forget myself. Days come and ages pass and it is ever He who moves my heart in many a name, in many a guise, in many a rapture of joy and sorrow."

"The day is no more. The shadow is upon the earth. It is time that I go to the stream to fill my pitcher. The evening air is eager with the sad music of the water. Ah, it calls me out into the dusk. In the lonely lane there is no passerby. The wind is up, the ripples are rampant in the river. I know not if I shall come back home. I know not whom I shall chance to meet. There at the fording in his little boat the unknown man plays upon his lute."

"Light, my light, the world-filling light, the eye-kissing light, heart-sweetening light! Ah, the light dances, my darling, at the center of my life; Ah, the light strikes, my darling, the chords of my love; The sky opens, the wind runs wild, the sky opens, laughter passes over the earth. The butterflies spread their sails on the sea of light, lilies and jasmines surge up on the crest of the waves of light. The light is shattered into gold on ev'ry cloud, my darling, and it scatters gems in profusion. The butterflies spread their sails on the sea of light, mirth spreads from leaf to leaf, my darling, and gladness without measure. The heaven's river has drowned its banks, and the flood of joy is abroad."

LEO ORNSTEIN
B. DECEMBER 11, 1895 IN KREMENCHUK, RUSSIAN EMPIRE
(NOW UKRAINE),
D. FEBRUARY 24, 2002 IN GREEN BAY, WISCONSIN

*Piano Quintet (1927)*

Allegro barbaro
Andante lamentoso
Allegro agitato

Leo Ornstein emigrated with his family to the United States in 1906 to escape the pogroms. The son of a cantor, Ornstein was a piano prodigy who studied composition with Glazunov at age ten and worked as an opera coach at age eleven. After his successful New York piano debut, Ornstein began to concertize with his own experimental repertoire. His savagely ultra-modernist works such as *Wild Men's Dance* and *Suicide in an Airplane* drew large and often unruly crowds. Recognizing that his radical works stood near chaos, Ornstein abandoned the concert stage and began to compose in a more coherent, tonal style. He accepted a teaching position at the Philadelphia Music Academy, where he produced his most significant works—among them the piano quintet, which is recognized as a masterpiece of the quintet repertoire. After his retirement in 1953, Ornstein drifted into obscurity. His music was rediscovered in the mid 1970s by musicologist Vivian Perlis, who inspired him to resume composing with his unique voice. He wrote his final work, Piano Sonata No. 7, at age 95. Both Ornstein and Elliott Carter, who at age 103 wrote *Epigrams for Piano Trio*, have been honored as the oldest published composers to continue creating new music.

Ornstein claimed that his fierce and opulent piano quintet "sprang into his head fully formed" like Minerva from the forehead of Zeus. Strongly influenced by the modernist harmonies of Ravel and Scriabin and the insistent rhythmic patterns of Bartók, the quintet develops forcefully with kaleidoscopic changes of atmosphere. The work has been heard as part of the Futurist movement, an early twentieth-century Italian phenomenon, soon spread to Russia, that strove to liberate artists from the "dead hand of the past." Technology, speed, and violence were reflected in its musical and artistic products.

The quintet's three movements are linked by their similar oriental atmosphere, achieved through modal harmonies and shimmering cascades of note patterns. The opening Allegro barbaro (fast and barbarous) offers homage to Bartók's 1911 piano work of the same title, a work of ferocious rhythmic drive and surprising contrasts. Ornstein's turbulent movement develops with numerous ostinato patterns, energizing note repetitions much favored by Bartók. The virtuoso lines of all instruments fall at the extremes of their note ranges and dynamic levels.

The Andante lamentoso (slow and lamenting) opens with a muted statement in the solo viola, then the cello, that suggests a cantor's evocation. At the middle section, the statements become more fervent as cascades of notes are heard fortississimo (*fff*) with soaring themes played in octaves by the strings. Tight clusters of notes animate the harmonies. Near the end the score indicates *morendo* (dying), and a descending piano line brings the movement to a quiet conclusion.

Allegro agitato, the "fast and agitated" finale, unfolds with numerous metric changes that impart a sense of unrest. At its fervent middle section, directed to be played *con fuoco e molto feroce* (with fire and very ferocious) the turbulence of the opening Allegro barbaro returns. Percussive tone clusters in the piano drive the momentum. In its final section the mood calms in a section played *tranquillo*. Changing to the major mode, the movement concludes *tristamente* (sadly) with a pianissimo dynamic.

QUINCY PORTER
B. FEBRUARY 7, 1897 IN NEW HAVEN, CONNECTICUT,
D. NOVEMBER 12, 1966 IN BETHANY, CONNECTICUT

*String Quartet No. 3 (1930)*

Allegro
Andante
Allegro moderato

A direct descendant of colonial theologian Jonathan Edwards, known for fiery sermons such as "Sinners in the Hands of an Angry God," Quincy Porter was the son and grandson of Yale professors. A student of the distinguished Horatio Parker at Yale, Porter later was mentored by Vincent d'Indy in Paris and Ernest Bloch in Cleveland. While continuing to compose, Porter served as both Director of the New England Conservatory and Professor of Music at Yale. A fine violist and violinist, Porter had vast experience as a quartet player. His nine string quartets, written over the course of his career, are considered his most important compositions.

Porter wrote his Quartet No. 3 in Paris, where he resided during his Guggenheim Fellowship year of 1930, and the work reflects the optimism of this early phase of his career. After the quartet won the Society for the Publication of American Music Award, the

*Washington Post* commented that the work was "independent of schools and unallied with any exoticism; although a poetic vein runs through its three movements, fantasy is kept on a rather tight curb."

A well-crafted and engaging work, the quartet reveals Porter's strong melodic gifts. Clear harmonies, fluidity of movement, and warmly sonorous scoring for all instruments are heard throughout. Porter commented that the opening movement is loosely structured in sonata form. This Allegro develops two subjects, the first of which is transformed into an ostinato figure that underpins the second idea. The second movement is a tranquil statement with mild dissonances. The third movement is a triple-time rondo with colorfully varied passagework.

RUTH CRAWFORD SEEGER
B. JULY 3, 1901 IN EAST LIVERPOOL, OHIO,
D. NOVEMBER 18, 1953 IN CHEVY CHASE, MARYLAND

## *String Quartet (1931)*

Rubato assai
Leggiero
Andante
Allegro possibile

The first woman awarded a Guggenheim Fellowship, Ruth Crawford Seeger used these funds to study in Berlin, where she absorbed the latest European trends and wrote her modernist string quartet. Returning to the U.S. the following year she married musicologist and social activist Charles Seeger, who reset her focus to folk music. As the committed mother of Mike and Peggy Seeger and stepmother to Pete Seeger, folk musicians and eventual social activists like their father, Ruth devoted herself to transcribing folksongs. After publishing the influential *American Songbook for Children* (1948) she returned to her own composition, but within a few years succumbed to cancer.

Crawford Seeger's string quartet, considered her masterpiece, develops with innovative organizational structures that influenced composers of the generation following, such as Elliott Carter. Her self-described system of "dissonant dynamics," in which each instrument changes its dynamic level individually so that a melody emerges or recedes from a dissonant background, is clearly heard in the third movement. Bold and concentrated in its gestures, this twelve-minute quartet develops with increasing energy and remarkable dramatic tension. The four movements are played without pause.

The fleet Rubato assai (somewhat flexible tempo) unfolds with dissonant harmonies loosely centered on C major. A slower viola soliloquy leads to the second movement, the rapid Leggiero (very light). Imitative writing and a playful staccato section animate this energetic movement.

The sustained and mystical Andante pulsates with dynamic gradations. Double stops, subtle dynamics, and ever faster tempos create greater intensity. The movement fades to a pianississississimo (*pppp*) conclusion.

The Allegro possibile (as fast as possible) immediately follows. After a brusque introduction, muted and scurrying passages support the forcefully declamatory violin line. Dialogues develop with punctuations from remaining players. Single forte notes in the violin bring the work to an abrupt conclusion.

SAMUEL BARBER
B. MARCH 9, 1910 IN WEST CHESTER, PENNSYLVANIA,
D. JANUARY 23, 1981 IN NEW YORK CITY

## *"Dover Beach" for String Quartet and Baritone, Opus 3 (1931)*

Samuel Barber composed his setting for Matthew Arnold's poem "Dover Beach" while he was still a student at the Curtis Institute. Although written during the expansionist era of Victorian England, Arnold's 1867 poem is deeply pessimistic. Material progress, in Arnold's view, does not protect society from conflict and war. Like the tide, the Sea of Faith, embodied in religion and other life philosophies, has ebbed. The moonlit world that lies before the lovers at the Dover Cliffs is beautiful but unreal—it is merely a land of dreams. The true world is a world of darkness "where ignorant armies clash by night."

The sonorous imagery of Arnold's poem lends itself to a musical setting. Barber, sensitive to the poem's nuances, strives to represent its mood through descriptive musical gestures—for example, rocking figures in the string parts represent the movement of light on the sea. The setting gradually builds to an impassioned conclusion at the poem's final stanza, where all preceding images take on their full emotional weight.

*Dover Beach*

The sea is calm tonight.
The tide is full, the moon lies fair
Upon the straits; on the French coast the light
Gleams and is gone; the cliffs of England stand,
Glimmering and vast, out on the tranquil bay.
Come to the window, sweet is the night air!
Only, from the long line of spray
Where the sea meets the moon-blanched land,
Listen! You hear the grating roar

Of pebbles which the waves draw back, and fling,
At their return, up the high strand,
Begin, and cease, and then again begin,
With tremulous cadence slow, and bring
The eternal note of sadness in.

Sophocles long ago
Heard it on the Aegean, and it brought
Into his mind the turbid ebb and flow
Of human misery; we
Find also in the sound a thought,
Hearing it by this distant northern sea.

The Sea of Faith
Was once, too, at the full, and round earth's shore
Lay like the folds of a bright girdle furled.
But now I only hear
Its melancholy, long, withdrawing roar,
Retreating, to the breath
Of the night-wind, down the vast edges drear
And naked shingles of the world.

Ah, love, let us be true
To one another! for the world, which seems
To lie before us like a land of dreams,
So various, so beautiful, so new,
Hath really neither joy, nor love, nor light,
Nor certitude, nor peace, nor help for pain;
And we are here as on a darkling plain
Swept with confused alarms of struggle and flight,
Where ignorant armies clash by night.

## String Quartet, Opus 11 (1936)

Molto allegro e appassionato
Molto adagio—Molto allegro (come prima)

In 1936 Barber received a Pulitzer Travelling Scholarship for composition and happily settled into a hunting lodge in the Austrian Tyrol to write his string quartet. Unfortunately, winter arrived early, and Barber was forced to leave the unheated lodge before finishing the work. "It has a hoodoo on it," he said of the third movement, which he never quite finished to his satisfaction.

The second movement endures as Barber's most popular composition through its orchestral transcription *Adagio for Strings*, which he created for Arturo Toscanini. Because of its noble and elegiac character the movement has actually—to Barber's dismay—become international music of mourning, having been played at the funerals of Franklin D. Roosevelt, John F. Kennedy, and Princess Grace of Monaco. Yet many listeners hear it not as an elegy but as a simple love scene.

The first movement (B minor) develops three themes—the first is bold and arresting; the second calm and chorale-like; the third a widely arched legato melody. The Adagio (B flat minor) is based on a sinuous, stepwise-moving theme that begins with serenity but gradually builds to a peak of intensity as each instrument plays at the upper limits of its range. A subdued coda gently ends the momentum. The third movement, an altered repetition of the first movement in a new tonality, proceeds without pause. The opening tonality of B minor returns at the brief coda.

AARON COPLAND
B. NOVEMBER 14, 1900 IN NEW YORK CITY,
D. DECEMBER 2, 1990 IN NORTH TARRYTOWN, NEW YORK

## Sextet for Clarinet, Piano, and String Quartet (1937)

Allegro vivace
Lento
Finale

Copland's sextet is his own arrangement of *Short Symphony* (Symphony No. 2, 1933), a work he wistfully referred to as "one of my neglected children" because of conductors' reluctance to program it. Copland freely discussed the frustrating performance history of the original orchestral version: "Several conductors had announced performances, but gave up because of rhythmic difficulties. Koussevitzky considered the piece for a year and a half. When I asked him, 'Is it too difficult?' he responded, 'No, it is impossible!'" Copland simplified the work slightly to create the sextet, which was premiered in 1939 at New York's Town Hall by a Juilliard graduate ensemble. Because of its many syncopations, cross rhythms, and shifting meters, the sextet remains a fiendish challenge for its performers.

Copland describes the work: "It is a bare fifteen minutes in length, but those minutes are concentrated in meaning. The work is written in three movements—fast, slow, fast—to be played without pause. The first movement's impetus is rhythmic, with a scherzo-like quality. All melodic figures result from a nine-note sequence—a kind of row—from the opening two bars. The second movement, tranquil in feeling, contrasts with the first movement and the finale, which is again rhythmically bright in color and free in form." Worked out through complex rhythmic formulations, the melodic material references the Charleston, Mexican popular dance tunes, and German film music.

LEONARD BERNSTEIN
B. AUGUST 25, 1918 IN LAWRENCE, MASSACHUSETTS,
D. OCTOBER 14, 1990 IN NEW YORK CITY

## Piano Trio (1937)

Adagio non troppo—Allegro vivace
Tempo di marcia
Largo—Allegro vivo e molto ritmico

American icon Leonard Bernstein has been described as a Renaissance man. Renowned as a much-recorded composer, conductor, and pianist, he also wrote influential books and essays that promoted music as a vital, living art. An inspiring teacher, Bernstein brought his messages into American life through televised lectures and Young People's Concerts. Despite a schedule of astounding complexity he remained dedicated to numerous humanitarian causes throughout his life. His impressive list of awards includes 21 honorary degrees, 13 Grammy Awards, 11 Emmy Awards, 25 television awards, 23 civic awards, honorary titles in 20 societies and orchestras, including Laureate Conductor of the New York Philharmonic and the Israel Philharmonic.

Bernstein wrote his piano trio during his junior year at Harvard, where he broadly studied humanities but also enrolled in Walter Piston's composition classes. That summer he had visited Mildred Spiegel, a pianist friend from his high school days, at York Harbor, Maine. She wrote: "He borrowed a farmer's truck and drove out to where I was playing with my trio. I was delightfully surprised. Later that year he wrote a piano trio for me and my friends, and we performed it at Harvard." Possibly detecting a few student elements in the work, Bernstein did not agree to its publication until 1979.

Bernstein's unique musical personality emerges in the ebullient melodies of his youthful trio. Although he had received little formal instruction in composition by that time, he had become a devotee of the neoclassicists Aaron Copland and Paul Hindemith, his summer teacher at Tanglewood. In his trio, Bernstein synthesizes current harmonic and structural idioms with his own free sense of rhythm. His theatrical sense of pacing is heard in the trio's dramatic alternations of slow and fast tempos, changes often highlighted by a trill, glissando, or new dynamic marking. Bernstein recycled several of the trio's themes in later compositions; the opening of the second movement appears in his first musical, *On the Town*.

## EXPANDING HORIZONS: NORTH AMERICA IN MID-CENTURY

IGOR STRAVINSKY
B. JUNE 17, 1882 IN ORANIENBAUM, RUSSIA,
D. APRIL 6, 1971 IN NEW YORK CITY

*Septet for Clarinet, Bassoon, Horn, Piano, Violin, Viola, and Cello (1952–53)*

Quarter note = 88
Passacaglia, ca. quarter note = 60
Gigue, eighth note = 112–116

After becoming a United States citizen in 1945, Stravinsky resided in Los Angeles and New York. Always an innovator, Stravinsky at this time experimented with the serialist procedures characteristic of Arnold Schoenberg, a fellow expatriate whom he knew in Los Angeles. Despite new procedures, these works share traits of his earlier compositions—energetic rhythms, melodies crafted from extensions of two or three note cells, clarity of form and scoring.

Stravinsky's vivacious septet offers homage to Schoenberg, whose own Opus 29 Suite, also for seven instruments, is constructed through twelve-tone technique. The entire septet unfolds with a variety of contrapuntal procedures, but the final two movements reveal Stravinsky's new style most clearly. The opening movement, constructed in sonata form, explores two themes, the second of which (heard in the piano as E sharp, F double-sharp, G sharp, A sharp, B) anticipates the tone row heard in the second and third movements.

The second movement, Passacaglia, follows the baroque form, here a ground bass that consists of nine variations over a foundation of sixteen notes; the concluding coda can be heard as a tenth variation. A contrapuntal tour de force, the movement develops with canons that are inverted (upside down), retrograde (backwards), and retrograde-inverted.

The final Gigue is a dancelike series of four ingenious fugues based on the Passacaglia's sixteen note sequence. Its first section is a three-voice fugue for strings; the second fugue is a piano repetition with a wind trio fugue superimposed to create a double fugue. The third section is a three-part fugue for strings; the finale is a double fugue for piano and winds with the note rows inverted. The smooth metrical flow belies the intricacy of this very intellectualized *gigue*.

GLENN GOULD
B. SEPTEMBER 25, 1932 IN TORONTO,
D. OCTOBER 4, 1982 IN TORONTO

## String Quartet, Opus 1 (1955)

Pianist and composer Glenn Gould was a musically precocious child who could read music before he read words. By the age of six Gould performed his own compositions at informal family and church gatherings, and at age ten he was enrolled as a theory and composition student at the Royal Conservatory of Music in Toronto. After a back injury at this time, Gould began to use a very low chair that allowed him to pull down on the keys rather than to strike them from above; it has been said that this position enabled him to achieve his trademark clear and rapid note execution. At age twelve Gould passed his final conservatory examination with highest marks and began his career as a professional pianist. Sought after as a soloist with a wide-ranging repertoire, Gould chose to give up live performance at age 31 to focus on recording projects. Although famous as a writer, broadcaster, and preeminent interpreter of Bach, Gould was less well known as a composer. Many of his works were unfinished, and except for a string quartet, his completed body of work is largely unpublished.

Gould began to write his quartet at age sixteen. As homage to J.S. Bach, extensive fugal passages form the pillars of each of its four essentially continuous sections. Much of this fugal treatment is stylistically baroque, but quotations are also taken from Beethoven's *Grosse Fuge*, Opus 133. Late romantic harmonies characteristic of the early expressionist Alban Berg prevail. Gould describes its F minor key: "It has a certain obliqueness, halfway between complex and stable, upright and lascivious, but gray and highly tinted." Since the quartet was pianistically conceived and its score lacks normal string articulation marks, the work is immensely challenging to interpret as an ensemble. Gould himself performed it as a piano solo.

Players who have studied the quartet with Gould offer valuable insights. Violinist Laura Andriani writes: "One of its greatest technical challenges is its proportions. The quartet starts out with the kind of minimal monotone landscape you get in Canada in the winter. This is followed by a series of long phrases, like a huge musical construction without movements, accompanied by metronome markings that underline the sense of time scale. The moods continuously change. It is very emotional.... It's like Gould was working in a musical laboratory, trying to isolate substances, combine them, observe the transformation—a process, not a final result."

LEON KIRCHNER
B. JANUARY 24, 1919 IN NEW YORK CITY,
D. SEPTEMBER 17, 2009 IN NEW YORK CITY

*Piano Trio No. 1 (1954)*

I.

II. Largo

Leon Kirchner grew up in pre-World War II Los Angeles, then a creative haven for artists fleeing Nazi Germany. Kirchner studied composition at Berkeley and UCLA with Schoenberg and Bloch, and in 1942 he won the George Ladd Prix de Paris for study abroad. He enrolled in the military instead, but eventually he resumed his musical training with Roger Sessions in New York. Esteemed as both a pianist and conductor, Kirchner was also Professor of Composition at Harvard from 1961–1989. He is most proud of the Harvard Chamber Orchestra, which he founded for the performance of traditional and contemporary repertoire.

Essentially a romanticist, Kirchner's works develop rhapsodically with asymmetrical rhythms and free thematic juxtapositions. Kirchner states that each composition is conceived as an organic whole; the various movements are interrelated both in motivic content and emotional atmosphere. Kirchner admired the harmonic richness of central European composers, and the listener hears their echoes. His music has been described as "a turbulent journey, impulsive and intense, with rapid changes that disguise its logical construction."

Kirchner wrote a statement for the trio's first recording: "It is my feeling that many of us, dominated by the fear of self-expression, seek the superficial security of current style and fad…. An artist must create a personal cosmos, a verdant world in continuity with tradition, further fulfilling man's 'awareness,' his 'degree of consciousness,' and bringing new vision and beauty to the elements of experience. In this way that Idea, powered by conviction and necessity, will create its own style and the singular, momentous structure capable of realizing its intent."

The densely compact trio develops with extreme contrasts of tempo, dynamics, and texture. Within a sixteen-bar span at its opening, Kirchner instructs the players: "lyrically and tenderly (soft) … powerfully (loud) … coming from nowhere, almost out of control (very soft) … a little faster, perhaps (very loud) … strongly marked (less loud) … relaxed and flutelike (very soft)." Rapid figuration in the piano connects the motivic ideas. Although the trio is organized by a progression of variations, an improvisatory atmosphere prevails.

TERRY RILEY
B. JUNE 24, 1935 IN COLFAX, CALIFORNIA

## "In C" (1964)

Conceived on a San Francisco bus and scored for an indefinite number of performers, *In C* ushered in the age of musical minimalism. Riley, who considers himself an improvisor first and a composer second, crafted fifty-three repeating phrases lasting from half a beat to thirty-two beats; each phrase is played in order but may be repeated an arbitrary number of times so that each performance differs. It is customary for one musician to play the note C in steady eighth notes to create a metronome, or "the Pulse." This concept, which modified the original arhythmic composition, was suggested by composer Steve Reich. The work has inspired composers such as Philip Glass, John Adams, and various rock groups such as The Who. *In C* is an early example of aleatory music, in which chance elements determine the realization of the performance.

Riley's mentor La Monte Young, creator of a series of drone compositions that doubtless influenced *In C*, states that "the rigorously sequential repetition and feeling of stasis in so-called minimal music are equally rooted in certain passages from Anton Webern's compositions. There is a convincing argument that this music constitutes a meeting of the East—with its drones and modes— and the West." Recorded numerous times with varying time frames and instrumentation, *In C* catapulted Riley to cult status. As *The Guardian* observes: "*In C*, Riley's most famous work, reflects the repetitive musical structures that he had heard in North Africa. It was defined by its interactions between diverse musicians that would produce differences every time it was played. Like so many of the greatest musical breakthroughs, *In C* is simple to understand but rich, subtle, and diverse when you hear it performed."

# FIFTEEN

# Innovation and Discovery in North America

A spirit of independent exploration guides North American chamber composition of the later twentieth century and millennium. World developments—scientific and technological advances, ecological and social concerns—have inspired many composers. Some, like Chris Rogerson, convey personal experience while others, such as David Ludwig (see both below), illuminate global perceptions through allusive musical language. Ethnic and jazz elements contribute energetic diversity. Often these infusions create a crossover genre, one that hovers between classical and popular fields. Women are at last well represented, and chamber music benefits from their performance presence as well as their compositions. Humor buoys many works, possibly the result of a postmodern relaxation with the creative process. Yet the chamber music of earlier eras continues to provide a source of inspiration and standard of craft, and often it is referenced as honored thematic material.

Many of the works in this chapter have been commissioned for specific professional ensembles, always the composers' most useful resource. Composers now communicate closely with innovative groups such as the Kronos Quartet and the Jupiter Quartet. Familiar with new music's often formidable technical requirements, these players help achieve desired effects as they engage with the numerous and necessary trials—and performers gain immeasurably from such entry into the composer's world. Pianist Gloria Cheng writes of her own interactive experience:

"The reason I love my involvement with new music is that it has led me to universes that I could never otherwise have imagined. Each is a very private universe conceived from a rich personal history, philosophy, and culture; each somehow traces indefinable facets of human experience; each invites a response from deep within me. Understanding requires openness, respect, humility, and a lot of patience. The more openness we can show in the face of a new encounter, the richer our lives become."

Commissioning groups throughout North America have offered valuable encouragement by funding compositions and expanding performance opportunities. Works included in this chapter have received recognition though premieres and subsequent performances; sincere apologies must be given for the countless significant ones that are not included due to space limitations.

Because of their original development of harmonic, rhythmic, and textural practices, composers now write ever more elaborate descriptions of their works. Their comments are directly quoted throughout the chapter.

## UNITED STATES

ELLIOTT CARTER
B. DECEMBER 11, 1908 IN NEW YORK CITY,
D. NOVEMBER 5, 2012 IN NEW YORK CITY

*String Quartet No. 5 (1995)*

Introduction
Giocoso
Interlude I
Lento espressivo
Interlude II
Presto scorrevole
Interlude III
Allegro energico
Interlude IV
Adagio sereno
Interlude V
Capriccioso

Trained by Walter Piston at Harvard and Nadia Boulanger in Paris, Elliott Carter began his remarkably long career as a neo-classicist. After 1948 he found his identity as an experimentalist engaged with issues of novel formal and rhythmic organization. His intricate creations are unique constructs of a sonorous world that reward the attentive listener with glimpses of rare beauty.

The fifth quartet's introduction and interludes (the odd-numbered movements) conjure the illusion of musicians rehearsing musical ideas. In the even-numbered movements, the players perform them as coherent statements. This alternation reflects

Carter's compositional process of first exploring fragments, each comprised of pitch and rhythmic units that he terms "characters," and then assembling them into polished phrases. These brief, concentrated sections frequently suggest the meticulous structures of Anton Webern.

Carter writes about his Quartet No. 5: "One of the fascinations of attending rehearsals of chamber music, when excellent players try out fragments of what they later will play in the ensemble, then play it, and then stop abruptly to discuss how to improve, is that this pattern is so similar to our inner experience of forming, ordering, and bringing to fruition—and then dismissing—our feelings and ideas. These patterns of human behavior form the basis of the quartet. Its Introduction and Interludes present the players, one by one, trying out fragments from one of the six short contrasting ensemble movements and at the same time maintaining a dialogue with each other. In this score the matter of human cooperation with its many aspects of feeling and thought was a very important consideration."

GUNTHER SCHULLER
B. NOVEMBER 22, 1925 IN NEW YORK CITY,
D. JUNE 21, 2015 IN BOSTON

An astoundingly versatile composer, educator, and classics and jazz performer, Gunther Schuller has made a tremendous impact on American music. After many seasons as French horn player with high-profile orchestras, in the 1950s Schuller became a jazz hornist with Miles Davis. During that time Schuller and pianist John Lewis founded the Modern Jazz Society, which gave its first concert at Town Hall. The protean Schuller began to combine jazz and traditional techniques to create what he termed "Third Stream" music. Gradually he evolved into one of his generation's most eclectic composers; as one critic noted, "Schoenberg's technique meets jazz meets Stravinsky's rhythms meets Haydn in ways that one could never imagine without the score on the table." Schuller created over seventy works for a variety of chamber ensembles, each a unique statement.

## String Quartet No. 5 (2014)

Very rhythmic
Scherzando leggiero
Intermezzo leggiero
Presto

Schuller describes his work, written for the Miró Quartet: "After an introductory 'explosion,' both rhythmically and dynamically, the listener encounters subtle allusions to jazz and swing; a leisurely waltz section (marked Valse lente); and sudden unexpected contrasts of intensity. It is as if the music is suddenly interrupted by sounds from another planet. I also indulge in a 'polyphony of rhythms,' where three or four rhythms occur simultaneously. Debussy was the first to do this, heard in his 1913 ballet *Jeux* (Games).

"The second movement opens with a melancholy solo viola that leads into a lighthearted sequence full of drastic dynamic changes. The strings execute a left-hand pizzicato section, a technique invented by Paganini that alternates between bowed and plucked notes to suggest a torrent of rain drops. The melancholy opening theme returns in both retrograde motion and inversion in the first violin.

"The third movement resumes the lighter mood as it plays around with rhythmic changes that suggest Balkan folk dance. I also take some basic thematic material and displace it into the 'wrong' part of the measure, much as Charles Ives did a lot in his music, and even Brahms in the late nineteenth century.

"The finale begins as a tumultuous Presto, later using a 'walking bass' borrowed from jazz, now played pizzicato by the cello.

Occasionally there are quarter tones (please do not think the players are out of tune). I end the quartet with classical rhythms; even Mozart could have written it in one of his boisterous moods."

GEORGE CRUMB
B. OCTOBER 24, 1929 IN CHARLESTON, WEST VIRGINIA,
D. FEBRUARY 6, 2022 IN MEDIA, PENNSYLVANIA

Crumb is known for classically grounded avant-garde works realized through innovative techniques and vivid sonorities. He frequently juxtaposes contrasting styles that range from Western art music to ethnic folk. Often described as hauntingly mystical, Crumb's works reflect his penchant for theatrical elements and symbolism. During his long tenure at the University of Pennsylvania, his significant students included Jennifer Higdon and Osvaldo Golijov.

*"Vox Balaenae" (Voice of the Whale) for Three Masked Players: Electric Flute, Electric Cello, Amplified Piano (1971)*

Vocalise (... for the beginning of time)
Variations on Sea-Time
Sea-Theme
Archeozoic (Var. I)
Proterozoic (Var. II)
Paleozoic (Var. III)
Mesozoic (Var. IV)
Cenozoic (Var. V)
Sea-Nocturne (... for the end of time)

Crumb describes his work: "The instruments are all amplified in performance. The work was inspired by the singing of the humpbacked whale, a tape recording of which I heard two or three years previously. Each of the three performers is required to wear a black face mask (or visor-mask). The masks, by effacing the sense of human projection, are intended to represent, symbolically, the powerful, impersonal forces of nature (nature dehumanized). I have also suggested that the work be performed under a deep-blue stage lighting.

"The form is a simple three-part design consisting of a prologue, a set of variations named after the geological eras, and an epilogue. The opening "Vocalise" (marked in the score 'wildly fantastic, grotesque') is a kind of cadenza for the flutist, who simultaneously plays his instrument and sings into it. This combination of instrumental and vocal sound produces an eerie, surreal timbre not unlike the sounds of the humpbacked whale. The conclusion of the cadenza is announced by a parody of the opening measures of Richard Strauss's *Also sprach Zarathustra*.

"Sea-Theme ('solemn, with calm majesty') is presented by the cello (in harmonics), accompanied by dark, fateful chords of strummed piano strings. The following sequence of variations begins with haunting seagull cries of the Archeozoic ('timeless, inchoate') and gradually increasing in intensity reaches a strident climax in the Cenozoic ('dramatic, with a feeling of destiny'). The emergence of man in the Cenozoic era is symbolized by a restatement of the *Zarathustra* reference.

"The concluding Sea-Nocturne ('serene, pure, transfigured') is an elaboration of the Sea-Theme. The piece is couched in the luminous tonality of B major, and there are shimmering sounds of antique cymbals (played alternately by the cellist and flutist). In composing the Sea-Nocturne I wanted to suggest a larger rhythm of nature and a sense of suspension in time. The concluding gesture of the work is a gradually dying series of repetitions of a ten-note figure. In performance the last figure is to be played 'in pantomime' (to suggest a diminuendo beyond the threshold of hearing)!"

MARIO DAVIDOVSKY

B. MARCH 4, 1934 IN MÉDANOS, ARGENTINA,

D. AUGUST 23, 2019 IN NEW YORK CITY

Davidovsky emigrated to the United States in 1960 with the encouragement of his mentor Aaron Copland. Originally an electroacoustics specialist who paired standard instruments with electronics, Davidovsky pursued purely instrumental composition in his later years. His significant body of work has been described by the *Los Angeles Times* as "clear and compelling, drawing the listener immediately into its personal, idiosyncratic world. It handsomely rewards repeated listening and study." A longtime professor at Columbia and Harvard, Davidovsky has taught renowned composers such as Chen Yi, Zhou Long, and Lei Liang.

## String Quartet No. 6, "Fragments" (2016)

Davidovsky writes: "The meaning of the word 'Fragments' as it relates to my Quartet No. 6 is ambiguous. Commonly, the word refers to broken parts belonging to 'something,' to some object; more importantly, it here means broken (and scattered) parts that, processed by some creative force, can aggregate to become 'something.'

"The piece begins by presenting a pointillistic sequence of events/gestures, one of which has a more defined rhythmic/ timbral dance-like character that will be transformed many times. The rest of the events are a set of 'elements' that do not offer the necessary pitch/rhythmic information to define them clearly as motives but can be described in basic 'expressive' terms—very fast, percussive, or lyrical. As the narrative unfolds, all these elements reappear in new sequences and contexts, constantly reprocessing, developing, and exhibiting distinct expressive personalities—as if each time impersonating a different character of the Commedia dell'arte, then attenuating and homogenizing the differences between them."

## PHILIP GLASS
### B. JANUARY 31, 1937 IN BALTIMORE, MARYLAND

One of America's most prolific composers, Glass first became known as a minimalist who created immense dramatic works (such as his 1976 opera *Einstein on the Beach*) from almost imperceptibly changing rhythms and harmonies. Once the darling of a small cult, the protean Glass gradually became part of the musical mainstream. He has continuously enlarged his musical language by incorporating elements from rock, ethnic music, and jazz, as well as the classical techniques absorbed from his early studies with Nadia Boulanger in Paris. His large repertoire includes music for opera, dance, theater, chamber ensembles, orchestra, and numerous films such as *The Hours*, for which he received a Golden Globe Award.

*Music from "The Sound of a Voice," arranged for Pipa, Violin, Cello, Flute, and Percussion (2003)*

In his chamber opera *The Sound of a Voice* (2003), Glass sets the dream and fantasy stories of David Henry Hwang to a score combining Asian and Western elements. Glass writes: "*The Sound of a Voice* explores how intimacy is achieved between people who have lived in seclusion. In the first part, an aging Japanese warrior arrives at the home of a mysterious woman who lives like a hermit deep in the woods. Has he come as her suitor, or assassin? Does she intend to love him or to imprison him forever, like the flowers she cultivates so assiduously? The battles of love become a deadly contest in this tale, blurring the distinctions between hero and coward, between victor and vanquished. In the second part, an elderly Japanese writer visits a mysterious brothel, which caters to men near the end of their lives by providing them with a means to relive their youth. The writer's initial contempt for the house gives way first to acceptance, then to regular visits. Ultimately, he finds his dreams and fantasies exposed before the elderly Madame, and he embarks with her on an ethereal journey beyond sex and love."

JOHN HARBISON
B. DECEMBER 20, 1938 IN ORANGE, NEW JERSEY

## *"Twilight Music" for Horn, Violin, and Piano (1985)*

Composer, conductor, and longtime MIT professor John Harbison studied composition at Harvard with Walter Piston and at Princeton with Roger Sessions. Praised for his deeply expressive and inventive works, Harbison cites his most important influences as the Bach cantatas, Stravinsky, and jazz.

Harbison writes: "*Twilight Music* shelters abstract structural origins beneath a warm exterior. Since the horn and violin have little in common, any merging must be *trompe l'oreille* (a trick of the ear), and they share material mainly to show how differently they project it. The two instruments meet casually at the beginning of the piece, and they part rather formally at the end. In between they follow the piano into a Presto, which dissolves into the twilight half-tones that named the piece. The third section, an Antiphon (a responsive verse), is the crux—the origin of the piece's intervallic character. It is the kind of music I am drawn to, where the surface seems simplest and most familiar, where the piece seems to make no effort, but some purposeful, independent musical argument is at work. The final section's image of separation grows directly out of the nature of the instruments.

"This piece was commissioned by the Chamber Music Society of Lincoln Center for performance by David Jolley, James Buswell, and Richard Goode. Such virtuosity as possessed by these artists allowed me to write with reckless subtlety for instruments which I heard meeting best under cover of dusk."

JOAN TOWER
B. SEPTEMBER 6, 1938 IN NEW ROCHELLE, NEW YORK

Joan Tower is one of this generation's most dynamic and colorful composers. Her bold and energetic compositions, developed with dynamic energy and novel structural forms, have won large, enthusiastic audiences. She has been active as founder and pianist for the award-winning Da Capo Chamber Players; a celebrated conductor; and longtime Professor of Composition at Bard College. Because of her knowledge of each instrument's potential, Tower's writing is both challenging and flattering for its performers.

## "Night Fields" for String Quartet (1994)

Tower describes her composition: "*Night Fields*, my first string quartet, is a one-movement work and lasts about sixteen minutes. The title, conceived after the work was completed, provides an image or setting for some of the moods of the piece: a cold, windy night in a wheat field lit up by a bright, full moon where waves of fast-moving colors ripple over the fields, occasionally settling on a patch of gold."

A darkly reflective solo violin line introduces the work, which gradually grows in fervency to suggest furious winds. The mood calms to convey the serenity of a broad nocturnal landscape.

## "Wild Summer" for String Quartet, from "Four Seasons/Four Composers" (2019)

The composer writes: "*Wild Summer* was commissioned as part of the Jasper String Quartet's homage to Vivaldi's *Four Seasons*. I was asked to represent summer. The first thoughts I had about summer were memories of when I was younger and going to school. Although I was expected to get a summer job, it was also a time for a vacation to finally be free and to have a really good time. Since I was a rather wild teenager, I vividly remember being intent on as much dancing, partying, and going after the boys as possible. This goal had an intense manic side to it that bordered on an anxiety, a possible failure of actually having a good time, sort of like the vacation you fantasized about that never quite worked out the way you expected. This nine-minute piece alternates between a driving, wild, and manic type of energy with a relaxed, meditative, slow feeling in between—a breathing and recuperating space (on the beach)."

## ELLEN TAAFFE ZWILICH
### B. APRIL 30, 1939 IN MIAMI, FLORIDA

Zwilich earned dual distinction as the first woman to receive a doctorate in composition from the Juilliard School, where her teachers included Elliott Carter and Roger Sessions, and the first woman to be awarded the Pulitzer Prize (for her 1983 Symphony No. 1). A prolific composer in virtually all media, she creates compelling works characterized by long melodic lines, sophisticated rhythmic treatment, and virtuoso writing. Her works, commissioned by groups such as the New York Philharmonic and The Chamber Music Society of Lincoln Center, have been described as reflective of an optimistic and uniquely humanistic spirit.

*Piano Trio (1987)*

Allegro con brio
Lento
Presto

Zwilich describes her work: "Many of my favorite works for piano trio are duos in which the two strings together balance the piano. In the interest of formal and aesthetic balance, I took a similar approach. I also decided to exploit the essential differences between the strings and keyboard, allowing some materials to arise from the nature of the piano and some to be generated by the nature of string instruments. Most often the material is taken up and reinterpreted by the other family; sometimes the material forms a basis for a dialogue with the other. Ultimately, however, the instruments are three equal voices of exploration.

"My ideal performers possess the kind of virtuosity that combines exhilarating athleticism with real musical values and feeling. In anticipation of that kind of performance from the Kalichstein-Laredo-Robinson Trio, this work was written in a 'white heat'—very quickly for me—and I feel it to be a particularly immediate and personal statement.

"The dramatic opening Allegro explores both the virtuoso and lyrical capabilities of the three instruments. The Lento, piquant in atmosphere because of its arpeggiations and pizzicati, opens with harmonics in the strings against rhythmic counterpoint in both hands of the piano. Strong rhythms drive both the Allegro and the final Presto. The brief and coda-like Presto is built on rapid scale figures that suggest Shostakovich."

## Quintet for Alto Saxophone and String Quartet (2007)

Quarter note = 66
Quarter note =132
Quarter note = 60, 126, 120

Zwilich writes: "My concept for chamber music is a conversation among equals, a dialogue that is unique to the parties involved. In this instance the alto sax brings a luscious singing quality and a certain sassy attitude to the mix, while the strings offer their amazing agility and variety of articulation, color, and phrasing. One of the great pleasures of writing (or playing or listening to) chamber music is that each player can be a virtuoso soloist one moment and a sensitive partner the next, and the 'electricity' becomes an agent of musical form."

## *Quintet for Piano, Violin, Viola, Cello, and Double Bass (2010)*

Quarter note = 60
Fantasy, "Die launische Forelle"
Quarter note = 120

Zwilich's quintet reveals an affinity for jazz and her keen musical playfulness. She comments: "My quintet (for the same instrumentation as the great 'Trout' Quintet by Franz Schubert) is in three movements, the second of which has a title roughly translated as "The Moody Trout." I couldn't resist using a very small quote from the Schubert song on which his quintet is based. I also took the liberty of allowing that movement to spin out musical images of a 'moody' trout. In all three movements the weight and character of the contrabass is an important element in the overall design. I'm especially interested in the possibilities offered by the contemporary contrabass player's virtuosity and artistry which allows the composer to reach for that chamber music ideal of equal partners."

CHICK COREA
B. JUNE 12, 1941 IN CHELSEA, MASSACHUSETTS,
D. FEBRUARY 9, 2021 IN TAMPA BAY, FLORIDA

## *"The Adventures of Hippocrates" for String Quartet (2004)*

Quasi Tango
Waltz
Ballad
Rock
Fugue

Corea's colleague Joel Evans offers commentary on this multi-dimensional composer, whose solid classical foundation supported his work across genres: "Chick Corea is one of America's foremost popular artists. Many of his compositions are considered jazz standards, and he has been described as one of the major jazz piano voices to emerge in the post-John Coltrane era. His career has been driven by his will to operate as a free agent and compulsively explore different avenues of music making. He is an important catalyst in the world of serious, mainstream acoustic jazz and one of the most influential figures in the last forty years.

"*The Adventures of Hippocrates* was commissioned for the Orion Quartet by the Santa Fe Chamber Music Festival in collaboration with the summer festivals at La Jolla and Caramoor. Corea's first and only string quartet is a 'serious' work rooted in his jazz background and twentieth-century styles. It is a suite of five contrasting movements that explore different tempos and rhythmic frames—including first a tango that directly quotes from Astor Piazzolla and secondly a lilting, nostalgic Waltz. The Fugue finale, played with 'a swiftly moving tempo,' shows his considerable contrapuntal skills. Throughout the entire piece there are jazzy syncopations, irregular rhythms, and sound effects like slapbass pizzicati. What Hippocrates has to do with it is not explained.

"Although Corea will not reveal the origin of his whimsical title, his aficionados believe that the work was inspired by a robot-like character named Hippocrates which appears in Ron Hubbard's 1954 science fiction book *To the Stars.*"

JOHN ADAMS
B. FEBRUARY 15, 1947 IN WORCESTER, MASSACHUSETTS

*String Quartet No. 2 (2014)*

Allegro molto
Andantino—Energico

A composer with strong roots in the minimalist movement, John Adams is known for operas such as *Nixon in China* (1987) and *Doctor Atomic* (2005), the subject of which is the Manhattan Project. His music is characterized by elements of Romanticism in that it develops humanistic themes with expressive climactic moments. He states: "I use the fabric of continually repeating cells to forge large architectonic shapes, creating a web of activity that ... knows light and dark, serenity and turbulence." Although repeating cells create a strong rhythmic/melodic framework, his music unfolds with surprising elements that create a sense of spontaneity.

The St. Lawrence String Quartet, who advised Adams as he composed Quartet No. 2, comments: "The quartet is based on tiny fragments—'fractals,' in the composer's words—from Beethoven. The economy here is strict. The first movement, for example, is entirely based on two short phrases from the Scherzo of the late Opus 110 Piano Sonata in A flat Major. The transformations of harmony, cadential patterns, and rhythmic profile go way beyond manipulations of Beethoven motifs in the earlier Adams work *Absolute Jest*, written for the St. Lawrence String Quartet and orchestra.

"This new work is organized in two parts. The first movement has a scherzo impetus, and it moves at the fastest pace possible for the performers to play. The familiar Beethoven cadences and half cadences reappear throughout the movement like a homing mechanism, and each apparition is followed by a departure to an increasingly remote key and textural region.

"The second part begins Andantino with a gentle melody drawn from the opening movement of the same piano sonata. Here the original Beethoven harmonic and melodic ideas go off in unexpected directions, almost as if they were suggestions for compositional free association.

"The Andantino grows in range and complexity until it finally leads into the Energico final area, a treatment of one of the shorter Diabelli Variations. This variation features a sequence of neighbor-key appoggiaturas, each a half step away from the main chord. Adams amplifies this chromatic relationship without intentionally distorting it. Like its original Beethoven model, the movement is characterized by emphatic gestures, frequent use of *sforzando* (abruptly loud), and a busy but convivial mood of hyper-activity among the four instruments."

STEPHEN PAULUS
B. AUGUST 24, 1949 IN SUMMIT, NEW JERSEY,
D. OCTOBER 19, 2014 IN ARDEN HILLS, MINNESOTA

*"Exotic Etudes" for Viola and Piano Quartet (2000)*

Energetic
Dark and Austere
Shimmering
Melodious
Vibrant

Prolific in all genres, including orchestra, opera, chamber ensemble, and solo voice, Paulus was appointed Composer-in-Residence of the Minnesota Orchestra and subsequently the Atlanta Symphony. During his residency its conductor, Robert Shaw, commissioned numerous vocal works for his eponymous chorale. A composer with a strong sense of lyricism, Paulus has received recognition for operas such as *The Postman Always Rings Twice* (1982). *Exotic Etudes* was premiered at the 2000 Tucson Winter Chamber Music Festival.

Paulus writes: "The work is an abstract instrumental character sketch casting the viola in a quasi-concerto role—the viola becomes a character with its distinct personality and is accompanied by violin, viola, cello and piano. The movement titles suggest a quilt-like work organized for balance, variety, and contrast. A wide range of contemporary techniques (pizzicati, angular melodies, mixed meters and unusual instrumental positions) test the musicality and agility of the performers. I hear each instrument as being equally important in its contribution to the work as a whole. The quartet always allows the solo violist moments of prominence that highlight its special statements.

"Each of the first four movements opens with a duet between the soloist and one of the quartet players. In the spirit of camaraderie, the opening movement begins with an animated duet between the two violists. The second movement explores the dark instrumental color possibilities of both cello and viola. The third movement capitalizes on the piano's ability to create a shimmering sound. Movement four plays to the violin's melodic and lyrical strength. All players join from the beginning in the final movement. In effect, each member of the quartet has introduced itself to the viola and has emphasized a particular quality of its own instrument."

PAUL DRESHER
B. JANUARY 8, 1951 IN LOS ANGELES

*"Double Ikat" for Violin, Piano, and Percussion*
*(1989, revised 1990)*

Part One
Part Two

After graduating from University of California branches at Berkeley and San Diego with degrees in composition, Dresher studied Ghanaian drumming, Hindustani classical music, and Balinese and Javanese music with various masters. Known for his ability to integrate diverse influences into his own personal style, Dresher has created experimental opera, live instrumental electro-acoustic chamber music, and numerous scores for theater, dance, and film. As Artistic Director of the Paul Dresher Ensemble, he has guided the creation of the American Trilogy, a set of music theater works that address different facets of American culture.

Dresher describes his hypnotic *Double Ikat*: "For several years, percussionist William Winant had been pestering me to write a piece for a San Francisco trio he was working with. After I finally heard the trio perform, I was truly inspired to create a work for them.

"The opportunity came when I was commissioned by ODC/ Dance (San Francisco) to compose a score for their new work, *Loose the Thread*. I took the opportunity to compose a work for both the dance and the trio. The version that resulted took its form largely from the choreography; I took the material from that work and recomposed and edited it into an entirely different form, strictly as a concert work.

"The title refers to a style of weaving common in South East Asia in which both the threads of the warp and weave are dyed to create the pattern or image. For me, the title relates both to the interrelationships of the three instruments and to the title of the choreographic work from which it sprang. The last section of Part Two of the work is an homage to North Indian sitarist Nikhil Banerjee, one of the finest musicians of this century, who died in 1986."

DANIEL ASIA
B. JUNE 27, 1953 IN SEATTLE, WASHINGTON

*Nonet for Flute, Oboe, Clarinet, Bassoon, Horn, Violin, Viola, Cello, and Double Bass (2010)*

Impetuous, contemplative
Moderato
Allegro, molto ritmico
Adagio
Allegro
Lively

An eclectic composer, conductor, educator, and writer, Asia is the driving force for the University of Arizona School of Music's American Culture and Ideas Initiative, a pedagogical worldview that sees the arts as tied to humanity's innovations and embedded in its survival. The recipient of a Guggenheim Fellowship and four NEA Composers Grants, Asia has composed extensively for chamber artists.

Asia writes: "The work was written for the Czech Nonet, the world's longest continuously performing chamber ensemble. Movements I, III, and V are less than a minute and are three takes on the same materials, which are boisterous and then melancholic. The presentations are quite different in character, as appropriate for their positioning in the work, with the materials being reordered as well as varied. The first, introductory in quality, with much doubling, and fanfare-like rhythms, is contrasted with an area of sweet repose. Movement III is much fuller harmonically and is contrasted by sharp syncopations and a strong jazz-like sensibility. Movement V, the third and final take on this material, is reminiscent of the first movement in its lean texture. At the same time, it is more rhythmically complex, with the two lines occasionally going their own way.

"Movements II, IV, and VI are the real meat of the work. Movement II, Moderato, is a set of variations. The mood is restrained but optimistic. It is punctuated by occasional cadenzas, the material of which sometimes invades or seeps into the variations themselves. The overall flow and structure of the movement is arch-like, with a building of energy from the beginning to the middle, then a gradual receding to the end. Movement IV is a gently lyrical adagio that is mostly meditative in quality. Whereas the other movements sparkle with quick and rapid changes of texture and color, this movement highlights different small groups. Movement VI is an all-out presto, full of devilish twists and turns. It combines rapid registral shifts, dizzying changes of texture, and wickedly abrupt dynamic changes. It provides a rollicking conclusion to the entire work."

BRUCE ADOLPHE
B. MAY 31, 1955 IN NEW YORK CITY

*"Machaut is my Beginning" for Flute, Clarinet, Violin, Cello, and Piano (1989)*

Composer and music scholar Bruce Adolphe has written inventive works for a vast range of chamber music's most creative artists. In 2009 Yo-Yo Ma premiered his *Self Comes to Mind*, a neuroscience-inspired work for solo cello and two percussionists; Adolphe collaborated with neuroscientist Antonio Damasio, who contributed its poetic text about the evolution of consciousness. In 2011 Adolphe composed *Reach Out, Raise Hope, Change Society*, a cantata on themes of social justice, civil rights, and freedom, and in 2019 he wrote *I saw how fragile and infinitely precious the world is* for mezzo soprano, cello, and recorded sounds from space (provided by NASA). He writes numerous works for young listeners as part of his education company, The Learning Maestros.

Adolphe comments: "The Da Capo Chamber Players asked me to recompose a canon written by Guillaume de Machaut, the most significant composer of fourteenth-century France. I happily undertook the project, and I looked at his clever and catchy little canon translated as 'My end is my beginning' with the idea of somehow arranging it for their ensemble. It turned out to be a fun assignment, a kind of game within a game. For Machaut's ditty is already an elaborate polyphonic toy, a retrograde ('crab') canon of exquisite design and mechanical interest. The rules of my game were to use only his notes and rhythms, either as they were, or as cells to generate familiar if somewhat mutated clones. The tinkerer in me enjoyed this, but I also had to give in to my romantic side, which contributed the dreamy passages which are like the hallucinations of elusive phrases by Machaut."

RICHARD DANIELPOUR
B. JANUARY 28, 1956 IN NEW YORK CITY

*"The Book of Hours" for Piano Quartet (2006)*

Morning
Midday
Afternoon into Evening
Night

Associated Music Publishers of America writes of Richard Danielpour: "He has established himself as one of the most gifted and sought-after composers of his generation. A distinctive American voice, Danielpour's music is made from large and romantic gestures, brilliantly orchestrated and rhythmically vibrant. His work has attracted an illustrious array of champions, and, as a devoted mentor and educator, he has also made a significant impact on a younger generation of composers. Much in demand across the globe, Richard Danielpour's music has been heard throughout the United States and abroad and his commissions read like a Who's Who of the world's leading musical institutions and artists."

Danielpour comments: "*The Book of Hours* represents the twenty-four-hour cycle beginning with morning or first light. That the cycle is itself a metaphor for the life cycle has always been of interest to me. Distinctly related to an idea (though not in musical material) is an earlier work of mine, *Psalms* for piano solo. The three movements in that work are titled 'Morning,' 'Afternoon,' and 'Evening.'

"As my friend the late Stephen Albert once said to me, turning fifty reminds one that there are a limited number of hours left in our lives. And so, having reached the half century mark in January 2006, I am not only constantly reminded of our mortality, but also the blessedness of being alive regardless of how good or bad a day we are having. This idea of course requires constant reminding. *The Book of Hours* was for me created to be one such reminder. It was also written to be a remembrance of one other idea—that all things live and die—and live again."

EDGAR MEYER
B. NOVEMBER 24, 1960 IN TULSA, OKLAHOMA

*Trio No. 1 for Violin, Cello, and Double Bass (1986)*

Allegro moderato
Andante
Moderato
Allegro vivace

String bass virtuoso Meyer is considered a stylistic chameleon. A highly inventive composer, he collaborates with a wide range of prominent musicians in both the classical and popular fields. His luminous, eclectic works draw from bluegrass, jazz, Bartók-tinged classicism, and a variety of folk and ethnic styles. Meyer is a long-standing member of the Telluride Bluegrass Festival's "super-group" that includes luminaries such as banjo virtuoso Béla Fleck.

Meyer writes: "This trio was written as the first of a set of three string trios for the Santa Fe Chamber Music Festival. The work can be split into two separate pieces between the first and second movements. The final three movements form a continuous structure that is held together by increasing activity and harmonies not fully resolved until the finale. The first movement is more self-contained. It is clear cut with a simple melody and a 'noodly' idea to contrast it. These two items are presented individually, then smashed together in the loud and busy middle section and pulled apart at the end of the movement.

"The emphasis shifts to rhythm in the last two movements. Performance techniques from outside classical music are used, including bowing patterns and pitch embellishments common to different types of traditional fiddle music. The finale is an energetic rondo."

WYNTON MARSALIS
B. OCTOBER 18, 1961 IN NEW ORLEANS

## *String Quartet No. 1, "At the Octoroon Balls" (1995)*

Come Long Fiddler
Mating Calls and Delta Rhythms
Creole Contradanzas
Many Gone
Hellbound Highball
Blue Lights on the Bayou
Rampart St. Row House Rag

Perhaps because he grew up in the richly diverse musical environment of New Orleans, trumpeter and composer Wynton Marsalis moves with ease between classical and jazz venues. In recent years composing has occupied more of his time. "I have always been interested in string quartets, especially those of Beethoven," says Marsalis. "However, my principal interest is 'How does it sound?' as compared to how the composition deals with issues of form."

The Chamber Music Society of Lincoln Center and Jazz at Lincoln Center commissioned Marsalis to create a string quartet for their landmark joint concert. The Orion String Quartet, who premiered the work, advised Marsalis about scoring to produce the maximum range of tonal effects. The resulting quartet's seven sections (a selection of four often performed as a group) evocatively develop rhythms and melodies inspired by Marsalis's early life in New Orleans. The quartet is significant for its breakthrough crossing of style and genre lines.

The string quartet is also a musical tribute to an old New Orleans tradition called the Quadroon Balls. Marsalis describes the background: "The balls were designed to introduce Louisiana's Creole young men to women with one black and three white grandparents.

The mixed ancestry was widely considered to provide these women with remarkable beauty. The next generation would be octoroon, so that's where the title figured. A ball is a ritual and a dance—everybody was in his finest clothing, and people from different strata of society came together in pursuit of pleasure and fulfillment. The music brought people together."

JENNIFER HIGDON
B. DECEMBER 31, 1962 IN NEW YORK CITY

One of America's most frequently performed composers, Higdon creates works appreciated by both critics and audiences as being warmly communicative and inspiriting. Her music has been hailed by *Fanfare Magazine* as having "the distinction of being at once complex, sophisticated but readily accessible emotionally." *The Times* of London praised it as "traditionally rooted yet imbued with integrity and freshness." She holds an Artist's Diploma from the Curtis Institute, a Ph.D. in composition from the University of Pennsylvania, and she has received several honorary doctorates.

*Piano Trio (2003)*

Pale Yellow
Fiery Red

Higdon writes: "Can music reflect colors and can colors be reflected in music? I have always been fascinated with the connection between painting and music. In my composing, I often picture colors as if I were spreading them on a canvas, except I do so with melodies. The colors that I have chosen in both movement titles and in the music itself reflect very different moods and energy levels, which I find fascinating, as it begs the question: can colors actually convey a mood?"

The two movements present a fascinating diptych. "Pale Yellow" is a meditative pastorale that creates a gentle prelude to the driving energy of "Fiery Red." Colorful piano glissandi and emphatic punctuations from the strings propel this movement of exhilarating ferocity.

## "Color Through" for Piano, Violin, and Cello (2016)

Wondrous White
Brilliant Blue

In Higdon's second piano trio she continues to ponder the questions posed in her first piano trio. She states that the movements of both piano trios can be combined to form the *Color Through Piano Trio* or *Piano Trio Color Through*. She reflects on the emotional properties of color:

"Wondrous White. The symbolism of white ... religious, bright, hopeful. And the immense use of white in all art ... start out as some form of white, in preparation for painting, and it is often used as a highlight, to lighten, and to create a glow. In fact, in scientific terms, white is the presence of all colors ... our eyes perceive the collection of all colors together as 'white.'

"Brilliant Blue. Blue represents so many different moods ... from the literal term of feeling blue to the blue sky. The recent discovery of a new form of blue made me think about all the different permutations a color has. And for me, the things that 'Blue' represents."

### AUGUSTA READ THOMAS
#### B. APRIL 24, 1964 IN GLEN COVE, NEW YORK

The American Academy of Arts and Letters states that "Augusta Read Thomas has become one of the most recognizable and widely loved figures in American music." Educated at Yale, Northwestern, and the Royal Academy of Music, Thomas served ten years as resident composer for the Chicago Symphony, during which time she premiered nine commissioned orchestral works and helped establish the MusicNOW series. A lyricist, Thomas is said to sing as she composes, and she dances to feel rhythms. A creator of viscerally felt works, she writes: "All the art that I cherish has an element of love, recklessness, and desperation. I like music that is alive, music that jumps off the page and out of the instrument as if something big is at stake."

## *"...a circle around the sun..." for Piano Trio (2000)*

## *"Moon Jig" for Piano Trio (2005)*

Thomas writes about her two companion trios: "The first work's title refers to George D. Kennedy, who is honored for his generous support of the Children's Hospital in Chicago. He gives energy to children in need like a circle around the sun, giving strength and warmth. The music starts with a G (for George) when, slowly, orbits of sonorous and fragile notes unfold and spiral outward creating a gracious and vibrant resonance. After sixty seconds, the piece bursts forth with a good deal of energy, like a sun-flare or like children scattering on a playground in all directions, and later returns briefly to the opening materials on the pitch G.

"...*a circle around the sun...* can be paired with *Moon Jig*; the two works can be played independently or in either order. Somewhat of a cross between 'Jazz' and 'Classical,' *Moon Jig* can be heard as a series of outgrowths and variations, which are organic and concerned with transformations and connections. The piano serves as the protagonist as well as the fulcrum point on and around which the musical force-fields rotate, bloom, and proliferate.... A multifaceted merging process finally results in one long sweep of music rushing in its highest registers of the trio, as if the Jig leaped skyward and moonward."

*"Murmurs in the Mist of Memory" for Eleven Solo Strings (2001)*

Ceremonial
Lullaby
Ritual
Incantation

From the composer: "Written for the International Sejong Soloists, the piece possesses a wide spectrum of nuance, at times lyrical, abstract, passionate, subtle, vivid, aggressive, colorful, floating, rhythmic, elegant, clean, or light. Each movement reflects a different aspect of the Soloist's performing technique—individual and collective—left hand as well as bow arm. The aim was to capture, concisely, a specific 'universe' or 'mood' in each movement in the short space of three or four minutes, such that the musicians would escort the listener through a mini suite of diverse expeditions into remembrances.

"Each of the movements is inspired by a short poem of Emily Dickinson. Each poem reveals impressions having to do with *light*."

*Poem 228*
Blazing in Gold and quenching in Purple
Leaping like leopards to the Sky
Then at the feet of the old Horizon
Laying her spotted Face to die
Stooping as low as the Otter's Window
Touching the Roof and tinting the Barn
Kissing her Bonnet to the Meadow
And the Juggler of Day is gone.

*Poem 1577*
Morning is due to all—
To some—the Night—
To an imperial few—
The Auroral light.

*Poem 1541*
No matter where the Saints abide,
They make their Circuit fair
Behold how great a Firmament
Accompanies a Star.

*Poem 1556*
Image of Light, Adieu—
Thanks for the interview—
So long—so short
Preceptor of the whole—
Coeval Cardinal—
Impart—Depart.

## PIERRE JALBERT
### B. 1967 IN MANCHESTER, NEW HAMPSHIRE

Pierre Jalbert has developed a personal musical language that draws inspiration from sources as varied as natural phenomena and ancient plainchant. The *Los Angeles Times* states that "his music holds the listener through a canny blend of instrumental colors and combinations, chromatic but not dissonant, and ultimately pleasing." Among his many honors is The Chamber Music Society of Lincoln Center's 2006 Stoeger Prize, given biennially "in recognition of achievement in the field of chamber music composition."

## *"Secret Alchemy" for Piano Quartet (2012)*

Mystical
Agitated, relentless
Timeless, mysterious, reverberant
With great energy

Jalbert writes: "With any new composition, there is a sense of discovery and mystery during the creative process. Though the piece is not programmatic, imagining the air of secrecy and mysticism surrounding a medieval alchemist at work provided a starting point.

"The first movement begins with this sense of mystery. String harmonics are used to create the rhythmic backdrop for melodic lines played by the cello and, later, the viola. The second movement is a relentless scherzo characterized by pizzicato strings, turbulent piano writing, and quickly alternating rhythmic patterns. The third movement is influenced by medieval music with its use of open fifths, chant-like lines played non-vibrato by the strings, and reverberant piano harmonies, simulating the sound and reverberation in a large cathedral. The fourth movement concludes the work with an energetic music characterized by strings playing fast measured tremolo figures (rapid movement of the bow back and forth on the string). These alternate with the piano's massive chords and occasional rapid melodic figures, along with muted tones emanating from inside the piano."

## *Piano Trio No. 2 (2014)*

Mysterious, nocturnal, desolate
Agitated, relentless

From the composer: "Written for the Morgenstern Trio, this work is in two movements of contrasting character. A couple of ideas inspired each movement: the first was the thought of a desert landscape at night, desolate and calm; the second came from an incident driving home in Houston. I was driving late at night on an elevated highway, which runs through the center of town. Everyone was going at a high rate of speed, some cars were weaving in and out of lanes. As I glanced at the downtown skyline, the buildings seemed to be going in slow motion, even though our cars were going very fast. This provided the impetus for the second movement. The music is not intended to be pictorial—it is absolute music. These were simply starting points, and the music itself eventually developed on its own terms."

### VALERIE COLEMAN
#### B. 1970 IN LOUISVILLE, KENTUCKY

Composer, flute virtuoso, and Imani Winds founder Valerie Coleman has contributed numerous works to the wind chamber repertory, many of which have been recorded with Imani by Naxos, Blue Note, El Music, and International Opus. In 2020 Coleman was named "Classical Woman of the Year" by *Performance Today*. A graduate of the Mannes School of Music, Coleman incorporates diverse styles into her compositions—jazz, classical, and politically motivated popular themes continuously interweave.

### *"Red Clay and Mississippi Delta" for Wind Quintet (2009)*

From the composer: "*Red Clay* is a short work that combines the traditional idea of a musical scherzo with living in the South. It references the background of my mother's side of the family that hails from the Mississippi Delta region—from the juke joints and casino boats that line the Mississippi River, to the skin tones of kinfolk in the area: a dark skin that looks like it comes directly from the red clay. The solo lines are instilled as personality, meant to capture the listener's attention as they wail with 'bluesy' riffs accompanied ('comped') by the rest of the ensemble. The result is a virtuosic chamber work that merges classical techniques and orchestration with the blues dialect and charm of the South."

## "Umoja: The First Day of Kwanza" for Wind Quintet (2001)

Commended by Chamber Music America as one of the "Top 101 Great American Works," *Umoja* originated from Coleman's earlier unpublished anthem for women's choir. An expanded version with the subtitle "Anthem for Unity" (2019) was commissioned and performed by the Philadelphia Orchestra, the first time a work by a living African-American woman has received this honor.

Coleman writes: "Umoja is the Swahili word for 'unity.' This work is a traditional call-and-response, and the call-and-response tradition was a way of passing on history, messages, stories, whatever it may be. As a composer, I'm a storyteller, so *Umoja* is going to take the listener on a story about unity, and I think this is a message that we need today, more than ever."

### KEVIN PUTS
#### B. JANUARY 3, 1972 IN ST. LOUIS, MISSOURI

Known for his distinctively textured musical voice, Puts has been praised as a lyricist whose contemporary idiom "allows the musicians to shine at their best, both in execution and expressivity" (*The Boston Music Intelligencer*). He has created a large body of works that have been commissioned, performed, and recorded throughout North America, Europe, and the Far East. Puts received his training as a composer and pianist at Yale and the Eastman School of Music, which emphatically stated: "Puts can now be described as one of America's most important composers, period." He is a member of the composition department at the Peabody Institute in Baltimore.

*Quintet for Piano, Violin, Viola, Cello, and Double Bass,*
*"The Red Snapper" (2005)*

Molto adagio
Scherzo: Prestissimo energico
Tema: Adagio e variazioni

From the composer: "The quintet (affectionately titled *Red Snapper Quintet*) was commissioned by Robert Freeman and his family in memory of his father Henry Freeman. The first bassist to graduate from the Eastman School of Music, Henry joined the Boston Symphony and served for twenty years, the last two years as principal bassist.

"The story behind the work's creation may be of interest. It was intended to serve as a companion piece to Franz Schubert's 'Trout' Quintet. To further develop this connection, Mr. Freeman commissioned poet Jack Brannon to compose a poem entitled 'Red Snapper,' the first stanza of which I was asked to set to music. I would then use this music as the theme for a set of variations somewhere in the quintet, since the fourth movement of Schubert's quintet is a theme with variations on his own song 'Die Forelle' (The Trout).

"This variation set became the third movement of my piece, and the intervals and general qualities of its theme are foreshadowed by a series of slowly descending melodies in the first movement. The second movement is a short but very virtuosic scherzo played prestissimo, and some of the music here found its way into the seventh and final variation in the third movement. A very high, fragile series of bell-tones opens the first movement and sets the mood for the entire piece. This material returns as a moment of reflection near the end of the work, and it came to me immediately after reading Jack Brannon's poem for the first time."

*Red Snapper*

It hangs above the pier's rank bustle,
Shimmering vermilion orb,
Trophy stunning as a second sun,
Gilt on the luster of day's last light.

A prize-star fixed by unseen wire,
The fish outshines its sun-scorched anglers
Proudly caught in gleeful portraits
Lit by dazzle from their catch's red glare.

Lordly luminary: bright-prismed oval
Rivets our gaze on its heavenly form—
Sublime crown of crimson armor
Declined below fins to silver eclipse.

No prisoner of the sky's pale void,
This god springs like mighty Poseidon,
Violet sovereign over blue-deep realms
It rules iridescent, vanishing free.

*Jack Brannon*

LERA AUERBACH
B. OCTOBER 21, 1973 IN CHELYABINSK, SOVIET UNION

Born in the former Soviet Union, Lera Auerbach defected
to the United States while still in her teens. She soon entered the
Juilliard School, where she studied composition with Milton
Babbitt and piano with Joseph Kalichstein. A virtuoso performer,
Auerbach continues the great nineteenth-century tradition of
pianist-composers. Also a prolific writer, Auerbach has won recognition for her volumes of poetry and prose, several of which are
required reading in Russian high schools and universities. She has
recorded for companies worldwide.

## String Quartet No. 4, "Findings" (2007)

Con moto, marcato
Andante (...from the silence of memories the theme is born?)
Religioso, dolce misterioso
Moderato (Michelangelo's trumpets?)
Allegretto (Dance of shadows?)
Andante (A carousel in the time of war?)
Agitato scherzando (Games in the Jewish ghetto?)
Recitativo andante
Misterioso lento
Moderato energico
Scherzando
Andante, ma con moto
Andante misterioso sognando (Faces of Time?)
Prestissimo (The wind of oblivion?)
Andante
Adagio molto, misterioso, ad libitum

Auerbach offers a narrative: "The score is a group of manuscripts found in the attic of an old house near Hamburg, where I stayed for a night unable to continue my journey because of a storm. The owner of the house, a small bed-and-breakfast type of place, upon hearing that I was a musician, asked me to look through a pile of music paper he had in the attic. Apparently, the house owner's father was a collector, but a collector of a most unusual sort. He would keep other people's memories: scraps of paper, broken dishes, old dolls with missing arms, empty bottles of unknown medicines, and other peculiar and completely useless things. His son, an old man already, was determined to clean up the mess and turn this attic into an extra bedroom. His father had died a few years ago and most of his collection no longer made sense to keep.

"The attic was in a chaotic state, full of strange objects, books, spider webs, mannequins, all covered in thick layers of dust. The old man opened one of the trunks and brought out a yellow pile of handwritten music pages. He asked if these could be of any use to me. I said I did not know. Then, he asked me to take the pages anyway and do with them as I pleased or he would simply throw them away. I took the pages.

"I saw, by the handwriting, that they had been written by more than one person. The pages were not numbered in any way—musical excerpts with no clear beginnings or endings. Some pages were half-eaten by mice, others torn, some had dark brown stains, possibly leftovers of wax or glue, and for the most part entirely missed any tempi or dynamic indications.

"I did not know what to do—it all made so little sense, yet simply to throw these pages away did not feel right. After all, nothing is purely accidental in life, and for some reason fate brought me to this strange house. So, I decided to call these musical fragments 'Inventions' in the literal translation: 'findings,' and to publish them together as such. I took some additional liberties and suggested some tempi as well as possible titles to some excerpts—just some images that came to my mind, but these could be ignored all together as they were not in the original manuscripts.

"Although these composers may have had very different skills and backgrounds, and may have lived during different times, perhaps even centuries apart, these short pieces formed a strange collection of unrealized musical dreams."

DAVID LUDWIG
B. 1974 IN BUCKS COUNTY, PENNSYLVANIA

Born into an eminent musical family that includes pianists Rudolf and Peter Serkin, David Ludwig was educated at Oberlin College, the Manhattan School of Music, and the Curtis Institute, where he was mentored by Richard Danielpour, Jennifer Higdon, and Ned Rorem. He holds a Ph.D. from the University of

Pennsylvania, where he was the George Crumb Fellow. Ludwig has written for many musicians and ensembles, including the Philadelphia Orchestra and the National Symphony Orchestra. His choral work *The New Colossus* was performed at the 2013 inauguration of Barack Obama.

*Piano Trio No. 3, "Spiral Galaxy" (2017)*

Spiral Galaxy
Galactic Halo
Sagittarius A*

Ludwig writes about *Spiral Galaxy*: "My third piano trio is inspired by our cosmic home the Milky Way: many of my pieces are motivated by some relationship to science and observation. In this trio I have used principles from math and physics to guide its musical ideas, shapes and language. And the individual movements of the piece are each in their own way a direct reflection on specific galactic features.

"The eponymous first movement 'Spiral Galaxy' begins with a fragmented series of notes that wind outward from a single starting point, growing gradually into an extended musical line, followed by a spiraling aria. The second movement 'Galactic Halo' musically describes the sphere of stars that radiates out from the galaxy. This movement is concerned with the slowly evolving colors and static canopy of the firmament, held up in the extended sonorities of the trio instruments. The last movement, 'Sagittarius A*' is an homage to the great black hole in the middle of the Milky Way, and for this I've written a swirling fugue that continually pulls downward. At the end of the movement comes the final draw of its gravity into loud disintegration, and then finally, the quiet serenity of oblivion.

"On a more (literally) poetic level, I was moved in writing this trio by the idea of the spiral, itself, and how that shape is a metaphor for the growing connections (and complications) of our lives.

Lines from two poems occur to me—one from Yeats: 'Turning and turning in the widening gyre,' and this from Rilke:

> I live my life in expanding rings
> That pull across over all existence.
> I may not complete the last one's ending,
> But I will try."

MICHAEL DJUPSTROM
B. 1980 IN ST. PAUL, MINNESOTA

## *String Quartet No. 2 (2018)*

Pesante
Largamente, expansive
Poco pesante—Giocoso, non troppo allegro

Michael Djupstrom has a special passion for chamber music, and he has received numerous commissions from leading ensembles for performances worldwide. He holds an Artist Diploma from the Curtis Institute, where he studied with Jennifer Higdon and Richard Danielpour. Fascinated by Romanian culture, Djupstrom has founded a concert series at White Bear Lake, Minnesota with a focus on its chamber works.

Djupstrom writes: "As with a few other recent works, my interest in the classical and folk music of Romania served as a springboard to launch work on this quartet. A few years ago I spent time in Bucharest exploring various facets of the city's musical culture (the Enescu Museum, Radio Romania, etc.). I used Romanian folk tunes as points of departure for selected melodic material in each of the quartet's three movements, although the piece sometimes developed in other directions during its composition, seemingly of its own accord. Nevertheless, especially in the final movement, something of the Romanian folk element shines through.

"The first movement has an overall slow-fast-slow-fast form with numerous small changes in tempo and character. In the slow sections a heavy dramatic melody alternates with a more lyrical, somewhat mysterious one. The fast parts are very rhythmic and folklike.

"The second movement is more simply structured in ABA form; a brief scherzo is embedded within the Largo framework. The third movement follows without pause. The finale is like a rondo in that a principal theme recurs several times throughout. Its short introduction is followed by the main Giocoso (playful) tempo."

CHRIS ROGERSON
B. 1988 IN AMHERST, NEW YORK

## String Quartet No. 4 (2019)

Fugue
Meditation

Trained at the Curtis Institute of Music, Yale, and Princeton, Rogerson includes Jennifer Higdon, Aaron Jay Kernis, and Steve Mackay among his mentors. His work has been praised by *The New York Times* for its "virtuosic exuberance" and "haunting beauty." A prolific chamber composer, Rogerson has collaborated with numerous quartets for works premiered in the United States and Europe.

From the composer: "This work is my fourth string quartet, written for an ensemble that I greatly admire, the Escher Quartet. The opening movement is based on two central ideas. The first is an introduction composed of fortissimo chords, and the second is a fugue subject, which is first presented in strict fugal fashion but then developed in wildly different ways throughout.

"The second movement is an extended meditation that counterbalances the intensity of the fugue. This past summer, I trekked for two weeks in a remote, mountainous corner of Afghanistan called the Wakhan corridor, hiking a similar route to the one Marco Polo took centuries ago. In this desolate but hauntingly beautiful place, sometimes called the Roof of the World, people live in extremely harsh circumstances. As I hiked across the steppe, I returned to this idea of timelessness again and again. I was reminded of a poem: 'What the Mountain Saw,' by the British poet Philip Gross.

"For all of my lifetime, Afghanistan has been a land shrouded in mystery—a place steeped in epic history, difficult to traverse, now seemingly impossible even to visit. Over the years, what had these mountains seen?

"I do not intend this movement to be a portrait of a place that I do not have full understanding of, nor a statement of any kind. But I do hope that the listener feels the same timelessness, the same stillness that I felt when walking across this vast and sweeping landscape."

## CANADA

### R. MURRAY SCHAFER
B. JULY 18, 1933 IN SARNIA, ONTARIO,
D. AUGUST 14, 2021 NEAR PETERBOROUGH, ONTARIO

Schafer's seemingly spontaneous body of work is rooted in the major trends of the 1960s—twelve-tone serialism, indeterminacy, innovative use of space, mixed media. Although he has focused much creative energy on works for musical theater, Schafer has written ten string quartets that offer a unique contribution to the genre.

The recipient of six honorary doctorates from universities in Argentina, Canada, and France, Schafer is a lifelong educator who has raised awareness of the environmental effects of sound. With the support of UNESCO, he founded and directed the World Soundscape Project; as part of its pioneering research into acoustic ecology, Schafer has inventoried sounds worldwide. A prolific theorist, Schafer has written many articles and books on the phenomenon of sound.

### String Quartet No. 3 (1981)

Slowly, but with great passion
Allegro energico
Slow, calm, mystical

Schafer choreographed his String Quartet No. 3 theatrically. As the rhapsodic first movement opens, the cellist plays alone on the stage. The remaining players slowly enter, and after all have assembled the music ends. Schafer notes in the score that this movement should offer "almost no convergence among the players, who occupy different points in space and play mostly unrelated material."

The Allegro energico is an intensely physical movement that requires vigorous gestures and vocalizations that Schafer describes as "rather like certain oriental gymnastic exercises." The final movement is a long unison melody colored by microtones and quiet humming at its conclusion. During its final moments the first violinist departs and the remaining players conclude the work with gentle chords.

## *Trio for Violin, Viola, and Cello (2006)*

The composer writes: "Everything moves smoothly at the beginning; the violin plays a melody in the Lydian mode to a simple accompaniment in the viola and cello, but after a few bars the mood becomes more agitated. It is this mood, aside from a few quiet intervals, that is sustained through most of this single movement work. The climax is reached with a powerful descending scale in the cello on the notes E flat (S in German notation), C, B natural (H), A, F, and E—followed by a surprising modulation into a Gustav Mahler-like adagio. This leads back to the gentle opening theme to bring the work to a close. Could the trio be autobiographical? The sphinx shakes his head."

CHRISTOS HATZIS
B. MARCH 21, 1953 IN VOLOS, GREECE

## *"Old Photographs" for Piano Trio (2000)*

Hatzis's music is inspired by early Christian spirituality, his own Byzantine music heritage, a broad range of world cultures, and various non-classical music genres such as jazz, pop, and ethnic music. Many of his works bridge the gap between classical and popular idioms. He has created works inspired by the Inuit, Canada's Arctic inhabitants, and by spiritual traditions around the world. In addition to composing and teaching, Hatzis has written extensively about composition and contemporary music.

Hatzis writes: "*Old Photographs* is a movement from my multimedia work *Constantinople*, composed for mezzo-soprano, Arabic singer (alto), violin, violoncello, piano, and electronic audio. A team of artists developed *Constantinople* into a music theater piece in partnership with the Banff Center for the Arts. Bringing together music, choreography, projected visuals, and stage design, *Constantinople* combined artistic elements that act as a metaphor in an exploration of age-old cultural and religious issues. *Old Photographs* is totally based on Western musical idioms and starts with a slow and introspective theme for solo piano reminiscent of the Romantic period. As the work progresses, the violin and cello enter, and the work slowly begins to drift in the direction of Astor Piazzolla's style of tango."

KATI AGÓCS
B. JANUARY 20, 1975 IN WINDSOR, ONTARIO

## *"Rogue Emoji" for Flute, Clarinet, Violin, and Cello (2019)*

Praised as "one of the brightest stars of her generation" by *Audiophile Audition*, Kati Agócs writes powerful, lyrical, and diverse works that have garnered honors such as the Lifetime Achievement Award from the American Academy of Arts and Letters. In its citation the Academy said: "The music of Kati Agócs unfolds with both drama and complexity.... It is music that seems to come directly from nature. It reaches the hearer through melody and clear design, with its soulful directness and its naturalness of dissonance." Agócs earned her advanced degrees from the Juilliard School, where she studied with Milton Babbitt, a serialist known for his vast sonic range.

Agócs writes of her quartet, which *Sparrow Live* described as "vibrantly colorful and hyper-emotional": "*Rogue Emoji* is a work for mixed quartet comprising six miniatures. This piece is structured in a series of microcosms of roughly equal length, each with its own strong texture and emotion. Each movement works with specific instrumental color combinations, largely contingent upon changes to the woodwind instrumentation. These six musical/

dramatic scenarios flow together with minimal pause to make a single formal/narrative trajectory about fifteen minutes in length.

"The first movement works with repeating patterns scored in vivid colors that are continuously warped and interrupted, leading to a central arrival and erosion with Doppler effects. The second movement is a melodrama with a lamenting quality. Its theme is introduced in the clarinet and later picked up by all instruments. The third movement is a quick mixed-meter dance embodying pure visceral energy. In this movement I pair the instruments in duets that respond to one another antiphonally. The opening theme recurs but is altered, and it finally goes wild in the second half ('berserk' is the marking in the score). The fourth movement is a meditation with solos that grow into cadenzas showcasing the individual instruments. In the fifth these are juxtaposed into a lyrical colloquy in which each plays a separate discourse, each in its own world. The sixth movement begins as an obsessive ostinato but is hijacked by a fugue that falls apart, surrendering to a return of the opening movement's energy; previously interrupted material now fulfills itself. The piece ends with a sense of affirmation, togetherness, and finding individual strength (and the ensemble's collective resonance) out of chaos.

"*Rogue Emoji* deals with the dichotomies of disconnection and unity; dissolution (falling apart) and regeneration; and communication (connection) and alienation. Beneath the work's light, humorous surface lies something deeper: an exploration of order versus control, and the embrace of chaos."

*Rogue Emoji* was commissioned by Hub New Music, a Boston-based ensemble committed to forging new paths in twenty-first century classical music.

# Useful Terms

**Adagio**: A slow and leisurely tempo.

**Allegro**: A fast and lively tempo.

**Andante:** A moderately slow tempo.

**Aria:** A solo song; in instrumental music "aria" implies an extended songlike passage often scored for one instrument.

**Arpeggio**: The consecutive articulation of ascending or descending chord tones.

**Atonality**: Broadly defined as "without key center," the term emerged in the early twentieth century as composers explored schemes that diverged from the prevailing diatonic (strongly tonal) harmony based on major and minor Western scale patterns.

**Cadenza:** A virtuoso solo passage, often improvised, derived from earlier thematic material; often heard near the end of a movement.

**Cantilena:** A lyrical melodic passage.

**Chromatic:** Literally "colorful," chromatic notes are half-step inserts between notes of the major or minor scale.

**Col legno:** The player strikes the instrument "with the wood" of the bow.

**Con sordino:** Played "with the mute," a device placed on the bridge to alter tone color by reducing vibrations.

**Consonance:** A harmonious combination of notes.

**Counterpoint:** Two or more themes woven together, either as points of imitation with each other or paired as a theme and complementary countertheme.

**Cyclic form:** Significant thematic material recurs throughout a work for structural unification.

**Diatonic scale:** The seven notes of the major or minor scale; the seven diatonic triads constructed from these constitute the basis of much Western music. "Diatonic" notes are derived from these major or minor scales.

**Dissonance:** A combination of notes heard as a discord.

**Exposition:** See "Sonata form."

**Expressionism:** A modernist movement originating in German visual arts that conveys heightened emotional experience, most often through atonality.

**Forte** (Italian "strong"): A loud dynamic. Louder markings include "fortissimo."

**Fugue:** Imitative counterpoint in which one instrument passes a theme to the next instrument(s) in succession to create a continuous statement. Counterthemes and devices such as rhythmic augmentation (lengthening of note values) and thematic inversion (the subject appears upside down) introduce complexity.

**Glissando:** A continuous tone produced by sliding from one pitch to another.

**Impressionism:** Influenced by French symbolist literature and painting, this early twentieth-century style conjures atmosphere through colorfully nuanced harmonies, scoring, and subtle shifts of rhythm.

**Largo** (Italian "broad"): a stately tempo, slower than Adagio.

**Minuet** (also Menuetto): A triple-time dancelike movement that appears near the center of a composition. A contrasting "trio" section alternates with the opening material, so called because it was originally scored for three players.

**Modernism:** An international arts movement that emerged at the beginning of the twentieth century. Largely experimental in its early phase, as the century progressed Modernism often resembled a collection of ideas rather than a coherent style. New performance venues—exhibitions, cafés, outdoor events— became laboratories for exploring modernist concepts. Three musical characteristics prevailed: the expansion or abandonment of tonality; extended technical requirements for its performers; and the exploration of novel sonorities. Modernism's dominance began to wane in the 1960s and 1970s as Postmodernism emerged—a populist reaction to cultural authority characterized by skepticism of grand theories and greater structural freedom.

**Motif** (also motive): A brief idea consisting of a few notes that can be expanded.

**Mute:** A mechanical device used to soften instrumental sound and alter tone color by reducing vibrations.

**Non troppo** (Italian "not too much"; sometimes ma non troppo, "but not too much"): A tempo modification, i.e., Allegro non troppo.

**Nonet:** A composition for nine instruments.

**Octet:** A composition for eight instruments.

**Ostinato:** An extended repeating figure or group of notes.

**Piano** (Italian "soft"): A quiet dynamic marking. Softer markings include "pianissimo."

**Piano Quartet:** An ensemble comprised of a violin, viola, cello, and piano.

**Piano Quintet:** An ensemble comprised of two violins, viola, cello, and piano.

**Piano Trio:** An ensemble consisting of a violin, cello, and piano, perhaps the most popular combination in chamber music after the string quartet.

**Pizzicato:** The string is plucked with the finger to achieve a short, emphatic sound.

**Ponticello:** The bow is drawn very near the bridge to emphasize the higher overtones and achieve a glassy sound.

**Presto** (Italian "quickly"): A very rapid tempo.

**Quintet:** A composition for five instruments.

**Recapitulation:** See "Sonata form."

**Recitative:** A rhythmically free style that imitates speech.

**Rondo:** Most often heard as a final movement, the form is structured as A-B-A-C-A, with A as the main theme, the B and C sections as contrasting interludes.

**Scherzo:** From the Italian "playful," a rapid triple-time movement often varied by a slower central section, the "trio," so called because it was originally scored for three players.

**Septet:** A composition for seven instruments.

**Serialism:** A post-tonal method of organizing elements—tones of the chromatic scale, rhythms, dynamics, and/or timbres—to create structurally unifying sets.

**Sextet:** A composition for six instruments.

**Sonata form:** The prevailing structure for the majority of first movements in the Classic and Romantic eras with its use continuing into the twentieth century. There are three essential parts. The exposition introduces the various themes, which are most often of a complementary character; the entire section is customarily repeated. The development manipulates the stated themes in a variety of ways—recasting them with new harmonies, recombining components of a theme with new material, or expanding thematic elements to create a related statement that is essentially heard as new. The recapitulation is a section of restatement; the original tonalities and themes of the exposition return, most often with alterations that enhance but do not change their character. The entire movement may be prefaced with an introduction and concluded with a coda.

**Song form:** Borrowed from vocal music, this A-B-A structure instrumental form is often heard in slow movements; the central section frequently varies ideas heard in the opening A section.

**Sonorism:** A post-1950s avant-garde approach that focuses on timbre, texture, articulation, and dynamics.

**Spectralism:** From the Latin root "spectrum" (plural "spectra"), a luminous merging of tone colors drawn from a continuous sonic range that finds its counterpart in the optical phenomenon of the rainbow. Using advanced computer software, the composer analyzes the spectra of overtones generated by resonating pitches and constructs a work incorporating these patterns.

**Staccato** (Italian "detached"): Each note is separately articulated with a short stroke of the bow.

**String Quartet:** An ensemble consisting of two violins, a viola, and a cello.

**Syncopation:** An expected accent is shifted to an unexpected beat within the measure.

**Tremolo** (Italian "trembling"): For string instruments, the bow moves rapidly back and forth on the same note; for other instruments, two notes alternate rapidly.

**Trill:** A note alternates rapidly with the note above to create an ornament.

**Variation form:** A theme is transformed rhythmically, melodically and/or harmonically to reveal different guises.

# Sources

**Primary Sources**

Recordings and scores are ideal starting points for exploring chamber music. University libraries and often urban libraries own comprehensive collections, and WorldCat can provide additional resources. YouTube offers expansive listening opportunities, and many compositions listed there play concurrently with their companion scores. Since YouTube offers a selection of performers, when possible one can compare different interpretations, all listed with their performance times (which can vary significantly). Other streaming media resources such as Spotify are also excellent. Concert attendance is invaluable.

Composers' commentaries on their music can be found in recorded interviews listed on their websites. Reliable biographical studies that include substantial quotations from composers also are important sources.

**Secondary Sources: A Selected Bibliography**

BACKGROUND

Cooke, Deryck, et. al. *The New Grove Late Romantic Masters: Bruckner, Brahms, Dvořák, Wolf.* Norton, 1985.

Cooper, Martin, ed. *The Modern Age: 1890–1960.* Vol. 10 of *The New Oxford History of Music.* Oxford University Press, 1974.

Griffiths, Paul. *Modern Music and After.* Third edition. Oxford University Press, 2011.

Ross, Alex. *The Rest is Noise: Listening to the Twentieth Century.* Farrar, Straus, and Giroux, 2007.

Sadie, Stanley, ed. *The New Grove Dictionary of Music and Musicians, Second Edition.* Oxford University Press, 2001. Signed articles for individual composers; excellent bibliographies.

Salzman, Eric. *Twentieth-Century Music: An Introduction.* Fourth Edition. Prentice-Hall History of Music Series. Pearson, 2001.

Whittall, Arnold. *Musical Composition in the Twentieth Century.* Oxford University Press, 2000.

Wilk, Christopher. *Modernism: Designing a New World*. Victoria and Albert Museum, 2008.
World Wide Web. It is impossible these days to ignore the internet as a fact source. Its level of sophistication and accuracy of information is steadily improving.

**CHAPTER ONE: THE TWILIGHT OF EMPIRES**

Magris, Claudio. *Danube*. Translated by Patrick Creagh. Farrar, Straus, and Giroux, 1989.
Rosen, Charles. *The Romantic Generation*. Harvard University Press, 1995.
Segel, Harold B., ed. *The Vienna Coffee House Wits: 1890–1938*. Purdue University Press, 1993.
SUGGESTED LISTENING: Wolf's *Italian Serenade* (Fine Arts Quartet, Hännsler); Dohnányi's Piano Quintet (Takács Quartet with Marc-André Hamelin, Hyperion).

**CHAPTER TWO: VIENNESE SYMBOLISM**

Auner, Joseph. *A Schoenberg Reader: Documents of a Life*. Yale University Press, 2003.
Moldenhauer, Hans. *Anton von Webern: A Chronicle of His Life and Work*. In Collaboration with Rosaleen Moldenhauer. Knopf, 1979.
Moskovitz, Marc D. *Alexander Zemlinsky: A Lyric Symphony*. Boydell and Brewer, 2010.
Simms, Bryan R. *Alban Berg: A Research and Information Guide*. Third edition. Routledge Music Bibliographies, 2019.
SUGGESTED LISTENING: Zemlinsky Quartets (Brodsky Quartet, Chandos); Schoenberg, Webern, Berg Quartets (LaSalle Quartet, Brilliant Classics).

**CHAPTER THREE: REVOLUTIONARY FRANCE**

Lesure, François. *Claude Debussy: A Critical Biography*. Translated and revised by Marie Rolf. Eastman Studies in Music. University of Rochester Press, 2019.
Nichols, Roger. *Ravel*. Yale University Press, 2013.
Walsh, Stephen. *Debussy: A Painter in Sound*. Knopf, 2018.
SUGGESTED LISTENING: Debussy and Ravel Quartets (Borodin Quartet, Chandos); Messiaen's *Quartet for the End of Time* (Tashi, RCA).

**CHAPTER FOUR: CZECH DIALOGUES**

Beckerman, Michael, ed. *Janáček and His World*. Princeton University Press, 2003.
Large, Brian. *Martinů*. Duckworth, 1975.
SUGGESTED LISTENING: The Prazák String Quartet has released numerous excellent recordings of Czech works; the Schönberg Quartet has an excellent CD of Schulhoff's Sextet and String Quartets (Koch); there is a fine reading of his Sextet by the Raphael Ensemble (Helios); the Tucson Winter Chamber Music Festival has premieres of works by Gemrot and Bodorová on YouTube.

**CHAPTER FIVE: HUNGARIAN QUESTS**

Antokoletz, Elliott. *The Music of Béla Bartók: A Study of Tonality and Progression in Twentieth-Century Music*. University of California Press, 1990.
Chalmers, Kenneth. *Béla Bartók*. Revised edition. Phaidon, 2008.
Dalos, Anna. *Zoltán Kodály's World of Music*. University of California Press, 2020.
Schneider, David E. *Bartók, Hungary, and the Renewal of Tradition: Case Studies in the Intersection of Modernity and Nationality*. University of California Press, 2006.
SUGGESTED LISTENING: Bartók String Quartets (Hungarian String Quartet, Deutsche Grammophon).

**CHAPTER SIX: FORWARD THINKERS IN GERMANY**

Kennedy, Michael. *Richard Strauss: Man, Musician, Enigma*. Cambridge University Press, 1999.
Luttmann, Stephen. *Paul Hindemith: A Research and Information Guide*. Second edition. Routledge Music Bibliographies, 2009.
Stockhausen, Karlheinz. *Stockhausen on Music*. Lectures and Interviews compiled by Robin Maconie. Marion Boyars, 2000.
SUGGESTED LISTENING: Hindemith's complete *Kammermusik* (Claudio Abbado and players of the Berlin Philharmonic, EMI). StockhausenCDs.com in Kuerten, Germany, offers a complete edition of recordings in which Stockhausen participated personally.

**CHAPTER SEVEN: POLAND ASCENDING**

Vest, Lisa Cooper. *Awangarda: Tradition and Modernity in Postwar Polish Music*. University of California Press, 2020.
Wightman, Alistair. *Karol Szymanowski: His Life and Work*. Routledge, 2016.
SUGGESTED LISTENING: Hyperion Records offers Szymanowski's works on CDs and downloads in a variety of formats.

**CHAPTER EIGHT: SOVIET UTOPIA**

Fay, Laurel E. *Shostakovich: A Life*. Oxford University Press, 2000.
Jaffé, Daniel. *Sergey Prokofiev*. Phaidon Press, 2008.
Nestyev, Israel. *Sergey Prokofiev*. Stanford University Press, 1960.
Roseberry, Eric. *Shostakovich: His Life and Times*. Hippocrene Books, 1982.
Volkov, Solomon, ed. *Testimony: The Memoirs of Dmitri Shostakovich*. Harper and Row, 1979.
Wilson, Elizabeth. *Shostakovich: A Life Remembered*. Second edition. Princeton University Press, 2006.
SUGGESTED LISTENING: The Borodin Quartet offers fine readings of the Shostakovich quartets (Melodiya).

### CHAPTER NINE: THE MEDITERRANEAN

Berio, Luciano, with Rossana Dalmonte and Bálint András Varga. *Two Interviews*. Marion Boyers, 1985.

Falla, Manuel de. *On Music and Musicians*. Marion Boyars, 1979.

Webb, Michael. *Ottorino Respighi: His Life and Times*. Troubador, 2019.

SUGGESTED LISTENING: Berio's *Circles* (Wergo) CD; Turina's works (Trio Arbós, Naxos).

### CHAPTER TEN: BRITISH SOUNDSCAPES

Carpenter, Humphrey. *Benjamin Britten: A Biography*. Faber & Faber, 1992.

Frogley, Alain, and Aidan J. Thomson, eds. *The Cambridge Companion to Vaughan Williams*. Cambridge University Press, 2013.

Holst, Imogen. *Gustav Holst*. Second edition. Oxford University Press, 1969.

Kent, Christopher. *Edward Elgar: A Thematic Catalogue and Research Guide*. Second edition. Routledge Music Bibliographies, 2012.

Moore, Jerrold Northrop. *Edward Elgar: A Creative Life*. Clarendon Press, 1999.

SUGGESTED LISTENING: Vaughan Williams chamber music (Maggini Quartet, Naxos); Gustav Holst *Kammermusik* (Ensemble Arabesques, Farao Classics); Elgar works (Goldner String Quartet with Piers Lane, Hyperion); Britten String Quartets (Doric String Quartet, Chandos); Adès *Arcadiana* (*Adès: Anthology*, Warner Classics).

### CHAPTER ELEVEN: CULTURAL FUSION IN LATIN AMERICA

Chávez, Carlos. *Musical Thought: The Charles Eliot Norton Lectures 1958–1959*. Harvard University Press, 1961.

Parker, Robert. *Carlos Chávez: A Guide to Research*. Garland, 1998.

Peppercorn, Lisa. *Villa-Lobos*. Edited by Audrey Sampson. Omnibus Press, 1989.

Schwartz-Kates, Deborah. *Alberto Ginastera: A Research and Information Guide*. Routledge, 2015.

SUGGESTED LISTENING: The Mexico-based Cuarteto Latinoamericano offers a large range of recordings by Latin American composers (Brilliant Classics).

### CHAPTER TWELVE: CHINA, TRADITION UNBOUND

Clark, Paul, Laikwan Pang, Tsan-Huang Tsai, eds. *Listening to China's Cultural Revolution: Music, Politics, and Cultural Continuities*. Palgrave Macmillan, 2016.

Jie, Jin. *Chinese Music*. Third Edition. Cambridge University Press, 2011.

SUGGESTED LISTENING: The Shanghai Quartet has recorded a variety of recent Chinese works in consultation with their composers (Delos).

**CHAPTER THIRTEEN: AUSTRALIA, INSIGHTS FROM THE NATURAL WORLD**

Kerry, Gordon. *New Classical Music: Composing Australia* (includes CD). University of New South Wales Press, 2009.

Skinner, Graeme. *Peter Sculthorpe: The Making of an Australian Composer.* University of New South Wales Press, 2007.

SUGGESTED LISTENING: The Tucson Winter Chamber Music Festival performances of Ross Edwards and Carl Vine premieres can be found on YouTube.


**CHAPTER FOURTEEN: AMERICAN PATHFINDERS**

Brown, Jeanell Wise. *Amy Beach and Her Chamber Music: Biography, Documents, Style.* Scarecrow Press, 1994.

Curtis, Liane, ed. *A Rebecca Clarke Reader.* Indiana University Press, 2004.

Magee, Gail Sherwood. *Charles Ives Reconsidered.* University of Illinois Press, 2008.

Pollack, Howard. *Aaron Copland: The Life and Work of an Uncommon Man.* University of Illinois Press, 1999.

SUGGESTED LISTENING: Amy Beach's Piano Quintet (Chandos); chamber works of Rebecca Clarke (Centaur).


**CHAPTER FIFTEEN: INNOVATION AND DISCOVERY IN NORTH AMERICA**

Carter, Elliott. *Collected Essays and Lectures: 1937–1995.* Edited by Jonathan W. Bernard. University of Rochester Press, 1997.

Taruskin, Richard. *Music in the Late Twentieth Century. The Oxford History of Western Music, Volume 5.* Oxford University Press, 2010.

Glass, Philip. *Words Without Music: A Memoir.* Liveright, 2015.

SUGGESTED LISTENING: Carter's String Quartets (Pacifica Quartet, Naxos); numerous premiere performances of North American works are offered on YouTube.